James Sharples, James Walter, Robert Cary

Memorials of Washington and of Mary, his mother and Martha, his Wife

Vol. 1

James Sharples, James Walter, Robert Cary

Memorials of Washington and of Mary, his mother and Martha, his Wife
Vol. 1

ISBN/EAN: 9783337715212

Printed in Europe, USA, Canada, Australia, Japan

Cover: Foto ©Thomas Meinert / pixelio.de

More available books at **www.hansebooks.com**

MEMORIALS OF
WASHINGTON

AND OF

MARY, HIS MOTHER, AND MARTHA, HIS WIFE,

FROM LETTERS AND PAPERS OF ROBERT CARY AND JAMES SHARPLES.

By JAMES WALTER,

RETIRED MAJOR 4TH LANCASHIRE ARTILLERY (BRITISH ARMY LIST),
AUTHOR OF "SHAKESPEARE'S HOME AND RURAL LIFE."

ILLUSTRATED WITH PORTRAITS OF WASHINGTON AND HIS WIFE, SEVEN PORTRAITS OF PROMINENT AMERICAN WOMEN OF THE PERIOD, AND PORTRAITS OF ROBERT FULTON AND PRIESTLEY, FROM PAINTINGS BY SHARPLES;

ALSO PORTRAITS OF

MARY WASHINGTON AND MARY PHILLIPSE,

BY MIDDLETON.

CHARLES SCRIBNER'S SONS,
743 AND 745, BROADWAY,
NEW YORK.

1887.

Entered at Washington, according to Act of Congress, in the year 1886. All rights reserved.

Each of the Portraits are also duly entered at Washington, and copyright thereby strictly secured.

PATRIOTS of every country will welcome with pride and gratification the following exquisite Sonnet from the pen of Francis Bennoch, the loved and gifted friend of Mary Russell Mitford, Nathaniel Hawthorne, and Longfellow. It has been suggested that the two final lines would serve admirably as an inscription for the Pedestal of the National Monument.

WASHINGTON.

BEFORE thy tomb, great Statesman, I have bowed
  In humble reverence, knowing well the zeal
    With which thou struggled for thy people's weal.
Struggled and conquered! Never tempest cloud
Could stay the lightning of thy heart, nor shroud
    That quenchless courage which made despots reel,
And men, down-trodden, of thy prowess proud!
  And now I gaze with rapture on thy face
So calm and deep in thought, transcending earth!)
    By SHARPLES limned,—where dignity, and grace,
And force combined to give a Nation birth,
  With power to speak and liberate the race!
Of FREEDOM's bravest leaders, there are none
Whose fame o'ershadows thine, HEROIC WASHINGTON!

                                        FRANCIS BENNOCH.

TAVISTOCK SQUARE, LONDON.

These Memorials are respectfully Dedicated

To the Nation so highly blessed in calling him her Son, whom no Climate can claim, no Country can appropriate,—the born of Providence to the Human Race, whose fame is Eternity, his residence the Creation.

In the formation of Washington, Nature may be said to have endeavoured to improve upon herself, and as though all the virtues of the Ancient World were but so many studies preparatory to the Patriot of the New.

Cæsar was merciful,—Scipio was continent,—Hannibal was patient, but it remained for Washington to blend them all in one, to exhibit in one glow of associated beauty the grace of every model and the perfection of every master.

As a General, he marshalled his Peasant into a Veteran, and supplied by discipline the absence of experience. As a Statesman, he enlarged the policy of the Cabinet into the most comprehensive system of general advantage; and such was the wisdom of his Counsels, that to the Soldier and the Statesman he added the character of the Sage.

      RANFOLD GRANGE,
   SLINFOLD, SUSSEX, ENGLAND.

CONTENTS.

CHAPTER I.

Arrival of the painter Sharples in New York in 1794, and again in 1809—Yellow fever prevalent—Cary's letters introducing him to the British Minister and Washington—English descent of the Washingtons—Sharples paints two portraits of Washington and one of his wife—Their despatch to England—One returns to America, and is exhibited before the Historical Society of New York in 1854—Article from *New York Albion* at the time—Great interest taken by Lord Lyndhurst in the Sharples and Middleton portraits 1

CHAPTER II.

THE SHARPLES PORTRAITS BEFORE THE NEW YORK HISTORICAL SOCIETY.

New York Historical Society minutes record as to the portrait loaned in 1854—Secretary Warner details its reception before the Society—Letter of the venerable Dr. Van Pelt, who remembered Washington, and testifies to his portrait—Letter from Washington Irving, referring to its accuracy, and asking permission to engrave it for his contemplated "Life of Washington"—Letter from the Poets Bryant and Longfellow, expressing admiration of the portrait—Letters from Washington Irving, urging purchase and stating that money cost is guaranteed—Letter from Colden to Macready in England—Macready replies with full history of the portraits—Letter from Dickens and Thackeray 13

CHAPTER III.

The three portraits return to New York in 1882, and are received at Century and Union League Clubs—David Huntington, Eastman Johnson, J. G. A. Ward, and Launt Thompson certify to their authenticity—The historian Dunlap and his account of the pictures—The *New York Evening Post* commends them to public notice—Ralph Waldo Emerson testifies and names Middleton's portrait of Mary Washington, to see which his efforts when in England were ineffectual—Letters from Nathaniel Hawthorne, Elihu Burritt, and Albert Gallatin—Speech of Daniel Webster on the portraits . . 25

CHAPTER IV.

Cary and Co., London, Washington's agents—Robert Cary more than a friend—Washington's fondness for English tripe—Letter from Washington expressing his own and Mrs. Washington's feeling in regard to the portraits, and as not favouring their being duplicated—Sharples formally introduced to Washington in Philadelphia by English Minister—Stays with the younger Franklin—Washington's great kindness—Introduced to Hamilton, who becomes his patron and friend—Emerson's efforts to see the portrait of Mary Washington duplicated—Artist life in New York—Voyage up the Hudson in 1809 41

CHAPTER V.

Sharples becomes "the fashion" in New York—Trumbull and the Hon. Mr. Jay make unsuccessful efforts for reproduction of the portraits for America—Letter from Trumbull urging same, and explaining their great value to the nation, also giving account of all the other existent portraits, contrasting them—Sharples paints Priestley in Philadelphia—Hamilton, Lee, and Washington meet in the painter's studio in Philadelphia—Affability and personal appearance of Washington—Sharples visits Lee in Virginia—Admirable criticism of the portraits by G. B. West, of St. Paul's 57

CHAPTER VI.

Washington's dreamy hours—Hamilton explains to Sharples that Washington fancies himself connected with the Methuen family, of Corsham, England—The Chief's profound knowledge of English history—Description of Corsham, its old mansion and church—De Witt Clinton's attachment to Sharples—His greatness, and public sympathy at death—Leading public men, through Washington and Hamilton, unite in guaranteeing commissions to Sharples—Biography of the guarantors—Washington, Hamilton, and Tobias Lear take supper with the artist 83

CHAPTER VII.

Mary Washington—Existence of an authenticated Portrait by Middleton—Its mutilated condition—Letter of Washington stating its injuries, how occurring, and desiring repair—The portrait sent to England for restoration—Royal Academician Bird undertakes it—The widow Sharples medium of communicating with the Custis family as to restoration of the painting—Bird completes it—Cary eventually pays the cost—General Grant views the portrait—His letter to the owner, expressing great thankfulness for the privilege extended him . . 103

CHAPTER VIII.

Attractive nature of female excellences—their qualities illustrated in Mary Washington—Good Parson Baker's teachings—Mary Washington's family descent—Source of her religious inspiration—The home of her youth—Her sponsors at baptism—Armorial bearings of her family—Washington and Franklin families originally residents in same part of England—Washington assists in removal of his mother to Fredericksburg—Her example under bereavement—Washington relates the advantages she received from Parson Baker's instruction—Remarks on his mother's portrait—Her bearing as a widow, and watchful care of her children—Her example meet for general imitation 117

CHAPTER IX.

Washington's pursuit in life directed by his mother—Mary Washington's life one of general privacy—Letter from Washington to his mother—Another letter assuring deference to her wishes—Mary's estimate of human greatness—Her interest deep though not over-sanguine of the triumph of America in the struggle—Her thankfulness at the success in passage of the Delaware—Her fervent gratitude in the surrender of Lord Cornwallis—Religious traditions bequeathed by Mary Washington—Her meeting her son after this eventful occurrence—The ball at Fredericksburg—Declines relinquishing her independent home—Her home happiness and abstemious life—Lafayette's visit—Washington's last visit and general submission to his mother . 139

CHAPTER X.

Washington's distrust of the French Revolution—His personal sacrifices during his terms of Presidency, 1789 to 1796—Imminent danger of the country during his second Presidency—Avails of the horrors excited by the French Revolution for praiseworthy purposes—Sharples' devotion to Washington—Washington's genius, evidenced in his conduct at time of the Declaration of Independence, retrieves the desperate condition of the country's affairs—The intrigues of Genet—Washington's message of December, 1793, on the country's foreign relations — Great excitement everywhere — Washington dignified and unswerving—Robert Cary tracks the designs and doings of Genet and other enemies in America—Pinckney's despatches make known England's desire for peace—Cary's great love and devotion to Washington 169

CHAPTER XI.

Mount Vernon Washington's goal of happiness—His visits there when a child—Lawrence Washington's marriage with Anne Fairfax—Their residence at Mount Vernon built by him— George as a boy visiting there—Joseph Ball's letter to Mary Washington, discouraging the sending George to sea—Early susceptibility to female attractions—Appointed public surveyor to Culpepper County—Excels as an athlete—Introduced to Martha Custis—Courtship, marriage, and early married life—Domestic habits—George Mason his neighbour and friend—The churches in which he worshipped, and their ministers—Martha Washington's children—Her daughter's death—Destroys her husband's letters—Lawrence at Mount Vernon—Sharples assists in improving the grounds—Washington and Lafayette—Able summary of Washington's character from Hunt's Merchant's Magazine. 196

CHAPTER XII.

Object of the Memorials—Washington joins Braddock—Early discouragements—Mary Phillipse—Rochambeau at Mount Vernon—English description of Washington—Rebukes Lund Washington—Labour in founding the City of Washington—Visits his mother at Fredericksburg—Declines State money aid—Course of life at Mount Vernon—Organization of Congress—Washington elected President—Proceeds to New York—Ovations *en route*—Sworn in as President—Seat of Government removed to Philadelphia—The Philadelphia mansion—Washington's English carriage described—also his presentation china—Equipages and plate described—Loss of valuable correspondence between Sharples and Robert Fulton greatly to be deplored—Eventful occurrences of 1794 and 1795—Jefferson's retirement—and requested resumption of office—Vaughan, a London merchant, presents chimney-piece at Mount Vernon 241

CHAPTER XIII.

Robert Fulton and Sharples, as artists and men of science, close friends during many years—Sketch of Fulton's steam and torpedo discoveries—Sharples' death—The unfinished oil portraits and sketches of female beauties left by Sharples—Vicissitudes through which many passed—Articles from the Boston papers—Testimony of the Rev. Henry Ward Beecher and Dr. Poole, Librarian of Chicago—The portraits' reception at Chicago, St. Paul, Cincinnati, and Philadelphia—Articles from the Chicago, Philadelphia, and Cincinnati papers—Testimony of Charles Henry Hart and W. G. Baker, of Philadelphia—Washington's high sense of duty in dealing with public appointments—Defence of Washington in the case of André from the charges preferred by historians—Washington's illness and death—Proceedings in the National Legislature consequent on his death—Rev. Dr. Bancroft on Washington 291

LIST OF PORTRAITS.

	PAGE
Profile Portrait of Washington	*Frontispiece*
Full-Face Portrait of Washington	13
Martha Washington	25
General Hamilton's Wife (née Schuyler)	41
Priestley	57
Miss Field	83
Mary, Mother of Washington	103
Miss Jay	117
Mrs. Van Ransalaer	139
Patrick Henry's Daughter	169
Angelica Peale	196
Robert Fulton's Wife (née Livingstone)	241
Mary Phillipse	246

 Writers of the time record how the young soldier, apparently invincible to the mortal weapons of war, was sorely smitten by the sly archer concealed in the bright eyes, blooming cheeks, and winning ways of Mary Phillipse. He lingered in her presence as long as duty would permit, and would fain have carried her away with him to Virginia as a bride, but his natural diffidence kept the momentous question unspoken in his heart, and Roger Morris bore away the prize.

Robert Fulton	291

 The pioneer in the application of steam-power to purposes of navigation. The first inventor of torpedoes and of submarine war vessels.

CHAPTER I.

Arrival of the painter Sharples in New York in 1794, and again in 1809—Yellow fever prevalent—Cary's letters introducing him to the British Minister and Washington—English descent of the Washingtons—Sharples paints two portraits of Washington and one of his wife—Their despatch to England—One returns to America, and is exhibited before the Historical Society of New York in 1854—Article from New York Albion at the time—Great interest taken by Lord Lyndhurst in the Sharples and Middleton portraits.

JAMES SHARPLES, the artist to whom the world stands indebted for the portraits of Washington and his wife, was an Englishman who studied in London under the eminent painter, George Romney. He paid two visits to America, the first occasion was in 1794, when the vessel on board which he, his wife, son, and daughter were passengers, was captured by a French frigate and taken into Brest, where they remained prisoners of war for some months. After his release he succeeded in getting out safely to New York, and resided in a house in Greenwich Street, and which was afterwards occupied by Bishop Moor. The date of his return to England is not known. Their second visit was in 1809, the voyage being made from Bristol in seven weeks in the brig *Nancy*, commanded by Captain Barstow. This vessel sailed from Bristol on the 1st of June, and reached New York on the 21st of July, 1809. They occupied a house in Lispinard Street, owned by a Mr. Knapp. There is now resident in Brooklyn, New York, a gentleman named Pope, whose wife is the daughter of the very captain who brought the family out, and who testifies as follows as to their arrival and occurring incidents during the voyage:—

"Brooklyn, April 3, 1882.
Our family retains a very pleasant remembrance of Mr. and Mrs. Sharples as often spoken of by my wife's father, Captain Wilson Barstow, with whom they came as passengers from Bristol in the brig *Nancy*, in 1809—indeed there seems to have grown up on the voyage a very strong feeling of mutual regard, as evinced in a letter of Mrs. Sharples. Mr. Sharples had offered a portrait of the captain to be made on the voyage, but this being declined, he painted for him in cabinet size a composition of Paul and Virginia, which picture we now have.

G. L. POPE."

Memoranda found among the family papers thus refer to their voyage and landing in New York:—

"On the 30th of May, 1809, political circumstances being favourable to our returning to America, as also the season of the year, we decided to embark in the packet from Falmouth, or in a brig at Bristol, the only vessel preparing to sail for New York, in order that my husband should execute Mr. Cary's commissions. We had some little hesitation which vessel to take, which was finally decided in favour of the latter, she being pronounced well-built and perfectly safe, the captain very skilful and of excellent character. We sailed from Kingroad, Bristol, on the 1st of June, and came in sight of Sandy Hook on the 20th of July. On the following day, early in the morning, we were opposite Staten Island, and within sight of New York, waiting for the port physician. We were disappointed in not seeing our old acquaintance, Dr. Rogers, who we regretted to learn was detained at home by indisposition. Dr. Baily came on board to examine the ship and people, and finding us all healthy, we were permitted to proceed to the city. Several newsmen also came on board to gain information respecting the politics of Europe, and we furnished them with papers. My husband and daughter Rolinda went on shore in one of their boats; the ship sailed up to the wharf. I remained anxiously expecting their return with information concerning our son James, whom we had left behind us in New York. My husband continuing absent some time, I began to apprehend either that some accident had befallen our son, or that he had left the city. Mr. Sharples and Rolinda returned without him, being a great disappointment, but their countenances indicated that all was well. We engaged apartments at Mrs. Williams', at whose house my son had boarded since his arrival in America. Mrs. Williams received us in the most kind and friendly manner, and gave us the most satisfactory intelligence respecting his conduct during nearly three years that he had been with her. She seemed to have a motherly affection for him, to be delighted to see his parents and sister, and talk with them about him. Previous to dinner we walked in the city, and called on Miss Templeton, who very cordially welcomed our return,-and in a way the most dignified and pleasing. After some time her mother made known to us that a week ago she had been married to Mr. Johnson. We engaged to take tea with them the next evening. On Sunday, the 23rd, Mr. Connard and Mr. Seymore accompanied us to St. George's Church. We were much struck with the beauty of its interior and decorations. Nine elegant glass chandeliers were suspended from the ceiling. On the 24th we went to see a house in State Street, which was to let. On going through it we concluded it would suit us very well. On inquiring the rent we were told it was a thousand dollars, besides taxes: this made us hesitate, and we concluded first to see a little more of the town and country. After dinner we went into the upper part of the town to examine houses that were to let, and went to Vauxhall Gardens. Dr. Miller called on the 25th, and expressed being much pleased at our return. He was easy and dignified; his conversation and manner were particularly pleasing. On the 26th, Mr. Charles Miller paid us a visit, and in the evening took us in a coach to drink tea at his country house in Greenwich. We were much pleased with our drive and visit. The houses on the island are delightfully pleasant, particularly those situated on the North River where the gardens are beautiful. On the 28th we called to see Bishop Moor, and found him living in the house we formerly occupied near Greenwich. The family were not at home. We afterwards called at Dr. Anderson's, Mr. Hodge's, and Mr. King's. Yellow fever was the prevailing subject of conversation; two cases had occurred in streets near ours, and every person manifested alarm. After much looking about, Mr. MacLain and other friends aiding our inquiries, we took a house in Lispinard Street, of Mr. Knapp, the owner. Governor and Mrs. Morris have been to see us, and took us to see Cooper in 'Macbeth.'"

This interesting letter shows the class of society in which the family had moved during their previous residence, and that their return was cordially welcomed. Sharples possessed some little private property, and was a man of culture, as well as versed in science. He had been led to America on the first occasion consequent on a sea voyage having been recommended for his health, and, as at the moment several commissions were offered him to paint officers of the army who at the close of the war had settled in America, and whose relatives in England desired portraits, he availed of the opportunity. Chief among such orders was a commission from Mr. Robert Cary, a merchant in London, who for many years had acted as mercantile agent for Washington in the sale of his tobacco grown on his estate.

"The house" of Cary and Co. had more than one client of the Washington family. In this connection it is interesting to go back to the period of the family first coming out to America, and to trace it from the year 1538 in England, such being the date when the manor of Sulgrave, in Northamptonshire, was granted to Lawrence Washington, of Gray's Inn, and for some time Mayor of Northampton, who, it is generally agreed, was born at Warton, in Lancashire, where his father lived. The grandson of this first proprietor of Sulgrave, of the same name, had many children, two of whom, John and Lawrence Washington, being the second and fourth sons, emigrated to Virginia about the year 1657, and settled at Bridges Creek, on the Potomac River, in the county of Westmoreland. The eldest brother, Sir William Washington, married a half-sister of George Villiers, Duke of Buckingham, and it is established that "blue blood" ruled in all branches of the family. Lawrence had been a student at Oxford; John had resided on an estate at South Cave, in Yorkshire, which gave rise, as Jared Sparks says, to an erroneous tradition among his descendants that their ancestor came from the north of England. The two brothers bought lands in Virginia; both were successful cultivators of tobacco, and transacted their home business through the Carys of London.

John Washington, shortly after his arrival in America, was employed in a military command against the Indians, and rose to the rank of colonel. The parish in which he lived was named after him. He married Anne Pope, by whom he had two sons, Lawrence and John, and a daughter. The elder son, Lawrence, married Mildred Warner, of Gloucester County, and had three children, John, Augustine, and Mildred.

Augustine Washington, the second son, was twice married. His first wife was Jane Butler, by whom he had three sons and a daughter—Butler (who died in infancy), Lawrence, Augustine, and Jane, the last of whom died likewise when a child. By his second wife, Mary Ball, to whom he was married on the 6th of March, 1730, he had six children, George, Betty, Samuel, John Augustine, Charles, and Mildred.

George Washington, the "Immortal," was born in Westmoreland County, Virginia, on the 22nd day of February, 1732, being the eldest son by the second marriage, great-grandson of John Washington, who emigrated to America, and the sixth in descent from the first Lawrence Washington, of Sulgrave, Northamptonshire, in England.

At the time of George Washington's birth, his father resided on the banks of the Potomac, in Westmoreland County, but he removed not long afterwards to an estate owned by him in Stafford County, on the east side of the Rappahannoc River, opposite Fredericsburg. Here he lived until his death, which happened, after a sudden and short illness, on the 12th of April, 1743, at the age of forty-nine, and was buried at Bridges Creek, in the tomb of his ancestors. His will proves him to have been possessed of large and valuable properties in lands, and, as these had been acquired chiefly by his own industry and enterprise, it may reasonably be inferred that, in the concerns of business, he was methodical, skilful, honourable, and energetic. His occupation was that of a planter, which, from the first settlement of the country, had been the pursuit of nearly all the principal gentlemen of Virginia.

Jared Sparks further tells us that each of his sons

inherited from him a separate plantation. To the eldest, Lawrence, he bequeathed an estate near Hunting Creek; this is the property now known as Mount Vernon, of worldwide notoriety, which then consisted of twenty-five hundred acres; and also other lands, and shares in iron-works situated in Virginia and Maryland, which were productive. The second son had for his part an estate in Westmoreland. To George were left the lands and mansion where his father lived at the time of his decease; and to each of the other sons, an estate of six or seven hundred acres. The youngest daughter died when an infant, and for the only remaining one a suitable provision was made in the will. It is thus seen that Augustine Washington, although suddenly cut off in the vigour of manhood, left all his children in a state of comparative independence. Confiding in the prudence of the mother, he directed that the proceeds of all the property of his children should be at her disposal until they should respectively come of age.

From knowledge of Washington's nobility of character, and great services to his country, and through confidential relations he had personally become greatly endeared to Robert Cary, a merchant in London, his agent, so much so that "I greatly covet the illustrious General, my loved friend's portrait by a competent painter who shall do justice to the noble subject." So wrote Cary at the time. His whole heart, as his purse, was in the matter, and we accordingly find Sharples sent over the seas to compass his yearning; "having satisfied myself," as he added, "by several interviews with my friend George Romney that Mr. Sharples, whom he recommends for the purpose, will produce such a work as will meet my wish, and be worthy of the greatest of all men."

Romney had become advanced in years, Sharples was his pupil, and we may be assured he would select one he deemed best, as an artist to do justice to the subject; Washington being then the admired of the whole world, and Robert Cary an old friend he was desirous to serve. Romney came out of Lancashire, so did Sharples; there were thus birth ties as well as professional associations between the master and his disciple; and although there is nothing to show that the latter was a man of great note among artists, yet it must be borne in mind " there were giants in those days" in England's portrait world, and no pretence is made that Sharples ranked among them. To have sent out either of the stars then shining in portraiture, who would have needed at least eight months' absence—seven and eight weeks being in those days no uncommon length of the voyage either way—was out of the question, for, although Millais' two thousand guineas fee for a single head had not yet cropped up, yet very respectable prices were earned; Sharples himself, as a junior unblessed by fame, charging fifty guineas and getting it,—this at a time when men of means were few and far between. His passage outward was paid, and even on his first visit he walked on shore in anything but an impecunious condition, as his wife states that he on landing went and made a deposit of over two hundred pounds in a New York bank, as a nest-egg. It is by no means certain that this comfortable start was to his advantage. Instead of setting to work, and knocking off his commissions, he would appear to have taken things easy. There remains nothing to show the precise date at which he commenced or finished his two portraits of Washington, one a full-face in military uniform, the other a profile, and one of Martha, Washington's wife, a profile.

All that is certain regarding his work at the time, is that the portraits reached England during 1797. Three years and more had thus expired in the interval of his landing and the pictures' arrival. There was no holding on to them for exhibition purposes after their completion. Washington and his wife each gave their first sittings at Mount Vernon; the General afterwards gave him two final sittings in Philadelphia, but Lady Washington sat to him only at Mount Vernon. All three pictures were taken to New York, and finished there by Sharples in his own house in Greenwich Street, and were at once sent off to England. Mrs. Sharples, in a letter to Mr. Cary, dwells on the advantage her husband would have derived from an exhibition of the portraits, and which she said had been "seen by nobody but General Hamilton, Governor Morris, General North, Mr. Van Ransalaer, De Witt Clinton, Chief Justice Marshall, Judge Hobart, the Barclays, Chancellor Livingstone, Judge Kent, the Jays, and intimate friends of the family visiting at Mount Vernon; whereas if we could have been permitted the opportunity to exhibit them in Philadelphia, and here in New York, it would have benefited my husband greatly."

The portraits have through unbroken continuity been since generally known of and seen by such public men of America as through occasions of going to England were enabled to avail themselves of such to visit Mr. Cary, who up to the time of his death always felt a pleasure in showing the three portraits to any persons desirous, as he was wont to term it, of "paying court to my distinguished guests." Use of the word "guest" would indicate some design on his part to be the instrument of their return to America, and yet he possibly felt that he could hardly present that which had been given to himself. Cary was a bachelor, full of chivalry, and there was nobody to inherit these heirlooms, excepting a younger unmarried brother and one sister. She had become Mrs. Edwardes, and will be seen to hold a trust of deep interest to every American heart, inasmuch as it fell to her lot to inherit the priceless treasure, the portrait of Mary, mother of George Washington, painted by an artist named Middleton. At her death the painting passed into the possession of her unmarried daughter, Eleanor Edwardes.

The full-face portrait of Washington, and the Peter Stuyvesant army painting by Heath and Parke—the latter work since reproduced in most artistic manner by the Autotype Company of London—came out from England, and were loaned to the New York Historical Society, and exhibited by that body in the University of New York in April, 1854, under the announcement that, after a stay at Irving's home, "Sunnyside," "It is brought back to America for the inspection of the country's patriots." Strong feeling was at the time expressed that these works, so truly national, should be worthily engraved. Mr. Astor, Mr. Irving, and others offered to provide funds.

The *New York Albion*, of which Mr. Young was for some years editor and proprietor, described the full-face portrait in that then popular journal, but which no longer exists. Mr. Young was brother of George Frederick Young, a London merchant of high position, and who sat in Parliament during several sessions. He, together with Mr. Washington Irving, Mr. Astor, and others, took great interest in the pictures when brought back to America in 1853, and the following article, from Mr. Young's pen, appeared in the *New York Albion* at the time :—

"Members of the Historical Society, artists, and persons generally to whom the subject is attractive, are invited to call at the office of this journal, at any time during the next fortnight, for the purpose of examining a portrait of George Washington, which undoubtedly possesses high merit as a picture, and which there is abundant reason to infer was taken from the life.

Prior to the War of Independence, the mercantile house of Cary and Co., of London, acted as agents and correspondents of Washington, then an officer in the British service. Original letters from him to them, evidently not isolated, are before us as we write, forming as it were pendants to the likeness in question. These latter for many years hung over the mantelpiece in Mr. Cary's private office in London, and belonged recently to a Mr. Le Marchant, whose father was in the confidential employ of the firm, and from whom these particulars were obtained. Sharples was a relative of Mr. Cary, and came to the United States on a tour for the benefit of his health, bringing with him orders and commissions to paint numerous portraits of officers and gentlemen, for their families in England. The connection, therefore, between the subject, the painter, and the original owner of the picture is obvious enough. Whether this Mr. Sharples is identical with the Mr. Sharpless—two of whose crayon sketches of Washington were in the Washington Exhibition at the Art Union Rooms—we cannot pretend to determine. The slight variation in the mode of spelling the name is unimportant. Perhaps the fact that Mr. Sharples came hither expressly to execute commissions may account—in view of their identity—for his only leaving such slight souvenirs behind him. The head itself reminds one of Stuart's; but it has, we think, a *latent* fire in the eye which is wanting in the ordinary likenesses, and is on the whole more full of character. It is painted with great vigour and breadth, and cannot possibly be mistaken for a copy."

The interest evinced in these portraits by the late Lord Lyndhurst was the first moving cause of their being brought into prominence. Closely on their arrival in England, his lordship stated they would unquestionably be adopted as the typical portraits of the Washingtons. The pictures, would probably have dropped out of knowledge at Robert Cary's death, but for his admonitions. Lord Lyndhurst was an American citizen by birth, who through vast abilities raised himself to the dignity of Chancellor of England. His father, John Singleton Copley, was born in Boston in 1738, and went to England in 1776, where he knew Sharples. Copley was self-educated, and before leaving for England painted Washington. Copley acquired fame, and was elected a member of the Royal Academy. Lord Lyndhurst was in the habit of buying up portraits executed by his father. Through his father and Romney he knew Sharples and his portraits of the Washingtons well. Robert Cary apprised him of the arrival of the tattered fragments of Middleton's Mary Washington, and that "Bird had them in hand." He went to see "the wreck," and took interest in the restoration. Lord Lyndhurst continually visited at Cary's, bringing American friends to see the portraits. He always asserted that Middleton's presentment of Mary made her, "the grandest and most lovely woman I ever looked upon," and that "every lineament of Washington's countenance is seen and traced in that of his mother." He remarked to Robert Cary, "I know no other such instance." Lyndhurst was the greatest orator in the House of Peers, and held his mighty powers until past ninety years of age. When he brought Daniel Webster—a fellow majestic intellect, to see these portraits—he observed, "Mr. Cary has done more for America than any other man, in having been the means of securing to the world these portraits." On a later occasion, when Mary's portrait was with the others loaned to his lordship for the gratification of some American friends dining with him, he observed, "Americans will some day come by tens of thousands to look on that portrait of the most beautiful of all women."

WASHINGTON

CHAPTER II.

THE SHARPLES PORTRAITS BEFORE NEW YORK HISTORICAL SOCIETY.

New York Historical Society minutes record as to the portrait loaned in 1854—Secretary Warner details its reception before the Society—Letter of the venerable Dr. Van Pelt, who remembered Washington, and testifies to his portrait—Letter from Washington Irving, referring to its accuracy, and asking permission to engrave it for his contemplated " Life of Washington "—Letter from the Poets Bryant and Longfellow, expressing admiration of the portrait—Letters from Washington Irving urging purchase, and stating that money cost is guaranteed—Letter from Colden to Macready in England—Macready replies with full history of the portraits—Letter from Dickens and Thackeray.

THE exhibit of the full-face portrait before the Historical Society was thus officially recorded in the Transactions of that body.

" Historical Rooms,
University of the City of New York,
April 5, 1854.

The portrait of Washington, kindly permitted to be exhibited at a meeting of the Historical Society last evening, attracted much attention, and was much admired by the members, who expressed great satisfaction in being afforded the opportunity of seeing this valuable picture.

I thought it might be interesting to the possessors of this valuable picture, to extract from the minutes the remarks of Mr. Wetmore and the Rev. Dr. Van Pelt in alluding to the portrait.

I am, very respectfully yours,
ANDREW WARNER."

"At a stated meeting of the New York Historical Society, held in the Chapel of the University of the City of New York, on Tuesday evening, April 4th, 1854, Mr. Wetmore called attention to a portrait of Washington hanging over the President's chair, stating that it possessed intrinsic evidence of being an original painting, and had been pronounced as such by our most distinguished artists, familiar with all the well-known portraits of Washington. It was said to be superior to the world-renowned portrait by Stuart, and that until within a short time all knowledge of the Sharples portraits in oils was confined to such American tourists to England as carried letters to the owners. Its history is briefly this: Prior to the revolutionary war, the mercantile house of Robert Cary and Co., of London, it is well known, acted as agents and correspondents of Washington, then an officer in the British service. This portrait for many years hung over the mantelpiece in Mr. Cary's private office in London, and belonged recently to a Mr. Le Marchant, whose father was in the confidential employ of the firm. The portrait was painted by Mr. Sharples, a relative of Mr. Cary, who came to this country on a tour for the benefit of his health, bringing with him orders and commissions to paint numerous portraits of officers and gentlemen for their families in England. It has been very kindly permitted to be exhibited to the Society, to gratify those who feel interested in such an historical relic.

The venerable Rev. Dr. Van Pelt, who was present at this meeting of the New York Historical Society, said he had in his childhood the good fortune to spend some hours in the society of Washington, and after giving a detail of his appearance, he pronounced the portrait to be an excellent likeness of Washington as he remembered him.

(Extract from the minutes.)

ANDREW WARNER, *Recording Secretary.*"

The Rev. Dr. Van Pelt recorded as follows :—

"Hammond Street, New York City,
April 22, 1854.

In compliance with request, I have the honour now to transmit my opinion of the portrait of Washington, which was exhibited in our New York Historical Society, at a regular meeting held in the University, on the evening of the 4th April last.

It gives me pleasure to state that I had the satisfaction —I would add, the honour and happiness—in my youthful school-going days, after the war of the revolution, and previous to his inauguration as the first President of the United States, of seeing and spending part of a day in company with General George Washington, justly styled ' the Great and Good Man.'

He was indeed eminently so, in the various relations of domestic and public life, as also in his death.

Taught from my earliest childhood to cherish and estimate highly the patriotism, principles, virtues, and character of Washington, in common with my countrymen, and having the privilege, I approached near to him, got by the side of him—he putting his arm around my neck, embraced me close to him, and talked to me ; taking the buttons of his military coat between my fingers, and intent in looking at him, I observed distinctly the features of his face—his bland, dignified, majestic countenance ; his erect, tall, towering person ; his graceful movements and amiable demeanour—so as even at present, in my advanced age, to perpetuate the knowledge, and leave in my mind and memory the impress of the contour of his face, his grave look, and stately appearance. Accordingly, in beholding the portrait as suspended in view of the members of the New York Historical Society, I pronounced it then, as I do now, an interesting picture of our immortal Washington, who, we are pleased to say, was 'First in war, first in peace, and first in the hearts of his countrymen;' and that it is, according to my remembrance, a faithful, excellent, lifelike likeness of the Great Living Original, worthy to be carefully preserved, and highly valued.

With best wishes, respectfully yours,
P. J. VAN PELT, D.D."

After seeing the portrait, Washington Irving thus wrote of it:—

"Sunnyside, April 13, 1854.

I have seen the portrait of Washington by Sharples. There is much more of life and animation than in that by Stuart, but the latter has more calm dignity. I should think it was taken several years previously, probably during the war, when Washington was leading a life of personal activity and mental excitement.

The mouth is different from that by Stuart, and approaches more to the natural shape of that taken of him when he was forty years of age, by Peale. A set of artificial teeth, which I believe he did not wear until after the revolutionary war, altered the shape of his mouth, drew it down at the corners, and lengthened the upper lip.

The Sharples portrait gives a better idea of the innate energy of his character; which, after he laid by the sword and assumed the toga, may have been somewhat veiled by the sober decorums and restraint of official station.

I think the portrait a very valuable one, and should like very much to have the privilege of having it engraved for the Life of Washington, should I ever complete and publish that work, which the booksellers have so often announced without my authority, and even before the plan of it had been turned in my mind.

I am, my dear sir, with high respect,
Your obliged and humble servant,
WASHINGTON IRVING."

The poet Bryant also bore testimony thus:—

"New York, April 26, 1854.

I have seen the picture of Washington by Sharples. It is a fine picture and most interesting, inasmuch as it represents Washington in the vigour of manhood, some years before Stuart's portrait of him was taken. The countenance expresses thought, resolution, sensibility, and a high degree of physical energy.

I regard the discovery of the picture as an event of great importance. W. C. BRYANT."

Two years later Longfellow wrote appreciatively thus:—

"Cambridge, September 22, 1856.

I have just returned from a long visit to the seaside, and find your friendly letter and the Sharples portraits (small photos had been sent to Mr. Longfellow), and hasten to thank you for them, and to explain why I have not done so sooner.

These portraits are very beautiful and very valuable. They are treasures which I highly prize, and which I shall guard with jealous care; and, as you request, will ever respect your interests, and on no pretence allow them to go out of my house.

If there was an artist here equal to the one who took the copies of the Sharples pictures, you should have one of me in the same style. But alas! that is not the case, and I shrink from subjecting myself to the process of Daguerre.

With greatest regard, yours faithfully,
HENRY W. LONGFELLOW."

Efforts were about this time made to purchase this portrait and hold it in America, but, as hereafter explained, a sale could not then be made. The Cary family had been advised to put the portraits in settlement, which tied them up for a time. Washington Irving thus urged the matter to P. M. Wetmore and Cadwallader Colden at the time :—

"Sunnyside, April 13, 1854.

DEAR MR. WETMORE,—I wish you would convey to the members of the Historical Society that Mr. Bryant and myself are equally anxious with them and others that these portraits and the Stuyvesant picture should not again leave the country. What, however, is there to do that has not been done?

Mr. Astor unavailingly stood forward as money sponsor, so that any idea of lack of funds being a difficulty is utterly erroneous. The owning family are described by Dr. Beale as ' English gentlefolks ;' and we can only hope that when the time comes for any disposal of the pictures, the spirit of that class may be evidenced.

I coveted having the portraits engraved for my purposed Life, but see clearly no such permission could be given.

Respectfully, your humble servant,
WASHINGTON IRVING.

P. M. Wetmore, Esq."

Irving also addressed Mr. Cadwallader Colden, a prominent citizen of New York :—

"MY DEAR COLDEN,—It is indeed matter for national regret that the Sharples Washington portrait cannot be allowed to rest in America. The Historical Society took it up in a very earnest way, and Dr. Beale, President of St. George's Society, helped all he could ; but as explained to Mr. Astor and Mr. Wetmore, the pictures cannot be sold for many years.

Mr. Astor generously offered to be security in a large sum for the three portraits and the Stuyvesant Army Procession, or to deposit a sum to accumulate until a sale could be made; but Mr. Astor's counsel advised that unless a price could *now* be agreed upon, any such course would be increasing the difficulty when the occasion may arise for the portraits' return to America.

James K. Armstrong, on behalf of Mr. Astor, has done his utmost. Bryant, too, and Mr. Charles Leupp and myself concur that the owning family have done all in their power to meet our wishes for the pictures to be owned on this side. All that we can hope for is that at some distant day this yearning of all patriots may be realized.

My dear Colden, with high respect,
Your faithful, humble servant,
WASHINGTON IRVING.

Cadwallader Colden, Esq.,
President, Cambrian Society."

Cadwallader Colden with like object thus addressed his friend Macready, the great tragedian, in 1856:—

"MY DEAR MACREADY,—Washington Irving, through Mr. Armstrong, has been told of the much trouble you have taken in seeing what chance exists for any negotiating the purchase of the Sharples portraits of the Washingtons. You will understand Mr. Armstrong's prominence in it when I name to you that he is one of the Astor Executors, and gives care to the family property affairs; he is also a warm friend of Irving. Both Mr. Astor and Mr. Aspinwall feared the difficulty could not at the moment be overcome; but it is pleasant to learn that some years hence their possession and transference to this country, their only becoming home, is by no means an impossibility.

You must have had several journeys on behalf of this mission. I will not call it a fruitless one, as it has made us acquainted with the obstructions, and, at the same time, the more than probability of the paintings being placed at this country's disposal at no very distant future. We are all much indebted to you, and I need not express the satisfaction we shall have in any definite arrangement for your many friends being honoured, educated, and delighted by your again holding its stage. Charles Leupp desires me to join his affectionate greeting with mine.

Ever your friend,
DAVID C. COLDEN.

W. C. Macready, London."

Macready's deeply interesting reply was as follows :—

"MY DEAR COLDEN,—Our dinner to Thackeray, at the London Tavern, on his departure to you, was in every sense a superb affair, worthy of the guest. It did me good to be of the party, and make the trial of drawing myself out of my crushing sorrows. I had a quarter of an hour's talk with him before the company assembled, and used the occasion to explain my efforts to get hold of the Sharples' Washington portraits. Thackeray will tell you they are owned by a friend of Charles Dickens, on the Cheshire side of the Mersey at Liverpool. Stanfield, Maclise, and myself were introduced by Dickens, and have all seen the pictures. Maclise says they are above mediocrity, and as is often the case, men of Sharples' capacity seize a likeness more effectually than a really great painter. None of us have been able to trace many portraits by this said Sharples; there are, however, some known to Dilke of the *Athenæum*, and Jerdan of the *Literary Gazette*, a great authority, and who, writing me, says 'he is known chiefly through his portraits of Washington and his wife, and also for a lot of oil sketches of noted American women of the Washington Court, some of whom were thorns in Martha's side. These sketches were brought home to England by Sharples' widow, and though evidencing great ability, are little more than indications for designed portraits. It would seem that he "rubbed" these on the canvases as a speculation, hoping some day for orders to complete. The story told by the widow is that all were to have been worked up in their turn, but Lady Washington resolutely set her face against the whole lot, and that her husband had been most liberally rewarded in a money acknowledgment from the General, to whom he had given an assurance that he would not carry them any farther.'

So says Jerdan, but we must remember he is a bit of a scandalmonger, especially in the case of so great a man. One of these outlines, said to be the portrait of General Hamilton's wife, and another believed to be the wife of 'The Patroon' of Albany, have since been worked up by Maclise, and more lovely women it would be difficult to dream of. If the beauties revolving in Washington Court, at Philadelphia and Mount Vernon, were as charming as Mrs. Hamilton and this said 'Patroon's' wife are represented, there should be no cause for wonder at the fascination power of the since female generations of America.

Wentworth Dilke, who was associated with Charles Dickens in starting the *Daily News*, has taken especial interest in hunting up memorials of Sharples, but so far all he has told me is that 'he was a quiet gentleman, well conducted, a Jesuit who sought not fame, and known chiefly through his very effective portraits of the Washingtons, also an admirable portrait of Priestley, painted in Philadelphia a year or two prior to his death. That his wife had brought to England unfinished portraits of Jefferson, the two Presidents, Adams and Madison, also of Hamilton and his lovely wife, and portraits of Robert Fulton and his wife, all outlined by him, but never completed.' Charles

Knight says he knows of several heads by Sharples, and that they evidence an artist of high merit in portraiture, though possibly unknown outside the walk of private connection.

Dickens has talked with Christy, the great auctioneer in art, about him, and learns that 'he painted very real portraits, in their day esteemed powerful, so far as resemblance to life was concerned; but inasmuch as that period was rich to an extraordinary degree in portrait artists, none but names of highest gifts came to the fore. A time that boasts of Gainsborough, Reynolds, Romney, Opie, Lawrence, and such like, dropped lesser stars; though to have been even an average man of such a day was to be an artist of more than capability, although possibly not ranking as a genius.'

Stanfield and Maclise agree as to the portraits having at Mr. Cary's death suffered a good deal from storage in a lumber-room; careful restoration has remedied this, and made them far better than Sharples left them. Young, Wallack, and Power have seen them. Wallack is more than a mere amateur in art, and he says, 'They are the portraits history will hold to!'

I would gladly have been of more help. I have made several journeys to Liverpool, but without succeeding. It is, however, satisfactory to know they are in safe keeping, and, as Washington Irving expresses it, 'they will come home some day or another.' Mrs. Hemans was charmed with all three.

Emmett seems labouring under the feeling that more may have been done. My chief and uppermost vexation is that Irving should be frustrated in his wish to have them engraved for his Life of Washington. Here is real sorrow, but it cannot be avoided.

How odd it is that these coveted pictures should be so

much identified with actors! Booth, when first playing at Covent Garden in 1817, visited Mr. Cary, and knew the portraits well, as also did Charles Kean and the Kembles. Sharples cultivated the friendship of stage professionals, and owned David Garrick's copy of Rowe's first edition of Shakespeare in six volumes, published in 1609 and the first biography. It was inscribed in Garrick's own hand, and he was very proud of its possession. John Kemble and Mrs. Siddons often brought friends to Mr. Cary in order to see the portraits, and always spoke of Washington as 'the Great Star of our Firmament.'

I lead a very quiet evening life here, sticking to old classic writers, and revelling more than ever in the great master whose words we have so feebly endeavoured to illustrate. Thackeray is charged with an infinity of messages.

Ever yours sincerely,
W. C. MACREADY."

Of eminent actors of our own time, Edwin Booth, Lawrence Barrett, Joseph Jefferson, Genevieve Ward, and Mrs. John Drew have been warm adherents. Henry Irving, of England, is also numbered among those adopting the creed of their sure recognition as the true national presentment. The veteran manager, McVicear, presented autotype copies to the Chicago Historical Society and other public institutions. One and all have patriotically presented the autotype reproductions to public schools in unison with the wish expressed by the poet Longfellow.

Dickens wrote, " I have had much pleasure in securing the good offices of Maclise, though the being successful is more due to Stanfield than my efforts. Certainly he has made pictures out of Sharples' sketches of American women of Washington's time, remarkable for their beauty and grace.

Maclise has been interested in these charming subjects, and he certainly has done wonders with them. I did not see them until months after he had taken them in hand. He calls them his 'American blazing beauties.' As to the Sharples portraits of Washington and his wife. When in Boston I saw the portraits by Stuart, so also others most in favour with American friends. None, however, excepting the Sharples, convey to my mind his capacity, benignity, dignity, or grace. These portraits are unknown in America, but when the people see them and are left to judge for themselves, they are safe to accept the Sharples as their national portrait. They care not as to the nationality of the artist, what they want is reality. When Washington was in the flesh his country had just secured its national independence. Art was comparatively unknown, and it is fortunate there are existing such presentments of the nation's founder; equally satisfactory is it they have until now remained in England. They would have been kiln-dried by 'furnace' power had they re-crossed the Atlantic. In good time the Americans will learn that the unnatural dry heat of their stoves in winter is wholly destructive of all paintings as of the fair countenances of their lovely women. Such portraits as those Washingtons are the charge of the whole human race, and should be cared for as the heritage of future ages. They should be placed out of the power of injury by fire or heat. A few winter seasons in an American private house would finish them and render them the utter wrecks others have already become.

"CHARLES DICKENS."

Thackeray also expressed himself :—

"I have only seen engravings of the Stuart portrait. It can never rank with the Sharples. It has too much austerity, and is wanting in life.

"W. M. THACKERAY."

CHAPTER III.

The three portraits return to New York in 1882, and are received at Century and Union League Clubs—David Huntington, Eastman Johnson, J. G. A. Ward, and Launt Thompson certify to their authenticity—The historian Dunlap and his account of the pictures—The New York Evening Post *commends them to public notice—Ralph Waldo Emerson testifies and names Middleton's portrait of Mary Washington, to see which his efforts when in England were ineffectual—Letters from Nathaniel Hawthorne, Elihu Burritt and Albert Gallatin—Speech of Daniel Webster on the portraits.*

THE deep interest excited in 1854 by the exhibition in New York of the first portrait, the full-face, and which, after remaining nearly two years in America, had been returned to England, rather increased than otherwise the general enthusiasm in the subject. Numerous applicants were ever afterwards seeking the owners in order to get a sight of it. This one picture had become free for disposal had it been desired; the other, the profile, and also that of Martha Washington, were not free for disposal until 1882, when all three were brought out to America. The three paintings, and also the Peter Stuyvesant, had been reproduced by the Autotype Company in London, and to meet the public wish these autotypes were offered for sale by subscription. On the three pictures arriving in New York, the first to welcome them was the Century Club, to which they were formally introduced by Charles Loring Brace,

E

one whose works of philanthropy are known throughout the world. David Huntington, President of the National Academy of Design; Eastman Johnson, the eminent portrait painter; J. G. A. Ward and Launt Thompson, the most gifted sculptors of the day, received them with great honour. All the leading artists of the city visited them during their few days rest at the Century. The members of the great publishing firm of Harpers were early to view them; so also among the first arrivals was the accomplished scholar and true gentleman, Charles Scribner, the eminent publisher.

After leaving the Century Club, the following official announcement appeared. The document was kindly volunteered by the distinguished artists whose signatures are appended. Such a document tells its own tale.

"In order for these portraits being exhibited to the American nation in becoming form, the eminent portrait painters and sculptors whose names are appended (than whom none higher could be cited) speak authoritatively as to the originality and authenticity of these historical works:—

'New York, April 12, 1882.

The Sharples portraits of Washington, a full-face picture and a profile, and that of Lady Washington, all three painted in oils and exhibited for several months in New York during 1882, bear every evidence of having been painted from the life. The full-face portrait was exhibited before the Historical Society of New York in 1854. The authenticity of these paintings has never been questioned by artists or others competent to form correct judgment.

(Signed)   D. HUNTINGTON,
President of the National Academy of Design.
EASTMAN JOHNSON.
J. G. A. WARD.
LAUNT THOMPSON.'"

From the Century Club, the three honoured paintings made a progress by special invitation to the Union League Club, where a Gallery Room had been set apart for their sole reception, the Peter Stuyvesant picture accompanying them. On arrival at these stately quarters they were formally and reverently received by S. P. Avery, Trustee of the New York National Museum, Eastman Johnson, and W. C. Riddle on behalf of the Club; Eastman Johnson decorating them with his own deft hands in festoons of maroon cloth hangings, and with a refinement of taste peculiarly his own. John Joseph Harper, and each member of the Harper house, and J. W. Parsons, the talented head of the Fine Art Department in Harper's vast establishment, paid them visits of honour and admiration, and at times the gallery of their abode was crowded with visitors.

During the time the portraits of Washington and his wife Martha were on exhibition in the Gallery of the Union League Club, the *New York Tribune* thus addressed itself to the subjects, their history, and the life of the artist who executed them:—

"Although there is a difference in the spelling of the name, we believe there is no reason to doubt that the Sharples who painted these portraits is the James Sharpless of whom our homespun Vasari William Dunlap gives so good an account in his 'History of the Arts of Design in America.' Dunlap tells us that James Sharpless 'was an Englishman, and being of a Roman Catholic family, was educated in France, and intended, like John Kemble, for the priesthood; but, like John, he preferred the fine arts. He married before coming to this country, and on the first attempt at passage was taken prisoner by the French, and with his wife and three children was carried to France, and there kept a prisoner for some months. When liberated, he made a more successful effort, and landed in New York about 1798. He visited all the cities and towns of the United States, carrying letters to persons distinguished, either military, civil or literary, with a request of painting their portraits for his collection. This being granted, and the portrait finished in about two hours, the likeness generally induced an order for a copy, and brought as sitters all who saw it. His price for the profile was fifteen dollars, and for the full-face, never so good, twenty dollars. He painted immense numbers, and most of them very valuable for characteristic portraiture. His headquarters was New York, and he generally travelled in a four-wheeled carriage of his own contrivance, which carried the whole family and all his implements, and was drawn by one large horse. He was a plain, well-disposed man, and accumulated property by honest industry and uncommon facility with his materials. Mr. Sharpless was a man of science and a mechanician as well as a painter.

In the first volume of the Hosack and Francis "Medical and Philosophical Register" will be found a paper on steam carriages, confirming this character. Mr. Sharpless had acquired property without meanness, and looked to the enjoyment of easy circumstances in old age, when he died suddenly at the age of sixty, in New York, of an ossification of the heart, and was buried in the cemetery of the Roman Catholic chapel in Barclay Street. His widow, her daughter and youngest son returned to England, and long resided near Bath, after selling the distinguished heads, among which I had the honour to be numbered, at public auction. The two sons, James and Felix, both practised their father's art in America. Felix resided and died in North Carolina.' Dunlap, vol. ii. pp. 71, 72.

Dunlap's account of Sharpless runs nearly parallel with that given by the owners of the portraits. The chief discrepancy, indeed the only serious one, between the two accounts is in the date of the artist's first visit to this country. The owners say 1794, and Dunlap says 1798, four years later, and only one year before the death of Washington. Further, the owners say that Sharples paid us a second visit in 1809, and that he died February 26th, 1811. Dunlap was a careless writer, and we believe is not much depended on for accuracy in details. The account given by the owners of the portraits seems to be founded on a better knowledge of the subject, and to be entitled to confidence. The difference in the spelling of the name is not of much importance. In America we are more precise and literal in our pronunciation of proper names and of words in general than the English. The impossible old story of the American who asked if Lord Chol-mon-de-ly (pronounced Chumley, and not in all syllables, as our countryman gave it) was at home, and was told by the porter that he was not, but that some of his pe-o-ple were, will illustrate the point. When Sharples was here, we perhaps read his name Sharpless, and then wrote it so—a process going on before our eyes on business signs all over the city. Dunlap does not tell us why Sharples came to this country, but the owners of the portraits give the object of his journey, that he came for the benefit of his health, and that being a friend of Mr. Cary, of the house of Cary and Co., merchants, of London, who before the War of Independence acted as agents and correspondents of Washington, then an officer in the British service, he was well provided with orders and commissions to paint portraits of officers and gentlemen for their families left at home."

The public journals of New York expressed the general gratification of the citizens at the opportunity of seeing the pictures. To reproduce the sentiments of a few is to make known the feeling of all. Take for example the following:—

(From the New York Evening Post.)

"Probably the fact of the existence of the Sharples pictures will be a surprise to most Americans of the present generation, but for many years past those best acquainted with the portraiture of the Father of his Country have either seen the works themselves or have otherwise known that in an English home were carefully preserved original profile and full-face portraits of General Washington, and one of Lady Washington, painted from life in oils, by Sharples, of which numerous crayon drawings extant by the same artist are reduced copies.

Apart from their immense value as portraiture, the works are interesting examples of painting—excellent in modelling and colour, indubitably life-like, most solid and clear in painting, and with really beautiful management of shadow, especially in the profiles. The full-face portrait is in military dress, and in the features is some corresponding elevation of expression—the majesty and high dignity of the accepted type. The profile of Washington, in plain clothes, is simpler, less glorified, and thereby strangely attractive. Mrs. Washington is quietly and gravely clad, in sweet matronly fashion, her dress minutely and delightfully given."

(From the New York Tribune.)

"As everything connected with the early history of the arts in this country is of interest to our people, these Sharples pictures, historically, must be reckoned of inestimable value. As paintings, too, they have been enthusiastically received by such judges as Mr. Daniel Huntington, President of the American Academy of Design, and Mr. Eastman Johnson and other leading artists. To our own apprehension it would seem that the difference between these portraits of Washington and the one in the Boston Museum of Fine Arts—a difference plain to every one, and so great as to have misled, apparently, both Mr. Irving and Mr. Bryant in judging of the time when they were painted—is owing merely to the difference in the character of the artists. The Sharples portraits are painted by a man in whom the mechanical, the technical, part of his art had always the upper hand. They are neatly, carefully painted. Dunlap's opinion that the full-face portraits by Sharples were never so good as his profiles, is not, to our mind, borne out by the present pictures. The profile of Mrs. Washington is certainly very clearly and even beautifully painted, and we are so glad to have it that we hardly wish to own to ourselves that it is wanting in life. It has exactly the immobility that is found in some of the early Italian portraits of the Umbrian and Florentine schools. All objections apart, what would we not give for such a portrait of Washington's mother? This calm, sensible, intelligent face, in which kindliness and firmness are equally conjoined, gives us a much more satisfactory notion of the wife of Washington than the Boston portrait.

The full-face portrait is an alert, characteristic head, and gives us an entirely different side of Washington from the one represented in Stuart's picture. As we have said, it seems to us to be painted in a different manner, too, from what we find in the profile. We cannot better express our own judgment of the picture as a portrait than by repeating the well-chosen words of Bryant: 'The countenance expresses thought, resolution, sensibility, and a high degree of physical energy.'"

(From the Independent.)

"The Sharples portraits of Washington and his wife prove more and more attractive as the effectiveness of their autotype duplicates becomes more known and their truthfulness realized. Our people need time to accustom themselves to the difference between the Stuart and other old familiar portraits, and the Sharples new revelation. True it is that they have always been known to certain of our literary visitors to England, and the reduced copies executed by Sharples himself, during his several stays in America, have been generally familiar; yet these oil paintings, first exhibited in New York in 1854, and now again allowed to gratify all patriots, seem to come upon us as a delight and surprise. We tenaciously pin our faith on Stuart and Peale, but, nevertheless, confess great allegiance to Sharples. Some of our ablest critics affirm that as time progresses future generations will adopt the rendering of Sharples as certainly that most to be desired. Few will deny but that these heads of the Father of the Country must win their way to all hearts. Everybody sees reality in them, and the truest evidence of their being painted from the life is their speaking vitality and vigour. Washington, doubtless, gave more actual sittings for these portraits than for any others, and the testimony of Mr. Custis, Mrs. Washington's son, in these emphatic words, 'The family always regarded the Sharples portraits as by far the best and truest representations,' is decisive. No other painter succeeded in giving us his calm dignity in union with his known determination and vigour of mind. Sharples gives us the Military Chieftain, the Patriot, the Statesman, the benign Christian Gentleman, all combined. Boston now for a short time receives these pictures, and will, doubtless, take up more than its proportion of the autotypes."

(From the New York Times.)

"The exhibition of the historic Sharples portraits of George and Martha Washington has been enjoyed by a great many persons of intelligence and artistic tastes. These remarkable portraits have remained the property of English owners ever since the time of their execution. Washington Irving, John Jacob Astor, and others endeavoured to purchase them, but succeeded only in having them brought to this country for a few months in 1854, at which time they were exhibited under the auspices of the New York Historical Society. The intrinsic merit of these portraits is obvious to any intelligent beholder. Irving held them in very high esteem, and in a letter now in existence, George W. P. Custis, Washington's adopted son, says: 'The Sharples portraits are the most truthful likenesses of Washington ever taken.' There are two pictures of Washington, one a full portrait and the other a profile, and naturally there is a great diversity of opinions as to the relative merits of the two. Painters and art connoisseurs seem to incline to the profile, possibly because no other original portrait of the kind is known to have existed. Comparisons between the Sharples and Stuart portraits of Washington are very favourable to the former. The portrait of Martha Washington is a superb and ideal picture of that revered lady. Artists and critics have, with scarcely an exception, expressed the warmest admiration for it."

The tone of the public press universally accorded with that of the many of America's greatest statesmen, poets, and literates who have from time to time visited these portraits in their home in England. Among the number have been Albert Gallatin, Daniel Webster, Washington Irving, Bryant, Longfellow, Ralph Waldo Emerson, and numerous others. The nation's essayist thus referred to what he styled "these great national paintings:"—

"I would willingly have crossed the Atlantic, if only to look on these portraits so priceless to our people. They are, indeed, our true Washingtons. Future ages will glory in their existence. There are those who assert that 'veneration' is quitting our national character, fickleness taking its place. If so, it is difficult of explanation, save through the frequent changes of government. Of this we may be certain, that whatever occasional aberrations may be manifested, the loyal and good of our people will never swerve in their devotion to him who must ever be the cornerstone of our fabric, and whose star will burn more and more resplendent as ages develop.

It has not fallen to my lot to get a look at the portrait of Washington's mother, and which I believe is a fine picture. I had always been under the belief that it was painted by Sharples, and owned by the same family as possess the portraits of our first President and his wife. Such is not the case. The portrait of the mother of Washington, though some eighty years ago owned by the same branch of the Cary family as possessed the Sharples portraits, has since passed away to a younger branch, and I have been unable to trace it. There is, however, no doubt as to its existence. Many of our people who know the owning family get access to its abode, which I hear is in Northamptonshire. Washington's mother's portrait, painted by an English officer named Middleton, must not be mixed up with the American female beauties outlined by Sharples, and, so far as four or five are concerned, finished by the eminent English painter, Maclise, and which are in the family here owning the Sharples Washington portraits.

These portraits must some day return to us. Well will it be for our women to see and know Martha Washington in the faithfulness she is rendered by Sharples, to realize that housewifery is a great duty, and that in her day it was deemed as creditable for women to spin and weave, as it was in the days of King Solomon, who in the Book of Proverbs describes an honourable woman: 'She layeth her hands to the spindle, and her hands hold the distaff.' 'She looketh well to the ways of her household, and eateth not the bread of idleness.' Or in the days when Homer made the use of the distaff and loom the employment of royal women :—

'Aleandra, consort of his high command,
A golden distaff gave to Helen's hand;
And that rich vase, with living sculpture wrought,
Which, heaped with wool, the beauteous Philo brought,
The silken fleece, impurpled for the loom,
Recalled the hyacinth in vernal bloom.'"

Nathaniel Hawthorne has written of them to General Cass, in 1854 :—

"My dear General Cass,—Thanks to Ticknor, I have had a long two hours with Sharples' beautiful portraits of Washington and Martha, in the quiet home where they live, seemingly as fresh as in the year of their execution at Mount Vernon. No wonder at Irving's entrancement, even under the distracting thought of such treasures being lost to their own country, their only fitting home. Our Boston Stuarts lose much of their charm when contrasted with these realistic, though possibly less artistic canvases. No man or woman ever had such China rose cheeks as Stuart bestowed on George and Martha. Such high colouring is outrageous. Sharples may not have been a great painter, and he seems only to have been known in England through his American work, but our people will bless the memory of Mr. Cary, who sent him out to paint Washington; and unborn generations will render him homage, for he has bequeathed them by far the best portrait of him whose fame and patriotism must fill the whole world to the dwarfing every of the greatest characters in history. At Sharples' death his wife carried to England numerous outline and unfinished canvases of lovely women, most of whom he met at Mount Vernon, at balls in Philadelphia, at the Patroon van Ransalaer's at Albany, and Chief Justices Marshall and Kent. Mean, censorious scandal-mongers have hinted at their frequent presence as the reverse of agreeable to Martha, but beauty ofttimes outlives envy. A lot of these canvas indications were brought to England by Sharples' wife at his death. Some are skeletons of portraits, others more advanced, but all much eaten by cockroaches during the long sea voyage, and when lying unclaimed in the English Custom House. These heads should be finished by a capable artist, as there is in many of them sufficient for facial perfectitude. Some display great loveliness, and all evidence that infinitude of womanly beauty and force of character marking the dames most in vogue at the Court of Mount Vernon. The President clearly appreciated good looks, and Martha herself had an eye in the right vein, evidenced in the noble stature and bearing of her husband."

Elihu Burritt, the philanthropist and apostle of peace, formerly Consul at Birmingham, and known as the "American blacksmith," author of "The Mission of Great Sufferings," "Visits to the Black Country," and other works on English country life, worshipping at the shrine of these portraits, thus recorded his impressions:—

"A helpful and most kind introduction from Lord Sandon has given me the happiness and great privilege of an entire week in the cultured home at New Brighton, Cheshire, where dwells the accomplished owner of the Sharples famed portraits of Washington. Near, indeed, are these to the heart of every American who has seen these inestimable works. I failed not in an almost unbroken audience during my stay. I felt, as it were, spellbound to the dining-room in which they hang, apparently searching all visitors with inquisitive glance as to whether of the new nationality away over the seas. It is beyond me to describe what I felt in the, to me, living presence of him whose fame is as wide as the world, and into whose form and presence God breathed the breath of an utterly unselfish public and private life. The words of Fox, uttered in the British Parliament in 1794, that 'he was wiser in his own policy than the ministers of his own country, or of any of the European Courts, and, as the illustrious man deriving honour less from the splendour of his situation than from the dignity of his mind, before whom all borrowed greatness sinks into insignificance, and all the potentates of Europe become little and contemptible,' —rose to memory, as did the burning exultation of Erskine only a year later, in a letter to Washington, yielding, if possible, a greater tribute to his august and immortal name. ' I have,' wrote Erskine, 'a large acquaintance among the most valuable and exalted classes of men; but you are the only human being for whom I ever felt an awful reverence. I sincerely pray God to grant a long and serene evening to a life so gloriously devoted to the universal happiness of the world.'

Before seeing these Sharples' creations, my imagination dwelt only on the Stuart portraits, the delight of my childhood, and cause of more than one pilgrimage to Boston in later life. But the Sharples haunt my memory as the Boston pictures never can again. The Sharples are more convincingly real, undoubtedly much more majestic. If, as some critics assume, the artist had not the technical skill, he clearly had a higher power of impressing than our Stuart; and yet, withal, they decidedly confirm the Boston portraits. Stuart's unnaturally high colouring evidences that the artist was indulging in a freak of fancy, whereas the Englishman was matter of fact, and yet thoroughly held in hand all the embodied dignified mien and greatness of his illustrious sitter. There is a grandness in the Sharples, a satisfaction in full, not to be found in the work of any of the artists who tried their hands on the Founder of the Republic.

Colonel Trumbull, himself an artist, and who may possibly have seen the portraits during execution at Mount Vernon, acknowledged their great superiority, and looked on their transfer to England as a calamity. Trumbull endeavoured to persuade Lady Washington to appeal to Mr. Cary for duplicates. Her refusal is explained in the very natural desire not to lower the originals in his estimate; her own portrait being a souvenir from herself. Sharples had returned to England; access to his original productions would be opportune. The money cost was collected; but Martha remained inexorable, and Mr. Cary may have been indisposed to gratify 'rebels.'

During my more than pleasant week's housing and constant associateship with these our should-be national belongings, I always felt they looked upon me as Columbia hailing, and as imploringly declarative of captivity. It should not, therefore, occasion surprise that Washington Irving, Bryant, Longfellow, Fenimore Cooper, Hawthorne, Emerson, Wendel Holmes, Ward Beecher, and others of our poets and literature-makers have, one and all, felt their delight tinctured with sorrow when face to face with these inestimable treasures. The truth that they are away from home, is a sad reality forced on every American heart. And yet how deeply grateful should the whole world (for Washington in all times will be its foremost and greatest character) be for the existence of these canvases, which the climate of England has retained in perfect health and freshness. There is thorough honest work and absence of art tricks in all three of the portraits. Sharples felt the greatness of his subject. He did his best, and it was more than a good best. As to Martha, in her simple home garb, she is what she wished to be, and what she was, a pattern to American women in all time. If ever they get back to their native land, it will be well if like care befall them; above all, let no ' demon stove ' be tolerated to dry up their blood."

When on his last mission to London in 1827-28, and which resulted in his obtaining full indemnification to American Southern citizens for injuries sustained in the violation of the Treaty of Ghent, Albert Gallatin tried to get permission for copies to be made, evidenced by the following letter to his friend King, who was, at the time, head of Columbia College, New York. Gallatin was President of the New York Historical Society.

" MY DEAR KING,—I have twice seen the portraits of Washington by Sharples. Mr. Cary, the owner, is most kind in allowing all Americans access to them. His deceased brother acted as Washington's agent, and esteemed him to a degree amounting to hero-worship. It is believed that Washington's English confidential relations were in Cary's keeping, and that he rendered him great political service in Europe, hence the more than friendship. He it was who traced treachery to its source, Cary getting hold of private letters written by General Gates and others to Genet.

It is clear to my mind that Martha Washington designed these portraits for British possession, and that she had a hand in Sharples being sent out to paint them. There never has been the smallest chance of their return to America, and my firm belief is that Martha quietly but determinedly opposed the proposal for copies being made.

What a glory for our New York Historical Society if we could persuade the present representative, Cary, to allow it to have copies. I am trying my best, but you had better not name this at any meeting.

My dear King, sincerely yours,
ALBERT GALLATIN."

No higher homage can be rendered the Sharples portraits than that bestowed by the most eminent of American statesmen, he whose greatness is so interwoven with the nation's dignity, and the occasion of whose death seemed as if some grand governing member of a system were stricken from its orbit, leaving emptiness and confusion where before was fulness of strength and controlling power. In the character of Daniel Webster's mind, few statesmen whom the world has seen could be regarded as of his type ; but an intellect like his, Milton's mighty hand has dragged into council when he says :—

> " With grave
> Aspect he rose ; and in his rising seemed
> A Pillar of State. Deep on his front engraven
> Deliberation sate, and publick care ;
> And princely counsel in his visage shone
> Majestic * * * * * sage he stood,
> With Atlantean shoulders fit to bear
> The weight of empires ; and his look
> Drew audience and attention still as night
> Or summer's noontide air."

Webster visited England in 1839. Speaking at a dinner of the Royal Agricultural Society, the illustrious orator said:—

"I have seen your great farms, the noble stock they breed and rear. I have seen England's rural life, and learned to love it. In America we want more beauty about our homes, and more real love for the country. I shall return overwhelmed at the deficiencies of memory to retail the impress of the many thousands of delightful localities of England. My mind is crowded out with the recollection of the places sacred to Liberty. Dear Old London! Its quaint Tower and surroundings, its history! Westminster Abbey is overwhelming—not only for what it is, but for what it is not. Smithfield, too, is full of glory. If ever Jacob's ladder rested upon earth, it was there, where bloody Mary made it the gate of heaven for so many martyrs. Bunhill Fields, I was too good a Puritan not to go there. I wanted to stand where Bunyan, Owen, Goodwin, and Defoe were buried. A visit to England is an education for youth; it furnishes matter for thought in future life, and teaches what so few understand, how to grow old decently. An ignorant, uncultivated old man is a poor affair; the tailor can pad out his wasted form, but nothing except early acquirements and good sentiments can make fine old age. In England our young people see attention paid to age and position; nowhere can the proprieties of life be so well learned. I trust England will graft on youthful visitants from America a little of its people's veneration.

It has been my privilege to visit a peaceful home where lives, in canvas life delineation, the man whose purity and greatness must fill the universe until the world shall be no more. Washington is there—and to the life—through the power of the painter Sharples. I have visited the shrine with a batch of youngsters; all are better for the pilgrimage."

WIFE OF GENERAL HAMILTON.
NÉE SCHUYLER.

Reproduced by the Autotype Company, London   From the original Oil Painting by Jarvi

CHAPTER IV.

Cary and Co., London, Washington's agents—Robert Cary more than a friend—Washington's fondness for English tripe—Letter from Washington expressing his own and Mrs. Washington's feeling in regard to the portraits, and as not favouring their being duplicated—Sharples formally introduced to Washington in Philadelphia by English Minister—Stays with the younger Franklin—Washington's great kindness—Introduced to Hamilton, who becomes his patron and friend—Emerson's efforts to see the portrait of Mary Washington duplicated—Artist life in New York—Voyage up the Hudson in 1809.

THE origin and growth of the more than friendship between Cary and Washington has been shown; how when Washington was serving as an English officer, Cary became his agent in London, his firm holding from many officers and their families, commissions of like kind. It is in no way strange that, out of business transactions of mutual dependence, friendships sprung up between the parties, having the ultimate effect of merging the mere mercantile agency duties with ties of closest family association and confidence. Sharing the lot of other illustrious men, the world's great patriot had secret enemies, puny as they were. Cary, as the friend of Burke, and enjoying the confidence of public men in Europe, laid bare their machinations.

Old Custom House records show that Cary and Co. received produce from over twenty families, many of them English officers who had relinquished their military callings, and in numerous instances had laid hold of the plough instead.

Others had adopted mercantile pursuits, as in the case of Barclay and Co., of New York, one of the oldest firms thus originally springing out of soldier origin. Mr. Barclay had held an officer's commission, and at the time there was quite a number of gentlemen sitting at the desk in " counting-houses "—offices had not then obtained admission into the vernacular of New York—and who, from varying causes, and under specially occurring opportunities, had with honour melted down their swords. The English War Office regulations did not then allow any donning of military uniform at the bidding good-bye to the service. There could be no dressing up with gold lace, or " buckling on of a rapier," after the relinquishment fiat had gone forth. Soldiering meant fighting with designated instruments of warfare, not with the goose-quill. In New Orleans there were half a dozen " old soldier firms," as they were characteristically nicknamed, and in Charleston several. Richmond, in Virginia, boasted of several of the new order; and it is an evidence of Washington's steadfastness of character and adherence to uninterrupted friendship, that through life he stuck to Cary and Co., in London, and to Barclay and Co., of New York; the one for the conversion of his tobaccos into hard dollars, and their due and safe transmission to his clutch, the latter for their transport over the seas in " good and safe bottoms."

Good Robert Cary was of the old-fashioned type. He managed all correspondence with clients in America in proper form and good style, and never huckstered in the matter of commissions. Copying-books had not in those days been evoluted. Fine thick water-lined laid foolscap was the medium of communication. None of your miserable modern paper from straw, but manufactured of linen rags and none other; free of slippery gloss, tempting the pen into tautologous meandering; each sheet bearing the maker's "water-mark" duly recorded thereon, as evidence of its worth in durability and toughness. "Whatman and Co," of Kentish renown, led the van of "true foolscap." Robert Cary and Co., and their ilk, would have no other; and each recurring spring, as a good ship was "entered out" for New York, a ream of this coveted papyrus was sent to Colonel Washington, with a supply of quill pens, and two pounds of sealing-wax of no other brand than Walkden and Co. Ink, too, there went, of famed fabricate, and three bundles of pink tape wherewith to tie the Colonel's bundles of documents. The list shows that a packet of "pounce" was included in the annual requirement. It will puzzle hurried men of to-day to translate "pounce." It was an article of finely granulated sand, for dusting on manuscript to prevent blotting—blotting-paper had not then sprung into life; and the head of the new nation was a man of almost unique care and neatness in all appertaining to his calligraphy. Robert Cary, to supply such wants, did not go into the next street to a stationer's shop; he opened direct communication with this notable J. Whatman, who, after specifying the weight per ream, sent it "up to London" by the weekly carrier.

But there were divers other things to be assembled for these annually recurring shipments. Home gastronomic comforts had to be thought of. Like Meg and Trotty Veck in Dickens' "Goblin Story of the Chimes," the General had a penchant for tripe. So important was the delicacy in his and Lady Washington's eyes, that Robert Cary was specially charged to ship him on one occasion no less a bulk than three huge earthen vessels, each of which is ordered to be "wicker bound," and recased in a cask to guard against fracture and spilling the precious contents. Cary, it is seen from Washington's warm acknowledgment, had been in the habit of sending him presents of the coveted Bristol pickled article. Two such jars had recently made safe travel to Mount Vernon, and as the Duke of Wellington would have done in like position of long distance from the provisioning base, the wary warrior looked ahead, backed by an admission made in explanation of the large consumption, that his molars were out of gear, three other such jars are requisitioned. The taste for pickled tripe of Bristol cure had been introduced from the West India Islands into New Orleans and other places. Quite a commerce had grown up in it, and among the sugar-planters it was a standing dish. The largest stone jars held about two gallons; there was a special pottery at Bristol for their make, and each jar had the curer's name burnt in on the frontal, in order to make sure of the contents being genuine. There were several favourite brands largely consumed in the West Indies; that of "Hamlin," brought to Barbadoes by the ships of Thomas Daniel and Sons, was the quality and brand preferred of Washington. Gradually, as there arose fondness for this tripe, direct imports occurred, and other English tripe-makers tried their hands; but for a century or more "Bristol tripe" held its way against all comers and home fabricators. New York and Massachusetts men went into the curing, but the oversea article defied them until cruel customs duties stepped in and ruthlessly swept away the monopoly.

The following highly characteristic letter of Washington, thanking his friend for a present of two huge jars of tripe, ordering as matter of business a further supply of the succulent dainty, declining on behalf of his wife and himself any meddling with duplicates of his or her portraits, and expressing their united opinions that the Sharples portraits are the best ever executed, is of deepest interest :—

"DEAR CARY,—Mrs. Washington joins me in warm

thanks to you for your considerate present of two large stone jars of pickled tripe, which reached Mount Vernon in perfect condition. I must ask you to arrange for four similar jars in wicker basket casing, packed in outer cask, to be shipped for my account direct from the curers in Bristol early in the season, when a vessel will be leaving that port for New York. If consigned to Messrs. Barclay, those gentlemen will give the little matter their unvarying care. Dental infirmity impels my caring for this necessary item in our domestic commissariat.

I have been solicited by Colonel Trumbull and others to request your permission for Mr. Sharples to execute copies in oils, size of the originals, of the two portraits of myself and that of Mrs. Washington, and to name that if Mr. Sharples thinks of returning to this country, a good opportunity would thus be found to bring them out. I cannot encourage any hope of commissions for expensive portraits in oils, such as these were. Our people cannot afford to pay the price. I shall ever value highly the friendship prompting the great outlay on your part.

It is agreed on all hands that his two portraits of myself are, so far as likeness goes, by far the best of the many made; hence the desire that the copies should be from the hand of the artist himself who painted the originals. In the instances of his frequent small pastel reproductions there is great inferiority. The copies I gave Judge Marshall are, perhaps, the best, but all are said to be very weak. My wife declines to join in asking your consent—I have undertaken simply to name it—to go beyond the mention would, it seems to me, be a clear impertinence.

In judging Mrs. Washington's seeming disinclination, it should be remembered that my having sat to Stuart has resulted in the country abounding in so-called 'originals.'

If it be your wish for the desired copies to be made, Mr.

Sharples should be required to enter into an undertaking they shall be painted in best manner of his capability; and in your interest he should be strictly confined to the execution of one copy only of each, and bound not to paint more; so also he should undertake not to remove the pictures from your residence.

Faithfully yours,
GEORGE WASHINGTON.

To Robert Cary, Esq.,
    Merchant in London."

A very general opinion has always existed that the First President did not personally favour the having copies of the Cary portraits made, and a good deal of remark, not always favourable to Lady Washington, has been vented, charging her with being opposed to the country getting permission for the execution of copies. All this is pretty much set at rest by the publication of the letter from the General, which, though treating of private family matters, conclusively shows that he would have nothing whatever to do in it beyond laying the request before Mr. Cary.

Lady Washington is made to avow her refusal to join in the request; she evidently desired that the English portraits should be real, and that no tricks should be played with them. The artist had been, in her estimate, liberally paid for his work, it had given satisfaction, and there should be an end of it. No blame can reasonably attach to her in the business. She doubtless had even stronger views on the matter than her husband. Stuart and others had been multiplying their presentments of her husband whenever the opportunity offered from a good-paying customer. Nothing may have been said as to actual "originality," but the inference conveyed with each such at time of sale was that the General sat for it, in other words that they were painted from the life, whereas only one of Stuart's many productions was original in the true sense. Martha stepped in here to hedge round and protect the Sharples portraits. She really wished that real worth should attach to them, and that they should be handed down to posterity unduplicated, and England for a while would be their safest home.

It was during a first stay in Philadelphia that Sharples' letter from the English Secretary of State, introducing him to Washington, was formally presented through the resident Minister, Mr. Hammond. There could not have been any need of this formality, as Mr. Cary's letter to Washington was more than sufficient to obtain the desired object. In common, however, with the routine style of the old merchant of those days, Mr. Cary did everything *en règle*, hence the formal document as advance-guard. No time was lost in Sharples being honoured with access to the illustrious chief, the object of his mission. The General did not formally wait the painter's appearing at Mount Vernon; he very considerately sought him out in Philadelphia, and expressed much gratification at his being domiciled in the house of " my friend, Mr. Franklin." He and Franklin were honoured by dining with " His Excellency" the following day, in the quarters he retained for occupation on occasion of his visits to Philadelphia, which were not unfrequent. At this family party, arrangements were made for his visits to Mount Vernon. As proof of Washington's liberality, and the nice delicacy prompting and attending his carrying out such acts, when Sharples came to settle with Franklin for a month's board—and it included that of his wife and two children for a like period—he was in tones of whisper informed that "everything has been settled by the General." The intimation was accompanied with hints advising calm submission, and with assurance that the liberal allowance of port wine had been included in the score, not omitting sundry bottles of archaic whisky. Sharples' noble portrait of Priestley was a product of like happy circumstances attending the perpetuation of the godlike lineaments of Washington. But for Cary and Benjamin Franklin, the world might have been without either.

Although, with exception of the Washingtons, no actual commissions were received by Sharples for portraits in oils until some considerable time after his settling down in America, yet he had made a beginning in his new walk of crayons within a month or so of entering on his new home, and had been honoured with a communication from Washington, stating that he would sit to him in Philadelphia whenever convenient to him to come over. A path, therefore, had been opened, and as graciously as it was promptly, cleared. After reaching that city, one of the earliest friends drawn to him through Washington was Alexander Hamilton, who instantly recognized his superiority to the artists then practising in portraiture. He at once saw the price was higher than either the means or inclination of the community would admit, and he frankly and with best intent said as much to Sharples. The newly-arrived artist would not reduce his charge, and Hamilton commended his spirit, adding, "They do not know a good portrait from vulgar, staring rubbish." May not the remark often in this our day be applied with truth? It was solely through Hamilton that Sharples entered on a beginning in his then new crayon style of portraits. The statesman saw in it a mode of solving the dilemma, and the start in the new rôle was made in Philadelphia. The first crayons were a Mr. and Mrs. Rush; after executing these, and fixing the price for such at twenty dollars each, the orders came in thick and fast. Through his "good, tender-hearted friend," as he terms Hamilton in his memoranda, "I have received over twenty orders," and "they are all so kind to me here in Philadelphia, New Brunswick, and Burlington, making me reside in their houses where I do the crayons, so that I am at no expense, and the money goes to fill up the hole made during my first two spendthrift months in New York." Although General Hamilton had found a bridge enabling Sharples to get over his first difficulty, he nevertheless felt that the crayon sketches were not his real mission. He was anxious he should leave behind him some worthy memorials of his residence in America. The Washington portraits were going away to their proposed home in England. Hamilton himself, Jefferson, the two Adamses, Madison and Mrs. Madison, Munroe, Clinton, and Robert Fulton and his wife, sat to him, though none had been finished. The lovely female portrait marked "Hamilton" among those sent to England at his death, and believed to have been his wife, shows how the painter's heart was thrown into this beautiful work. Hamilton appreciated it. There were at the time a number of beauties in Philadelphia. Public men of the day, following the taste of their great chief, seemed to have fixed their choice on the fairest of the land, and of these there appears to have been no lack.

Alexander Hamilton will occupy one of the highest places in history. The elder Adams and Jefferson attained the presidency in his day. Every research of criticism, every ray shed on the annals of those times, only the more indicate to those living in an hour when we can see the past as its truth is, that beyond all the men of the first chapter in the country's history—Hamilton, as statesman, was the first, nor yet alone as statesman, when memory warms in the thought of what his oratory was, and the chronicles of bravery would be incomplete without his name.

The administration even of Washington was moulded by him, and when the correspondence of the first President is carefully studied, it will be seen that Washington leaned on him more than on any other for counsel. What more vivid illustration of this than in the fact that Washington in sympathy, by the force of associations formed in the camp, by the memories of inestimable kindness shown to him in the saddest hour, was strongly predisposed when the question came before him of active friendship to France, or cold, calm neutrality towards her—a question argued by Jefferson for France, and Hamilton against her, yielded his mind to the truth so powerfully spoken by the latter, and risked even his popularity by the avowal of neutrality.

All, or nearly all, the other great men of that era became President. Hamilton rose only, in office, to a position in the cabinet, and yet we can see that Hamilton is now, in whatever constitutes real, praiseworthy fame, second only to the man of whose administration he was the great counsellor. He, it may be, felt that the Presidency had been as fairly earned by him as by Adams or Jefferson, but he felt also—for he had before him in English history many illustrations of the truth—that the power of office is the illumination of evening, the night of intellect, the enduring sunlight.

On the occasion of Emerson's last voyage to England, when visiting with his daughter in the family of Mr. Flower, at Stratford-on-Avon, he was very desirous of seeing the portrait of Washington's mother by Middleton. All efforts to trace it then proved unavailing, though had application been made at the American Legation, the place of all others seeming most likely to give the desired whereabouts, the mystery would have been solved. In order for a correct understanding of the past and present state of the holding of the various Sharples Washington portraits, it is best to explain that some time after the death of Robert Cary, the three portraits passed out of his brother's hands; so also the painting of Washington's mother changed hands, and they were for a short period dispersed. Their value to America caused their after purchase by one family, and, with the exception of the Mary, they have never since been separated. The portrait of Washington's mother ran great risk in being for a short time under divided family holding. It is, however, now controlled by the same family as the other pictures, although for a period of years Mary Washington's portrait was separated from the others. All four of the pictures have remained in London for some years, though the entire four have never been assembled together under one roof. The blessed mother, subject of her son's deep anxiety for so many years, got spirited away to the neighbourhood of Northampton, where she rested peacefully for some ten years; next for the honour of extending hospitality to her was the city of Bath, where for a short time she dwelt in obscurity, since which she has found a quiet, appreciating home in Sussex. A few years prior to Mr. Cary's death these paintings, second in historic value to no other portraits in the world, came near a rude scatter, and would probably have been irretrievably lost, the younger Cary, the inheritor, being entirely ignorant of his elder brother's close association with Washington. Through sagacious timely advice the family decided not to part with the portraits; each therefore took one, the portrait of Mary, by Middleton, falling to Mrs. Edwardes, Robert Cary's sister. Good advisers, conscious of their ultimate value, have since been always ready with best counsel, though there have been days of darkness when the perils of separation seemed imminent. By family arrangement the two portraits of Washington and that of his wife may practically be said to be now in one possession, Mary Washington in another holding; though all four of the pictures are for the time being free to make the home voyage back to their own land should their possession be desired.

The occasional unknown whereabouts of the portraits during the last seventy years is easily explained. Nobody having control over them heeded or could serve any object in bringing them into notoriety. For a time they may be said to have had no owners. After this period of doubt and neglect, the whole were with much foresight acquired by one and the same person. There were, however, clauses in a family settlement of the pictures preventing their sale, so also their being engraved, until an interested minor became of age. It was this specific, though as it proved, happy provision, that stood in the way of Washington Irving having them engraved for his "Life of Washington." Irving was deeply anxious for this permission. His first application was made in 1854, and was followed up by frequent communications during the succeeding ten years. He tried every means to get over the legal difficulty, but eventually admitted that the hoped permission to engrave the portraits could not be given. The three portraits were not freed from this settlement until 1882, when arrangements were made for their exhibition in New York, Washington, Boston, Philadelphia, Chicago, St. Paul, and Cincinnati. Autotype copies were executed and subscribed for in those cities, and the paintings then again returned to England. Middleton's portrait of Mary Washington has never left England since transmitted there, as is believed, prior to Washington's death, for repair and restoration, and as it appears in charge of Sharples, most probably under specific instructions from Washington himself.

The portrait of Hamilton's beautiful wife—a lovely picture—and the artist's gentle, unobtrusive manner had won her husband's heart, and doubtless his Chief's earnest request for his interest in Sharples' behalf, served to stimulate Hamilton's earnest zeal, all combined, made him the more than friend he proved himself. Washington headed the signatures to a list of commission guarantees. It was evidently his intention to have a portrait additional to that commissioned by Mr. Cary. Hamilton is credited with an earnest desire to possess one of the Chief he served so faithfully. It is suggested that a series of portraits were intended for some public institution in Philadelphia. Whether they were ever painted, and if so, what became of them, is a mystery. So far as is known, none of Sharples' portraits in oil, beyond the Washingtons, the Adamses, Madison and his wife, Hamilton and his wife, Munroe, Jefferson, Clinton, Robert Fulton and his beautiful wife, Priestley, and the seven ball-room beauties finished by Maclise, exist. He evidently found painting in oils tedious, and so he began, but rarely finished anything. Crayon portraits brought in more money. It is more puzzling to divine what has become of the innumerable Lawrences, or Sir Joshuas, than of any work that may be presumed to have come from Sharples' hand during his few years' resting in America. What has become of the portraits executed by Gainsborough, who painted in Washington's day, and whose easel was a fertile one? So coveted, in large degree consequent on scarcity, their value realized is almost fabulous; single portraits commanding eight and ten thousand pounds. At the moment of well-timed effort, the helping hand so cordially extended by Hamilton to Sharples, the new artist from England, came the crayon-venture success, and his hands had exercise to their fullest capacity. Portraits in oils, to be meritorious, were creations of toil, and open to endless criticism as to likeness; the crayon products were expeditious of execution, and, in almost every instance, staring likenesses.

Artist life in New York was not free from the struggles usually the lot of venturers on new ground. In the early stages of his first settling down in New Amsterdam he found expenses accumulate upon him, without any paying work in sight at the moment. Robert Cary, with the thoughtful consideration marking every act of his friendship with Washington, had armed him with a letter of introduction from the English Foreign Secretary to Mr. Hammond, the Minister to America, and to the New York Consul; and he had procured him a letter from an important personage at the Hague, introducing him to Mr. Van Ransalaer, the Patroon at Albany, also commendations to Chancellor Livingstone and Schuyler families. With the exception, however, of having made the acquaintance of the Consul and Mr. Barclay, Washington's agent, he for two months after landing made little progress beyond that of purchasing furniture and shaking down in his new house, which was near Greenwich Street, in the neighbourhood since designated the Battery. As before stated, Bishop Moore afterwards occupied the house. Even in those days rents were what he described to his friend and patron Cary as "pretty smart," as he seems to have paid for his house one thousand dollars per annum, besides taxes. This was anything but a small beginning, and as he afterwards admitted, a somewhat "imprudent plunge without sitters in view." He started, however, with a goodly balance of two thousand dollars in the bank—an amount soon reduced by purchase of furniture requisite for one sitting and three bedrooms. Friends were not slow in gathering round him—warm-hearted friends, too. "The artist from England" was socially well received, through the influence of the Consul and Mr. Barclay, and everything promised well, save actual commissions, of which there were none. He had brought with him a portrait of Burke, and also one of Erskine; these were purposed evidences of his capability, but clearly in advance, so far as money outlay went, of the community in which he had settled. These two portraits drew around him what he called a "large audience." "Everybody asks us out to tea;" and it was expected that the portraits of the great statesmen should accompany them on every such occasion. There seems to have been continual gatherings of these evening soirées, and among the New York "upper ten" of that day, whose lines were as sharply marked as in after-times, everybody delighted to revel in the society of Mr. Sharples' Edmund Burke and Erskine.

The English artist, through his introductions and by the unflagging forethought of General Hamilton, became known to wide circles in New York, Philadelphia, and Baltimore. His company was greatly sought; of this we have direct evidence from Washington and Lady Washington. He was in the habit of paying long visits at Governeur Morris's residence at Morrisania, which he speaks of as "a large, elegant house, superbly finished, and delightfully situated near the Sound and the junction of the Haarlem and East Rivers." He thus describes Governeur Morris's country residence: "On my visit to Morrisania, to paint Mr. and Mrs. Morris's portraits, my wife and daughter were both invited, and accompanied me. The great attention of this delightful family seemed beyond all bounds. Their agreeable conversation, the various amusements of viewing prospects, pictures, sculpture, tapestry, plate, china, glass, &c., contributed each day to interest us, and to make the time pass very swiftly. At dinner we had three courses every day, on a magnificent service of silver; dessert on the most exquisite French china. The library here is most extensive; and the beauties both of nature and art excite greatly my admiration." It is remarkable that he uses the words "paint the portraits." Such terms would hardly apply to pastels or crayon drawings.

That Sharples was a great favourite, and mixed in the best society, is beyond all question. Thus we find him writing of the Van Ransalaers:—

"We started from New York by steamer for Albany, to visit our old friends the Patroon family. Found many old acquaintances on board. There were 120 passengers; these filled the deck. Mr. Chancellor Livingstone met us at Red Hook landing, and expressed himself in warmest terms, begging us to pay them a visit, and urging that we could not refuse and pass them by for the Van Ransalaers. When we reached Albany there were numerous kind friends offering us the hospitality of their homes. Mrs. Beezley and Mr. Dexter were each most pressing. The Morgans we also found resident in Albany. We were fellow-prisoners at Brest with the Morgans for many months, having accepted Mrs. Van Ransalaer's warm invitation, we could not entertain the Morgans' earnest entreaty. The yellow fever was raging at Albany, and we were glad to find the Van Ransalaer's place about a mile out of the town. Nothing could exceed the affability of Mrs. Van Ransalaer, and the kindness and hospitality of the Patroon, her husband, was beyond all bounds. Two days after we drank tea at Chief Justice Kent's. In every house, however, the only topic of conversation was the yellow fever, and not liking to remain in a neighbourhood infected with such deadly sickness, we determined to shorten our visit, and return to New York. Mrs. Van Ransalaer was much affected on our intimating this determination, adding, however, 'Much as I deplore it,—for I need the companionship of loved friends at a time when much fortitude is required,—I think you are quite right. You have no duties to detain you here; but do come and see us, if God should see fit to lift the dreadful illness from our midst.' We returned to New York by sailing packet. The cabin very airy, and a great contrast to the crowded steamboat; wind favourable, soon succeeded by a calm, so that we could only move with the tide; when contrary, we lay at anchor."

CHAPTER V.

Sharples becomes "the fashion" in New York—Trumbull and the Hon. Mr. Jay make unsuccessful efforts for reproduction of the portraits for America—Letter from Trumbull urging same and explaining their great value to the nation, also giving account of all the other existent portraits, contrasting them—Sharples paints Priestley in Philadelphia—Hamilton, Lee, and Washington meet in the painter's studio in Philadelphia—Affability and personal appearance of Washington—Sharples visits Lee in Virginia—Admirable criticism of the portraits by G. D. West, of St. Paul's.

OUR English artist, who so immediately felt at home in America in 1794, at once drew around him the *élite* of New York and Philadelphia. Originally educated in a Jesuit college and intended for the Romish priesthood, and being, moreover, a man of much ability and generally accomplished, characterized by Jefferson as "a delightful converser," he became "the fashion" in the "best circles." Among his earliest made friends was Colonel Trumbull, who had served as aide-de-camp to Washington, and, having taste and ability in art, had sheathed the sword to ply the brush; and had voyaged to England to study under Benjamin West, having been aided in such object by appointment to official duties in connection with Mr. Jay's embassy. Robert Cary actively engaged himself in behalf of Washington, in moving among public men with the object of averting war. Intimacy with Burke helped him. His labours, though prosecuted in privacy, were none the less earnest, causing daily personal communication with Mr. Jay. Sharples was a visitor at his house. He there became acquainted with Trumbull, through mutual love of art, and, ultimately, they were friends. The newly arrived semi-military artist derived much valuable assistance by thus entering on his new pursuit, and it was owing, in some degree, to this intimacy that Sharples undertook Cary's commission to voyage out and paint his friend Washington. It would appear that he first saw the portraits in London, and at once concluded how desirable it was that Sharples should execute copies for America, and thus urgently pressed him in the following letter to Mrs. Sharples, found among her papers at her decease. The artist's wife is selected as a medium of communication, being deemed more likely of successful intercession with Mr. Cary, Mrs. Washington being adverse to the suit.

"It is much to be hoped you will induce Mr. Cary to change his determination, so as to allow your husband to duplicate his portraits in oils of the General and Mrs. Washington. The small pastels are but poor ideas of the original oils, and we are unable to see why Mr. Cary should have permitted their reproduction after this manner, and yet disallow the original oils, which all here remember with such satisfaction. It is a pity consent had not been given before the three portraits left for England. Mrs. Washington, as you know, was really the cause of the difficulty; why she raised it, is passing strange. Had she solicited Mr. Cary, he would have felt flattered. Her reply to all endeavours of inducement was that it would lessen the value of the portraits in Mr. Cary's estimate. All blame her. Many will never forgive her desire for English exclusive possession. Martha's blue blood often crops out.

Mr. Sharples is aware I was in Europe when his oils of the Washingtons were finished. I saw them first in company with the Hon. John Jay at Mr. Cary's, in London.

It was a revelation to us both I shall never forget, they being his first canvas work seen by me. We both told Mr. Cary of their national import, but dared not then intimate to him the importance of duplicates being painted for America. The matter of Sharples' charge need not be considered. Mr. Jay is ready with the cost, to which several are more than willing to join. Even if you had made a special return visit to America—and I trust you will return—there would have been no chance of getting the General to go through any sitting ordeal repetition, so we are quite satisfied to put up with duplicates, and trust Mr. Cary will loan him the pictures for the purpose. The General, after so numerous occasions of torment by artists, many of them utterly unworthy of the great subject, and incapable of appreciating the honour conferred, became a most unwilling sitter, and vowed to Gilbert Stuart he would never again go through the penance process. His portrait is much admired, but to my eye it is not the General, and I regret to say he is making numerous others, for none of which the General accorded a sitting. We must not, however, be hard on Stuart; the inducement is such as few of us could withstand. The General felt in durance with Stuart, who told me he knew not what to say or do to get the desired expression, and if he had, the chances are that nervousness would have prevented him seizing it. Only fancy using a model to get Washington's majesty of form, and yet this was resorted to, although none approaching him could be found. The General admitted to Stuart that 'although your husband had been accorded many long sittings, and that he yielded to sit for two portraits, although only one had been arranged for, yet the occasions had been rendered convenient,' and that 'Sharples' rapidity of work and master hand had interested him throughout.' He added: 'Sharples had the advantage of entertaining me with amusing newly-imported anecdotes of public men in England, and especially of the King, so that I never felt his sittings tedious or encroaching on my time; indeed, I looked forward pleasurably to our daily meetings at Mount Vernon, and his interesting conversation kept up during the whole time of work. Sharples was a clever man outside his art occupation, and had some novel ideas on the subject of artillery, which he always broached, yet with exceeding modesty; at the same time his brain worked with his lips, and he was evidently a good mechanic. He talked well and worked well at the same time, no common endowments.'

For myself, I had long despaired of his giving me another sitting. Had such been afforded, I should have devoted it to studies for future hoped-for work, rather than any formal portrait. This clear determination towards all artists makes us doubly anxious that the country should possess your husband's portraits of him. We cannot get the life originals, but we may, through Mr. Cary's assent, get the next best thing—copies by the hand that produced them from the life. The country has more than enough so-called 'portraits of Washington,' four-fifths of them destitute of the faintest resemblance. Many of those for which he so humanely sat come under this category; the workers were so dazed in his presence, they knew not what they were about. How greatly under these circumstances all future painters will be thrown back on the Houdon bust for a true conveying of our subject's grand head and sublime features! There is a completeness about the Houdon bust—an entirety, as it were—that nothing else carries, and it is certainly remarkable that deftness in clay modelling has in Washington's case achieved that which the brush has yet failed to produce. When Jefferson, in Paris, presented in 1785, Charles Willson Peale's portrait of Washington to Houdon, and which had been expressly painted for the purpose of conveying to him the form and features of his subject, he at once declined it, and at great personal sacrifices came out to Mount Vernon to see the great original himself. Our gratitude to Franklin for having brought him out is great. In looking at the Houdon, how few of our people know the fact, that Houdon actually took a cast of the face, and worked out a model of the face from this. So also he eschewed all resort to other forms of men for retaining the majesty of the original. He took the closest measurements of every limb, and, being from the heart impressed with the world's future estimate of the man, has left it a work worthy of the subject and the artist. Had he followed our people's wish, we should have had something very secondary. It is no mere individual opinion that the Houdon bust is our best Washington, and I am expressing the feeling of all who have seen your husband's renderings of the great subject, that they are by far the ablest canvas attempts. They are both inspired by lifelike and with individual grandeur and dignity beyond any other representations. They are far away from home, but the day will come for their rule in the world's heart, as true presentments of Washington!

The Pine, Stuart, Savage, and Willson Peale portraits, and, as I trust, some of my own humble productions, will be subjects for reference to future generations of artists, for their designed work, illustrative of the military achievements and struggles of our people's great master-mind in the country's early infancy. But we need more, or future painters will be deficient in realistic work of reference. It is in hope of this supply we turn to Mr. Cary. Sharples, in being welcomed and quartered at Mount Vernon, was, out of respect to his sponsor, placed in like position, and had extended to him all the advantages enjoyed by Houdon, Stuart, myself, and others, and we all admit his diligent availing of the great opportunity and privilege. I am thus particular, in order that Mr. Cary may know why duplicates of the Washington portraits are desired by us. Personally I am much interested, as they would afford authentic material to fall back upon for public work I have in contemplation, and there exists little else I could avail of with satisfaction. I do not believe the General will ever again sit to any one; it cannot be expected of him. Stuart will hardly produce anything more of real value, and I fear the General will not seek to influence Mr. Cary to give the needed permission. He has promised to name the matter, but we fear he will not go beyond a slight allusion, as any referring to portraits of himself he regards as savouring of vanity, and is most distasteful. Apart from any other feeling, the continued multiplying of copies by men in whom confidence has been reposed has disgusted him, and it is to be feared he looks on the whole fraternity of artists as birds of a feather. Lady Washington does not favour the duplicating Mr. Cary's portraits; she will discourage rather than help it. Both she and the General desire the existence of authentic portraits that have not been multiplied, and she favours England as their suitable resting-place. Having herself defrayed the cost of her own portrait, she holds to have a voice in the matter. She knows how the President has, throughout his public life, been harassed and bored in sitting for portraits, the great majority of them worthless. One of the Peale family had proved a very vampire on his time, and it says much for his amiability and patience that he so enduringly submitted to tyros palmed upon him by injudicious friends. In so new a country it was not probable artists should have been so soon raised up equal to the great call; we ought, therefore, to have brought out from England a Lawrence or a Gainsborough for this especial emergency. Mr. Cary, in sending Sharples out, did a great national service, and it is hoped he may see public good in granting the favour sought. I have gone into the matter thus minutely, feeling no one else will take it up on right grounds, and also with the knowledge that Lady Washington will oppose copies of the portraits being made. I address myself to you, knowing Mr. Sharples will not urge it with the force needed to induce Mr. Cary's consent; and, being yourself an artist, you will sympathize in our wish to have the duplicates.

Mr. and Mrs. Morgan and their two children, who were with you passengers from Bristol, and your fellow-prisoners at Brest, are living near the Patroon at Albany. Mr. Van Ransalaer, Chief Justice Kent, Chancellor Livingstone, Mr. Charles Wilkes and Mr. Jay have subscribed the same amount as Mr. Sharples received for the three portraits. As an artist myself, I feel strongly on the matter, as they are by far the best portraits. So if you determine again to come out, tell Mr. Cary the sum Mr. Sharples is to receive,—it may induce him to assent. The portraits must be painted in England before leaving, and without any trusting to recollection.

General Gates died the very last winter he spent in New York. He had long been weak and emaciated, but never ill nor suffered pain. Always had expressed a wish his wife might survive him, and she was with him in his last scene. (America can never forget its indebtedness to Cary in serving Washington as he did in the Gates and Genet perfidy. Sharples' wife was a friend of Mrs. Gates, but Sharples never would tolerate her husband.)

Stuart had not painted Washington prior to the time of Sharples' first visit, or he would certainly have seen it, and it would have been referred to by the sitter himself in their many conversations. The only mention of Stuart, traceable in papers left by Mrs. Sharples, is Colonel Trumbull's remarks on his portraits, and the annoyance felt both by

Washington and his wife that these should have been so indefinitely multiplied; and a letter from General Gates' wife, which contains this remarkable statement :—

"Mrs. Washington, it is well known, does not like Stuart's portrait of her husband; he has made him too fierce, and then the nose is altogether what the artists deem 'out of drawing,'—the distension of the nostrils, if I may so express it, is most unnatural. Then there is what Mrs. Washington, I hear, calls 'a sponginess in the nose' he has given him, and which nobody but the man who painted it ever saw. I do not think the General will ever sit to him again. And why should he endure more sittings? Mrs. Washington does not want any more portraits of him, and will not have any other than your husband's in the house. The subject of sitting for another portrait will never be named to him."

A wide margin must be given to this evident bit of woman's spite on the part of General Gates' better half. Her husband had proved himself a secret enemy of the great patriot, and had been, more or less, concerned in the plots to undermine the public estimate of his military capacity; nor had he rested here. Letters from him to public men in England and France had been unearthed by Robert Cary, and his more than complicity clearly established. Washington's nobility of heart stayed all exposure of the traitorous hypocrisy, and even went the length of forgiving, if not altogether forgetting it. It was not so with Mr. Cary or Sharples, who, knowing his Judas hypocrisy, ever afterwards despised him according to his deserts. Mrs. Gates would speak disparagingly of Stuart's portrait, but she would hardly be the depositary of Martha Washington's feelings in regard to it. The nose, as the mouth, were then, as now, in all probability objective features.

It is no part of these memorials to underrate Stuart's portraits of Washington, or to question the judgment leading to their hitherto adoption as the national ideal. Time alone must determine whether they can hold their ground against the Sharples. Most of the so-called originals by Stuart are mere recollections of the portraits painted from the few sittings given him by Washington. The Sharples portraits, so far as the general public goes, were until recently unknown in America, excepting to the few leading poets and public men travelling abroad, who knew of their whereabouts and sought them out. The pictures themselves were packed off to England instantly after production, and all that remained to the country were some pastel drawings made in the first instance from sketches executed with the original oil paintings before his eyes, but which, through multiplication, and in absence of the originals to guide him, grew weaker and weaker, until like Stuart's portraits they became mere results of recollection. The evidences of rapid change in the national feeling need no seeking. Boston, the city rightly priding itself in its possession of a genuine Stuart, has admitted, in free and honourable manner, that the Sharples portraits are "more real," "more human," than the Stuarts. New York, from the first moment of seeing them, never faltered in its judgment. Philadelphia, Chicago, St. Paul, and Cincinnati, the only other places in which the original paintings were exhibited, gave similar verdicts.

Stuart, as a portrait painter, is far more highly appreciated in England than in America. His portraits of Benjamin West, and several others by him in the National Portrait Gallery in London, are superb. The writer of these Memorials does not seek to place the two artists on a par. However greatly Sharples excelled with the Washingtons, Stuart was unquestionably the greater artist.

Trumbull was a frequent visitor at Sharples' house in New York. On Sharples going to Philadelphia to paint a portrait of Priestley, the eminent philosopher and electrician, he was accompanied by Trumbull, and they boarded there together during the few weeks devoted to the execution of that portrait, a very excellent work. The Priestley portrait, according to memoranda left by Mrs. Sharples, was painted at the advice and through the interest of Benjamin Franklin's son, who, strange to say, remained to his death a zealous loyalist, and to the last publicly avowed, as his earnest conviction, that "the United States would have developed more rapidly, had they continued under the British flag." The Priestley portrait was entirely a speculation, believing that it would lead to orders from families in Philadelphia and Baltimore. The portraits of Robert Fulton and his lovely wife, a daughter of Chancellor Livingstone, were commenced in Philadelphia, where they both came for the purpose of the sittings. Death, however, overtook the artist. Bird finished Fulton, and Maclise his wife. Both are now finer works than Sharples would have completed. The several portraits named in this volume, and portraits of Mr. and Mrs. Brown—the former being partner and one of the early projectors of the eminent banking firm of Brown Brothers—are the only paintings known in the shape of oil portraits executed by him in America. He evidently pitched his money key too high, as there does not seem to have been any response to his Priestley effort, although certainly it is a portrait of great merit. Yet in a new community in which money hardly yet abounded, the art prices of the Old World would not unreasonably be prohibitive. Nothing in oils bearing Sharples' name is now known as existent in either the neighbourhood of Philadelphia or Baltimore, though this must not be taken to determine that he did not paint any in those cities. Such works, sharing the fate of many portraits of ancestors, may long since have found their entry into brokers' shops, as preparation to the final bourne from whence none return. It is not clear whether the Brown portraits had been actually commissioned; the good banker would probably desire them finished off-hand, instead of Sharples' delaying habit. They were never finished by Sharples, the uncompleted canvases being among Mrs. Sharples' effects at the time of her death—good evidence of the Brown family never having seen them.

It would appear, from papers left by Sharples, that Benjamin Franklin had for several years, when in England, endeavoured to persuade him to visit America, and it was doubtless through this connection that their friendship occurred. Priestley had just then declined a chemical professorship in Philadelphia; he had gathered together a well-furnished library and chemical laboratory, and did not wish to have his mind disturbed from his all-absorbing electric experiments carried on in the midst of a hoping but incredulous community. It was not then demonstrated that lightning could talk, except in the sonorous bass which had resounded from the earliest time through the arch of the sky. A poet had said of his brother poet, that he—

"With the thunder talked as friend to friend;"

but it was one of those bold poetic licences in which the imagination outstrips, and sometimes foreshadows the reality. As yet it was a secret that men in the most remote corners of the globe should hold instantaneous converse by electric speech. God had broken His thunders over the world; but the still small voice of the lightning was as yet inaudible and unknown. Franklin and Priestley were gradually evolving light out of darkness, but could hardly have seen how soon electricity should articulate our own language, or write with the instruments of our own alphabet. As when Cadmus toiled his slow and weary way, bearing the letters of that alphabet from Phœnicia to Greece, how far from him was the thought that, in after time, the lightning's fiery tongue would speak them, through still greater distances, in an instant of time!

Amid all the angry strife for the immortal honours of this invention, the name of Priestley will be for ever linked with those early electric discoveries leading up to the development of the mighty revolution so soon to follow. Little did Sharples know, when painting the great chemist's portrait, that the element his absorbing study was so soon to revolutionize the world.

It was in 1752 Franklin made his celebrated experimen with the electric kite, by means of which he demonstrated the identity of electricity and lightning. His letters on electricity contain a number of facts and hints, which contributed greatly to reduce this branch of knowledge to a science. His discovery of the positive and negative states of electricity, manifested by the friction of glass and sulphur, and his demonstration of the identity of electricity and lightning, were both events of magnitude, and were calculated to call attention to a new field of labour and research, where so much fame was to be won. The honours paid to Franklin were sufficient to stimulate the ambition of all enlightened minds. The practical application of the lightning-rod in shielding the habitations of men from the destructive thunderbolts of heaven, was a crowning triumph; but in addition to this public benefit, if no further contributions had been made of the subtleties of the electric fluid, mankind would have remained ignorant of those grander marvels which have since been revealed. America was, at that time, in a state of colonial dependence upon Great Britain, and Philadelphia an obscure place, scarcely known abroad, and was first introduced to the notice of the world by this novel and philosophical kind of kite-sailing.

To the glory and advantage of America, the first steps in her progressive career were not belligerent and revolutionary, but intellectual and scientific. The public mind was awakened to activity in the interests of knowledge, ere popular zeal was animated in the cause of liberty. In this particular, Franklin unquestionably took the lead. He was printer, editor, practical philosopher, maximizer, and tutelary genius of the domestic household, warming it within by his fireplaces, and protecting it without by his lightning-rods;— in all these capacities he was eminently conspicuous before the commencement of the revolutionary struggle which settled his claim to that magnificent compliment bestowed upon him by Turgot :—

"Eripuit cœlo fulmen sceptrumque tyrannis."

Dunlap tells us that Sharples the painter was of an eminently scientific cast of mind; though fond of his art, he was equally devoted to chemistry; and so it can readily be understood how he came to paint the charming head of him at whose shrine he worshipped so devotedly. The probability is that he never offered his grand portrait of Priestley for sale, but preferred retaining it as a souvenir of the happy days spent in his company in the good city of Philadelphia. And now that Franklin, the friend of both, and through whom they had been brought together, had in ripe old age passed away from the world, the tie would be the stronger. Franklin had seen a good deal of Sharples in London, and, now that a warm friendship had grown up between the philosopher's son and the painter, the family tie had become one of great strength.

"There is a general feeling almost amounting to awe in regard to the great patriot in the minds of all who have personal intercourse with him." So wrote Franklin to Sharples.

"Franklin is not alone in this feeling as to the Chief. I

could share it," recorded Sharples, " but for the unreserved manner in which he has always so graciously unbent on occasions of honouring me with his presence in sittings. He has always made me feel at home; I generally concluded his desire was that I should enter into my work free from any of the embarrassments others have experienced in his presence. He asked many questions regarding you, and was pleased to learn anything I could tell him as to your home and manner of life. Chiefly, however, he liked to hear of the King; spoke of him always with great respect, and especially of his exemplary domestic life. Edmund Burke and anything I could tell him as to his personal appearance, and the opinion of Englishmen regarding him, was gratifying if eulogistic of Burke, whom he seemed to look upon as the greatest of all men. Erskine, too, was a subject of his warmest admiration; and oddly he would change the conversation to Lady Huntingdon, and here I was sadly at fault, for I knew very little of her or the peculiar views she held, although he was at home in her whole history and doings.

It is the fashion to speak of Washington's so-called reticence, but any one who had been with him, and to whom he unbent, would know that it was the silent manner of a deeply thoughtful mind that never gave utterance merely with the mouth; there was contemplative thought—every word had its purpose and a meaning. I never knew him repeat a question that he had before asked. He appeared to have, as it were, a present consciousness of all ever inquired into in previous conversations, and never referred to the same point in the public or personal character of public men in England, on which he had at any time before conversed. His comprehensive, orderly mind had retained all he desired, and it was engraven on his mind; and he had great faculty of making this known, so that one did not venture on the smallest prosiness—a common fault with the many, but which he never could have tolerated. He never named to me, or in any way alluded to public men of France. He made you feel that he was talking to an Englishman, and that he dwelt on them alone, and it is presumable he would consult other sources if desirous of conversing as to our amiable neighbours.

When on horseback in the streets of Philadelphia he rode a splendid animal of great power, and without any whip or stick in his hand; and indeed he needs a horse of great strength, as his weight is greatly in excess even of tall men's average. I never saw a horse so proud of his rider as the animal on which I encountered him; neither have I ever looked on a more graceful rider, or one who held such seeming unexercised power over the animal. Horse and man seemed as one: there was grandeur in both. He drew up to shake hands, and in my confusion my hat fell off, which caused him to bend forward as if with desire to pick it up. I was terribly put about, but the great Chief at once removed my embarrassment. Franklin tells me he does not like being in Philadelphia or any other city; Mount Vernon is his one home of rest and happiness.

General George Henry Lee, who has visited me several times here in Philadelphia during my progress with Priestley's and the Fulton portrait, is a fine fellow, his whole-heartedness beyond description. He and General Hamilton are great friends, and he wishes me to paint his portrait; but it is no use my making too many beginnings, or it will all end in my finishing nothing. General Washington is with him in Philadelphia, and both came yesterday to meet General Hamilton, and stayed some time during my work. It was not easy to ply the wretched brush in the presence of three such men. There was no occasion for my saying anything,

Generals Lee and Hamilton did it all. The former is one of the most brilliant conversationalists I have ever met; General Hamilton speaks well and always to the point, and evidences more what painters would call 'background' knowledge. I have never ventured to start any historical subject in conversation in which he did not prove himself at home, and as to public affairs of the 'old country,' he knows more, and that soundly and thoroughly, than any man I have ever met at home in England. He is a great man, and must have been everything to Washington. I shall never while life lasts get over the having the three in my little room together. Washington insisted on my keeping on at my work; I did so after a fashion, but it was only a mere pretence of work, an entire absence of mind from its actuality. Generals Hamilton and Washington were both very real and solid in all they said, General Lee full of vivacity; but whenever General Washington spoke, I observed they both seemed in wrapt attention. The Chief was conversing, and not a word bordering on interruption was uttered; both, as it were, hung on his words, as it appeared to me, with a something far higher than what we know as respect; and I noticed that after I had opened the door for their departure, and they had descended the steps into the street, they had both advanced some steps forward ere General Hamilton or General Lee covered their heads. Mr. Custis was to have met them at my rooms, but a messenger arrived begging them not to expect him, as he had been thrown by an untrained horse, happily without any injury being sustained. For several days after the Chief's visit to me in company with such men, kindly drawn by none but the purest motives of help, I seemed lost and unable to get anything done but a few crayon portraits; but these yielded good money, often, when I am in humour to work, as much as six pounds in a day. I did nothing to Priestley for a week. Franklin was at home when the Chief and his generals called; he kept out of the way, and I was glad of it—not that I need to have presumed on any intrusion, for he held Washington in awe. This always seems strange to me, being no Republican; the son of one of its greatest propounders, he himself a zealous Royalist,—yet he says, 'I look on Washington as something more than human. What a magnificent head and form it is!'

When in my room with Generals Hamilton and Lee, the Chief again brought back my attention to the condition of the portrait of his mother, so long hanging in his bedroom. His great desire was that I should undertake what he called 'putting it to rights.' I would do anything in my power even to give the smallest pleasure to this more than noble man, but I dreaded meddling with what he regarded with such reverence and sanctity. It cannot be called a picture: the jagged hole is some five inches in diameter, and the face, though uninjured through the same cause as the hole, has suffered through exposure to stove heat, and is peeling off. I tell him it had better go to England, and that in the hands of Opie or Romney it would be made a good picture. It is just this, what he called 'transmogrification,' he seems to fear."

The English artist little knew that strange feats have been accomplished both by dexterity in repair and through the power of transfer of paintings from one canvas to another, and even to the making several pictures from one, and yet each to be an original and genuine. A remarkable instance of this kind occurred in the case of a work of no less an artist than the celebrated Charles Landseer, entitled, "The Eve of the Battle of Edgehill," now in possession of the Corporation of the Town of Liverpool, which owns on behalf of the citizens a somewhat extensive and valuable gallery of pictures, and annually apportions from the city rates such money as can be spared towards judicious purchase of pictures to be added to it. The work by Landseer referred to was painted in 1845, on a commission from Mr. Henry Graves, the well-known print publisher of London, and it was subsequently engraved by Frederick Bromley, and published by Mr. Graves in 1852. While the picture was being painted, Sir Edwin Landseer, who was very partial to his elder brother Charles, and endeavoured to advance his interests in every way, inserted, as he had done on several other occasions, two dogs—one a spaniel, near the despatch bags, and the other the large dog, near the table. After publishing the plate, Mr. Graves sold the picture intact to a picture-dealer, who, being a sharp man of business, caused both the dogs to be cut out of the canvas, with the object of making two separate pictures of them. Fresh canvas was cleverly inserted, and the dogs were copied by another hand unknown to either of the brothers Landseer. Reference to the Landseer catalogue, compiled by Algernon Graves, shows that the larger dog, which now bears the title of "The Sentinel," had the background represented by a portion of an old castle wall, filled in by Henry Bright. This picture once belonged to Mr. Nunneley, and was disposed of at his sale at Christie's in 1872. It afterwards passed into the possession of Mr. Eaton, M.P., the present owner. The other dog, the spaniel with the despatch bags, was also sold at Christie's in 1879. It was described in Christie's catalogue as "A Spaniel and Despatch Bags," originally forming part of the joint picture of "The Eve of the Battle of Edgehill," by Charles and Sir Edwin Landseer. The original mutilated picture, now in the Liverpool Corporation Gallery, was sold at Christie's in 1868 for £231. "The Battle of Edgehill" picture is a curiosity and an example of the picture-liner's skill rather than of the work of the Brothers Landseer. In order to restore the picture's damaged reputation, the Arts Committee of the Liverpool Corporation endeavoured to purchase the two missing dogs by Sir E. Landseer, with the object of their being reinserted in their original places.

In a later letter addressed to Mr. Cary, Sharples wrote:—

"I have carried out my visit to General Henry Lee, at Shalford, in this same State of Virginia. Until he told me, I was not aware of your receiving his tobaccos. This aristocratic house is comparatively a modern structure, the original mansion having been burnt down in the time of Thomas Lee, who was President of the Colonial Council and Governor of the State, and the first man of American birth placed in this post by the British Government. All Thomas Lee's sons have been eminent men, and distinguished themselves, as you well know, in the events of the War of Independence. Richard Henry Lee, the great orator in the Senate; Francis Lightfoot Lee, whose name is found in the Act of Independence; and beside these there is Arthur Lee, the Minister to France. The whole race seem worthily destined for greatness. The noble man who has so honoured me is just such as you would single out to render such service as he rendered in causing the surrender of Lord Cornwallis." (When the house was burnt down in the time of Queen Caroline, Her Majesty, it is said, wrote him an autograph letter, begging to be allowed to contribute towards its restoration, and she did so.) "The existing house was largely built of the bricks of the old mansion, and which, partly on account of their having originally been brought from England, caused them to be availed of for the purpose. I have never experienced such hospitality as in his noble home, and have never before enjoyed the society of so brilliant a man. Most of the fittings of the residence are from

England, and the whole place and its surroundings proclaim culture and extreme refinement. The silver used at table is old and beautiful, and the china displayed in all the rooms most exquisite. There is, however, the usual drawback; the family portraits here, as generally elsewhere, are the productions of fifth-rate men, and detract sadly from any good pictures brought from Europe. Generally they are staring likenesses, which causes their toleration. A man with the judgment of General Lee knows perfectly well the artistic character of these ancestral remains, but he found them here, and has too much respect for those who lived before him, and whose heritor he is, to banish them to more fitting chambers; nevertheless, they spoil everything. The general has urgently inquired whether good portraits can be made of some of them so as to preserve the likeness, but I discouraged him. He offered me such a commission if I thought it could be done well. I dissuaded him from it; I could not undertake it. I have already entered on engagements I shall not live to fulfil, and, apart from this, it would not pay me to do it so long as I can find employment in the crayon sketches, many of which I have made for General Lee. He saw your Washingtons, and kindly told me he never envied any man a possession as he did you those. I told him I had done my best, and was glad they were gone out of the country, as all chance of painting others from them disappeared with the pictures, and therefore all temptation was out of sight. I assured him they were painted in less than half the time I should have bestowed on any others, but that I had not been my own master in regard to them. The Chief, I knew, was impatient and weary in sitting, and I was driven to work hard on them; the knowledge of what you, my kind, good friend, have done for me, forced on their execution. I would like to paint General Lee in oils; but I am in a vein of making money in the crayons, and it is time I should save a little for my family, which oil portraits would not enable me to do. Fifty pounds is the utmost obtainable. I am as slow in oils as the opposite in the crayons, and none of the public men I have done in these decline my reproducing them for friends; so I am constantly getting orders, and indeed have more than I can well get through. I have a number of oils rubbed in, waiting to be worked on when I get leisure."

Public attention was called to the portraits through the following admirable article from the able pen of Mr. G. B. West, then editing the St. Paul's magazine, *At Home* :—

"Nothing could be better fitted to inculcate the lessons of patriotism and unselfish devotion to the cause of our dear Fatherland, than the constant contemplation of these glorious faces of George Washington. Without them the study of American history lacks its best and greatest illustration. Without them it is impossible for the youth of the country to appreciate and understand the godlike character whose great heart, military genius, ability as a statesman, and self-abnegation, all rounded and sanctified in a life of beautiful and touching Christian faith and purity, accomplished more in the creation and establishment of the grand fabric of this Republic, than all the other causes and conditions bearing upon its birth and career in the family of nations. There is an apparent harmony between the life and services of Washington and the character of the man as depicted in the Sharples paintings, and this cannot be honestly said as to any other of the various pictures purporting to represent the features of the great patriot. That the Sharples are correct representations of the living original, we have the opinion of Washington himself and of Lady Washington, in letters yet extant; and if that were not enough, the evidence of the aged Dr. Van Pelt, of New York, who saw the full-face portrait in that city in 1854, on its former visit to this country. Dr. Van Pelt had known General Washington in life, and declared that it was a perfect picture as he remembered the General.

It is well that the Father of his Country should be remembered by the millions whom his achievements have made the possessors of the priceless boon of civil liberty; and it is well that the children of the nation should have his bright example continually held before them for imitation. The mind cannot conceive of a nobler object-lesson in the study of our country's history, in the study of the evolution of government by the people, than these very portraits hanging on the walls of every school-house in the land. It was Longfellow's ardent wish that they might be so possessed, and he earnestly longed, to the end of his great and useful life, that the original pictures might find a final home in the hero's own land.

Washington Irving, Longfellow, and others of our departed great, have said that they never appreciated George Washington until they had seen and studied the Sharples portraits. Nearly the same sentiment has been expressed by all Americans who have seen the famous paintings—that they had no tangible idea of what the Father of his Country might have been in life until happily a view of the Sharples portraits was vouchsafed them. Now we see how George Washington could possess the more than Spartan courage and almost godlike self-abnegation he displayed in refusing the crown a victorious army offered him. The heroism of Oliver Cromwell in declining the shadow of a sceptre whose political substance he wielded starkly beforehand, is often held up to admiration by the worshippers of that grand and rugged, if not in all things praiseworthy character in the history of our mother country; but Cromwell's circumstances were of such nature that he knew he might enjoy the essence, the homage, and the power of royalty, while it might be destruction to him to usurp the title. In the case of Washington there was not any serious obstacle to his assumption of the purple if he had chosen to assume it. The great nations of the world of his day, who respected and admired him, would have been better pleased to see the government of the nation just born, in the hands of a wise and politic soldier-statesman, than to accept the possibilities of future trouble through the example of a successful republic. The ruling elements in the colonial society of the day were aristocratic, and the tone of our high officialism, civil and military, was eminently so. The crown of a constitutional monarchy was not an unreasonable reward for the illustrious leader who had carved it out with his sharp sword and timely counsels, and there was not a doubt as to the universal heartiness with which the acceptance of that crown would be approved by the whole people, excited to almost adoration of the hero who had just won for them their battle over the most powerful nation of the world. But the crown was rejected, just as a third presidential term was rejected, *pro bono publico*, and out of the purest and noblest motives that ever actuated man. The character we have known through the media of the Stuart portraits would scarcely have objected to sit upon a throne. George Washington as he crosses the Delaware in a face borrowed from Stuart, would have accepted after only the show of reluctance he might regard as decorous, and consistent with his great solo act of attitudinizing for the centuries. George Washington as he sits on horseback in Union Square, New York, would have reached for the crown before it was offered. There is much which is fine and worthy of admiration about the Stuarts. We do not wish to appear lacking in respect for a type that has been accepted so long and trustfully as the real face of Washington by millions of our countrymen; but it has always conveyed to us an impression of deportment rather than character; of something made up for appearance on the great stage of history, rather than the counterfeit presentment of the most remarkable man, in many respects, to be encountered among the records of the human race. There may be people who can satisfy themselves that in the Stuart pictures they recognize at once the warrior; the sagacious leader at the council board; the polished, dignified chief magistrate; the conscientious vestryman, alive to the interests and busy in the little affairs of his parish; the practical, shrewd country gentleman, wise in his generation as to fodder, critical of the tobacco market, and holding decided views respecting the sacredness of fenced land; and finally the devoted son and husband, happier in his little home circle at Mount Vernon, than the most exalted monarch could ever dream of being on a dozen thrones. There are others, less fortunate, who cannot detect any of these elements of a many-sided character in portraits which, if true likenesses, ought to reasonably express some of them; but they are to be seen and recognized in all their beauty and harmony in the sweet, high-bred, calm, tired face of the Sharples pictures. In the full-face there is just a suggestion of a 'far-away' look, as if the donning of the uniform brought back scenes of carnage, disaster, and a continent of dark fears and cares—thoughts of Conway's cabal, of trusted Arnold's treason, of Lee's jealousy, and all the trials and crosses that the great heart had borne for his country's sake. It is a face built for command. Intense determination lingers latent around the mouth, and high emprise lurks in the eye. You gaze intently at it, and realize for the first time how with gentle grace its owner could stop in the streets of his capital and doff the laced hat in return for a poor woman's courtesy; how with that kind mouth set hard and eyes streaming with tears of pity and sorrow, yet speaking an inexorable purpose through the mist, Washington could send to his dreadful death the gallant, noble, but hopelessly doomed André. In all the pictures with which the nation has been familiar, there is lacking all this vivid personality so speakingly present in the Sharples. Who would for a moment imagine the Stuart Washington going out from camp into the woods, and dropping on his knees to pray for help in the impending battle? You can see him do it in the Sharples Washington, and you can see him get into his handsome coach and drive off to church behind the white horses, whose hoofs, we are told, were carefully blacked every day, and even stop on the way to tell a neighbour that he 'will see him on the morrow relative to that matter of the oats.' In short, there is not a thing about the life and character of George Washington mentioned in the books, incongruous with the noble Sharples pictures, and there is not a single one that is to be reconciled at all to the Stuarts. In the Stuarts, we have Washington the uniform; in the Sharples, Washington the man."

Hawthorne is mainly correct as to the sketches of portraits of female beauties made by Sharples with intent to finish at his leisure. The opportunity of finishing never came; and at his death his wife bore them away to England. Altogether there were ten of these canvases. Seven were left in a more advanced stage than the remainder, and the fair subjects of these seven were Mesdames or Misses Peale, Van Ransalaer, Hamilton, Fulton, Field, Jay, and a daughter of Patrick Henry, the great Southern Orator. At this distance of time, with the very slight information there exists in guidance, the names of the others cannot be ascertained. All were recognized charmers of their several localities. At the period of the sketches being made, balls took place in New York, Philadelphia, Baltimore, Richmond, and Alexandria; the leading families being generally known to each other, they all met as friends. Only very meagre memoranda existed among Mr. Cary's papers as to these sketches, beyond the fact of their purchase from the widow Sharples, together with the other portraits, at the time of realizing her husband's effects after her return to England. He had been working on some of them during the winter of his death, having had offers of considerable sums for them by families in New York. It is clear, therefore, that he intended to finish them. How it came that they were not completed during the period of his first visit, there exists no record. Probably their origin and commission was a private arrangement among the gentry attending the balls graced by the special aspirants, for whose hands in the graceful waltz there would be no lack of gay cavaliers,— whether of North or South need not now be asked,—though future generations of men and women, gentle and simple, will be ever fond of looking at the Sharples delineations of these lovely ones, and through them read what manner were they who held sway in the Court of Washington. If it be not heresy to suggest, may it not be through jealousies of rival charms, that Sharples' completion of the beauties was never carried out? This seems the reasonable explanation of their being in the artist's possession in an unfinished state at the time of his death, and their transmission to England as part of the deceased's belongings. He attended some of the balls, and was by no means indifferent to the charms of lovely women. Macready alludes to them in his letter to Cadwallader Colden; he had seen them and bore witness to their charms. It was probably Macready's influence that caused Maclise to work up the portraits as he did.

MISS FIELD.

CHAPTER VI.

Washington's dreamy hours—Hamilton explains to Sharples that Washington fancies himself connected with the Methuen family, of Corsham, England—The Chief's profound knowledge of English history—Description of Corsham, its old mansion and church—De Witt Clinton's attachment to Sharples—His greatness, and public sympathy at death—Leading public men, through Washington and Hamilton, unite in guaranteeing commissions to Sharples—Biography of the guarantors—Washington, Hamilton, and Tobias Lear take supper with the artist.

WASHINGTON, like most men, had his hours of dreamy romance, few as were the opportunities of indulging them. Without, as it would seem, any but imaginative basis, he connected himself with an old English family in Wiltshire, whose home is in a most sequestered spot, hoary of time and noted for its possession of a mine of wealth in shape of fine paintings of charming class. Finding that Sharples was intimately acquainted with this seat of his mental romance, he indulged it to the full, and with a result adding to its fervour. The memoranda of the artist are quite extended on this favourite hobby-horse, and thus refer to it:—

"General Hamilton had, before my going to Mount Vernon on my professional visit, confided to me that Washington was always happy if he could meet any one acquainted with those parts of England where he fancied some of his family had dwelt, and also that he believed his people had originally been connected, or sprung out of the family of Methuens, of Corsham, Wiltshire; that he expended a good deal of money in books, and in causing researches to be made, but could not in any sufficient manner satisfactorily trace any Washington dove-tailing. He had named to his Chief that I could tell him all about Corsham Court and the Methuens, and I ascribe much of the successful opportunities afforded me for my subject painting to the influence it afforded—so also to the ready compliance as to a first early sitting, and especially to his afterwards consenting to further sittings in order to produce the profile picture. I shall always feel that the old house of the Methuens at Corsham, and of which I could talk to him from personal knowledge, did more in securing me my great advantages than any other help. Lady Washington told me that the General was always in great good-humour after his sittings to me, and had told her he looked forward to them with real pleasure, as I could take him to Corsham Court."

"Washington's profound knowledge of English history astounded me. No more satisfying proof need be given of his extraordinary retentive memory power. He quoted freely, and I doubt not correctly, from old Saxon Chronicles. One morning on which he had called at the cottage in which I had been domiciled in order, as he so kindly and graciously said, 'To have the pleasure of your company and conversation in a before breakfast walk,' he had been led to speak of the Saxon blood in England's royal family. 'It was in the summer time of 1067,' remarked the Chief, ' soon after the Battle of Hastings, that Edgar the Ethling fled from England, with his mother Agatha, his sisters Margaret and Christina, Merleswayne and several good men, and went to Scotland under the protection of King Malcolm, who received them all. Then it was that King Malcolm desired to have Margaret to wife; but the child Edgar and all his men refused for a long time, and she herself also was unwilling. Eventually their scruples were overcome, and Malcolm obtained the lady as his bride, remarking that, "Full oft the unbelieving husband is sanctified and healed through the believing wife."'

Quoting, as he observed he had, the Chronicles from memory, he then continued to say that it was through the daughter of Margaret that the royal family of England traced their Saxon descent. "Here am I, with home so far away, at Mount Vernon, taking in draughts of my country's history from the great one who has written the chapter destined in future ages to afford its most perfect example of patriotism. My having lived near the village of Corsham, and for years known the glorious mansion called 'The Court,' in which had for centuries dwelt the family of Methuen was, he told me, an indescribable delight to him. It was from Washington's own lips I learned the history of this family of Methuens, with which he hugged the hope, if not full belief of descent. With the royal Saxon refugees in 1607, at the Court of Malcolm Caenmore (or the Great Head), came a person of distinction, of German nationality, who had faithfully served the royal family in their exile. On this gentleman King Malcolm bestowed the barony of Methuen, in Perthshire, in acknowledgment of his services, and from this place his descendants have obtained their surname."

During Queen Bess's days John de Methuen fled from persecution, and came to the court of the English queen; from him the Wiltshire Methuens are descended. Paul, the eldest son of John de Methuen, enjoyed the favour of Queen Elizabeth; he married in the family of Rogers of Cannington, Somerset; his grandson, Paul Methuen, became a maker of broadcloth at Bradford, and by coaxing over Flemish workmen, improved the staple trade of that district; his eldest son John represented the borough of Devizes in parliament,

1690—1702, he was also Chancellor of Ireland and Ambassador to the Court of Portugal, where he died 1706. Britton, the antiquarian writer, says he was buried in Westminster Abbey. But by far the most remarkable man of the family was Sir Paul Methuen, K.B., the son of John Methuen, born in 1672; he was at various times Ambassador to the Courts of Vienna, Morocco, Lisbon, Madrid, and Sardinia. Voltaire, in his "Age of Louis XIV.," calls him "one of the most generous, brave, and most sincere men his country ever employed in an embassy." Sir Richard Steele pays him the highest eulogium in the dedication of the seventh volume of the *Spectator*, as a statesman, a man of taste, and a patron of literature. Of his taste the grand collection of paintings at Corsham Court, which he made, answers for. Sir Paul was never married, declaring "that the blessing of wedlock was too great for him to enjoy." Many anecdotes are told respecting his high chivalrous character and courage. He died April 11th, 1757, and was buried by his father in Westminster Abbey.

Like many other of our venerable English village churches, that of Corsham seems to defy the usual wearing of time. It is much as it was when Sharples described it to Washington at Mount Vernon. So also with its almost unrivalled collection of paintings. The time, let it be hoped, may some day come when in America shall exist such treasure mansions; but let their builders and after-guardians beware that nothing but destruction can inevitably befall any painting or water-colour drawing in any private or public place where exists what is called the "furnace heat" of America. It must prove even more destructive of the thin paint film left on canvas through delicate artist's touch, than it is of the human countenance, which it ofttimes reduces to a sad pallor in a few short years of injurious action. If ever the Sharples national portraits get to America, for their own sakes, if not for that of the world, let them be guarded from "furnace heat"—they are not of the tribe of Shadrach, Meshach, and Abednego—rather expose them to long below zero, than roast them.

It is not out of character, or inappropriate to exalted living memory of Washington, to name that the Court at Corsham has in no degree lost any of its charms since the day when he hung on Sharples' descriptions of it in that room at Mount Vernon, where the accomplished artist was striving his best to steal for all mankind the face and form of him whose unalloyed patriotism should chain the admiration of the whole world. It contains one of the grandest collections of paintings housed under the roof of any one private residence in Great Britain. The old mansion being inadequate to contain the splendid collection of paintings, part of which remained in the family London residence, and in order to bring the whole together at the Court, Paul Cobb Methuen greatly enlarged the mansion, from the designs of the architect, John Nash; the park and pleasaunce he greatly improved under the direction of Humphrey Repton, so gifted in landscape gardening. Still, all was not as it should be, and in 1844 great alterations were made; the north front of the house was rebuilt under the architect Bellamy.

The glory of Corsham Court is the magnificent collection of paintings it contains, a list of which almost forms a volume. The house is open to be viewed on prescribed days. The apartments in which these grand works are shown are the grand hall, the state drawing-room, state bed-chamber, the cabinet-room, picture-gallery, music-room, drawing-room, and dining-room: the old masters are here grandly represented by their works. No rubbish palmed upon the unlearned, but the real article everywhere.

Dwelling on all that had transpired during his sittings to Sharples, the artist had made very careful record of these, to him, "most eventful days of my existence." He wrote that on two mornings the Chief, on taking his seat, remarked, "'Well, my friend, tell me more of Corsham and the Court, if your memory serves you.' I never knew any one more thoroughly enjoy a descriptive relation, than he did of anything concerned with Corsham. I am convinced he believed himself of the Methuen race. From wandering during years of youth in its churchyard, I knew by heart all the quaint inscriptions on its gravestones, and some of these were singularly odd and impressive. I made a pencil sketch of the church to best of my memory. It had a nave, chancel, three aisles, besides a chapel on the north side, and a tower surmounted with a spire. On one side of its south porch are the letters E. M. H., 1631, and the same initials are on the east and west. My memory enabled me to quote the remarkable inscription over the porch, and which runs thus:—

> 'In this Chvrch Porch
> Lyeth ye body of William
> Tasker Gent, who choose
> Rather to be a Doore Kee
> per to the House of His
> God then to Dwell in
> the Tents of Wickednes
> He departed this life,
> Jan. the 20 An 1684
> Aged 69 yeares.'

He listened with deep interest to the recital of these lines, and before leaving the room after the sitting, asked me to write them out, word for word, in the lines, spelling, and capitals as over the church porch. He begged me also to endeavour to make for him at my leisure, so far as memory enabled, a rough sketch of all I could remember of the church and court-house, and on my presenting them at the following morning's sitting, he seemed as though he could not give expression to his thankfulness. I had not then been long at work when I told him I had called to mind a queer inscription on a gravestone in this same churchyard. I related to him that in England gravestones were not always reliable evidence as to length of days of the individual in whose honour erected. In the case of Sarah Jarvis, she of Corsham longevity is represented not only to have reached her hundred and seventh year, but to have been endowed with 'fresh teeth' not long before her passing away.

'In Memory of
Sarah Jarvis
who departed this Life the
11 Day of December 1753
in the Hundred and Seventh
Year of her age.
Some time before her Death
She had Fresh Teeth.'

He enjoyed this wondrously. I had again to resort to the copying out, and General Hamilton told me how greatly these narrations had increased his interest in Corsham and the Methuens."

The old Methuen mansion at Corsham, with its art treasures, must have been doubly dear in the memory of Sharples, and he, as he wrote, "warmed up" in relating all these matters to Washington. Romney, his old master, as well as his friend Opie, would ofttimes have been there to study its grand pictures. Wolcot, too, who had drawn Opie from obscurity in 1780, would without doubt often be of the party; for they were all three close friends of Sharples, and, as artists, would gather round the Corsham treasures to drink at the fountain of inspiration. It was hither the father of Sir Thomas Lawrence brought his talented son, and in proof that he took advantage of his visits, Sir Joshua Reynolds immediately on seeing his early performances exclaimed, "You have been looking at the old masters, I see; but my advice is this: study nature, study nature." Young Lawrence was born at Bristol, from whence his father removed to Devizes, where he became landlord of the Bear Hotel. It was for a long time a moot point what profession the talented boy should follow, for he excelled both in the capacity of a painter and elocutionist. It was a favourite pastime of his father's to introduce his son to the guests who stopped at his house, on the road from London to Bath, and make him recite; in this way the lad first made the acquaintance of Garrick and Mrs. Siddons. Ultimately, the profession of a painter was decided on, and his splendid success shows the wisdom of this course.

These and such-like were the themes discoursed of by Sharples to Washington.

Knowing Washington's deep interest in Corsham, although it could hardly extend beyond the realm of sentiment, yet one feels that this venerable English church and surroundings he had never seen, possess, to say the least, a charm for all who venerate him. In the case of Sharples it was passing strange Washington should have found one who knew the place almost as a home, and could impart to his imagination the touch of reality needed to rouse him almost to enthusiasm. If either were now in the flesh, and wandering thither to consult the old gravedigger now holding office, respecting this phenomenon, he will gladly tell the tale, "Az ow the ould lady ad long kep er bed, an zo wen opple time wur cum, she zed to er datur, 'I sh'd like sum opples to yeat,' and er datur zed, 'Lor a-massey, mothur! wat be taakin about, you can't yeat um, vor you got no teef;' and the ould lady zed 'Rost-um,' and zo th' ded, an she yeat um aal up. An zo wen opple time wur cum agen, she zed to er datur, 'I sh'd like sum oppols,' and er datur zed, 'Lor, mother, you can't yeat um, vor you got no teef;' and th' ould lady zed, 'Breng em yer,' an zo ;h' ded, an th' nex day th' wur aal gon, and er datur zed, 'Wur be th' oppols gon to, mothur?' an she zed, 'I yeat um aal;' an she zed, 'You couden, mothur, you got no teef;' and th' ould lady zed, 'Put yer vinger in me mouf, and zee wur I hant;' and zo sh' ded, and she ad vour, but sh' diden liv long ater.'"

This is the Wiltshire vernacular, word for word, as the veteran would this very day translate and explain the tombstone. Reader, laugh not at the idiom of the gravedigger (the word "moonraker" is a relic of the grand language, the term is in England applied to men of Wiltshire birth, one of whom in bygone days is presumed to have believed the moon's reflection in a pond to be a cheese, and set to work endeavouring to rake it out.) We are proud of a remnant of that language spoken by our Wessex forefathers, that in which the glorious King Alfred spoke and wrote; the language of kings centuries before the Norman adulterated it with the coarse French he spoke. In the graveyard, close under the church, are two or three stones of a peculiar obelisk shape, which are gravely asserted to mark the burial-place of a witch; near at hand are two stone coffins, taken up from beneath the floor of the church during a late restoration—these are shaped for the reception of the head, and drained by a hole in the centre. Now, while on the subject of stone coffins, we must not pass over the stir caused among antiquaries by the discovery of one near this same Corsham in the year 1722, and respecting which the

Rev. Gilbert Lake, B.D., the Vicar of Chippenham, wrote to the celebrated antiquary, Thomas Hearne, as follows:— "Nov. 17, 1722. I cannot but let you know that a day labourer hereabouts, as he was cleaning a ditch, the sixth of this Month, lighted upon a Stone Coffin. All the bones of a humane body were in it, and, as I am informed, they were large ones: but what they were I cannot say: for when I went on Tuesday last to see it, I found few, and those the smallest bones belonging to a body, remaining. The country folk had, I conceived out of covetousness and ignorance, carried off the skull, with a complete set of fine teeth in it, and the largest bones belonging to it. The place where this Coffin is now to be seen is three Miles from hence (Chippenham), in the Parish of Cosham (a place I find twice taken notice of by Leland in his Collect): 'Tis but one ground distant from the great Road to Bath. It lies East and West, as the bodies of Christians do now a days."

Besides the church—which is dedicated to St. Bartholomew—Corsham possessed two religious houses, one a friary, afterwards used as a parsonage, the other a nunnery, which was converted into a public-house. At one time, near the church, stood a gaol and an old court-house; an ancient market cross once graced the town, all of which was indiscriminately swept away at about the period when Washington was trying to master, through the sketches and oral description of his artist friend, that which until then had been but an outline dream of the imagination. The market-house, which was then built, has lately been considerably altered and usefully improved. Corsham can boast of being the birthplace of a poet—Sir Richard Blackmore—a physician of some eminence, but chiefly remembered by his literary work. The adjoining hamlet of Pickwick was the remote means of furnishing Charles

Dickens with a name for his immortal hero. One night the guard of the down mail from London to Bath picked up a baby, and bestowed on it, as a surname, that of the place where found. The boy throve, grew up, and flourished; in time he, as proprietor, horsed the coaches running from the White Hart, Bath, to the White Horse Cellar, Piccadilly. Dickens, struck with the name he so frequently saw painted on the coaches, adopted it, which will, no doubt, live so long and wherever the literature of England is known.

It has been named that Washington esteemed highly Sharples' scientific attainments, and that during sittings for his portraits their conversation was not confined to the news and topics of English higher-circle life, but was frequently directed to the subject of the most recent artillery practice and invention. The artist had novel ideas, and fancied he could invent a gun that would eclipse all artillery then existing. To say the least, the General was struck with his notions, and saw "something" in them beyond speculative theory.

De Witt Clinton had early become attached to "the English artist," and realized his knowledge and practical experience outside of art matters. He had made a commencement of Clinton's portrait in oils, but never completed it, the more profitable crayon work having taken him from the higher walk; and it had been set aside with the Priestley, Jefferson, Adams, Hamilton, and the fair beauties who a year previously had been "rubbed in" on canvases, hoped for as a stock that would yield fame and likewise dollars.

Clinton is largely answerable for having lured the painter from the pursuit of his profession. At his and Governor Morris's instigation he was induced to accompany the commissioners appointed by the Legislature of the State of New York for exploring the country from Lake Ontario to the navigable water communicating with the Mohawk

River, in order to report on the expediency and practicability of uniting these waters by a canal. According to a memorandum made at the time he did not altogether fall in with this idling of time, but his devotion to Clinton overcame his objections, and he abandoned for the time his money-making crayon portrait creation. He wrote, "I could not resist his urging; he has been such a real friend, his truthfulness of heart is so marked, and the earnest way he has appealed to me have triumphed over my own and the objections of my wife, and I am off. Governor Morris is to be of the party, and also Mr. Van Ransalaer, whose charming wife says I must go."

It says not a little for Sharples' ability and discernment that he entirely realized De Witt Clinton's greatness, and that in him the State of New York had within her people a statesman to whom, above all party—beyond all party—the admiration, the confidence—the enthusiastic support of the State was given, and who if he now lived would, there is little doubt, as concentratedly be the man of New York, as these millions could bind their united devotion to the cause of any one among their vastness. When Clinton lived, the State was not the giant Commonwealth which it now is. Had it been, his eminent adaptation for greatness would have been even more generally recognized than it was. In person and in mind, the nobility that is of nature was demonstrated. Always a victor—victorious while all who clung to his fortunes failed—he was triumphant because the people saw that he was worthy to be, in all fields of action and duty, the representative of New York, and as such, repeatedly she presented his name as her own—whose name was identical with her own.

Thus heralded, it was apparent that not New York alone was to be the scene of his talent. The name of Clinton was associated with the presidential nomination. It had been prematurely presented once, but the error time had repaired.

While his name was rising on the popular voice—while the glowing success of internal improvement had turned to it the gaze of all the States who desired to garden their wilderness—destiny wove for him the robe of death in place of that of power. What an evening was that, when the very heart of the city of his residence thrilled, as the tidings of his loss was uttered by one mourner to another, and grief was the language of the heart—not of official proclamation.

As with the great Webster and Clay, the presidency never put its purple on him. Not even the rank of a Cabinet Minister, though offered him, was ever possessed by him. And now, who thinks that De Witt Clinton is less illustrious now, because he failed to be the occupant of the White House? James Monroe was President, almost without opposition, for eight years. Good and useful as he was, who remembers his name before that of Clinton, when recalling the men whose names are the wealth of American annals? More and more is the appreciation of Clinton, because his mind was the ruler in his day, without the adventitious aids of office.

Such of the artist's letters addressed to Robert Cary in London as have been found, and the leaves torn out of his memorandum-book and sent to his wife in Philadelphia during his stay at Mount Vernon, evidence the deeply interesting character of all memoranda of Sharples that have come down through Mr. Cary's papers, and it must ever be a subject of regret that no thorough search had been made among his wife's letters at the time of her death; such would probably have brought to light much that he had communicated to her of conversations with Washington during the moods of communicativeness generally ruling on occasions of the General sitting to his favoured artist friend. There is nothing to show the actual date of Sharples' presence at Mount Vernon, whether he had stayed there once only or oftener; but inasmuch as the Washington portraits were received in England before the close of 1797, and it is known from his letters that he was there in the autumn of 1795, the presumption is that he paid one visit only of any duration, and which extended into a fortnight. He had sittings before, and these were given in Philadelphia. All doubt on this point of the General sitting to him in Philadelphia is removed by the fact of Washington, Hamilton, and Lee meeting together at his rooms as recorded by himself. The probability is that Sharples worked on the full-faced portrait in Philadelphia, and went to Mount Vernon more as a visitor than in any professional character. The General would be in uniform when in the city. The profile painting was clearly the outcome of Mount Vernon, and, as is stated, consequent on the artist being so deeply impressed with what he termed "his magnificent appearance in evening dress." In the first instance this was painted to gratify himself, but afterwards paid for by Washington, and presented by him to Mr. Cary.

In addition to portraits of noted men arranged for at the suggestion of General Washington, and for which the artist would receive his full terms, a number of prominent men, zealous and devoted friends of Washington, subscribed their names for portraits in oil, to be painted at the artist's convenience; so that he seems very early to have left the day of anxiety altogether a matter of the past. The original of this requisition exists in shape of a leaf from a business memorandum-book of Hamilton's, on which is inscribed the names of public men who would appear to have thus made themselves responsible each for his portrait.

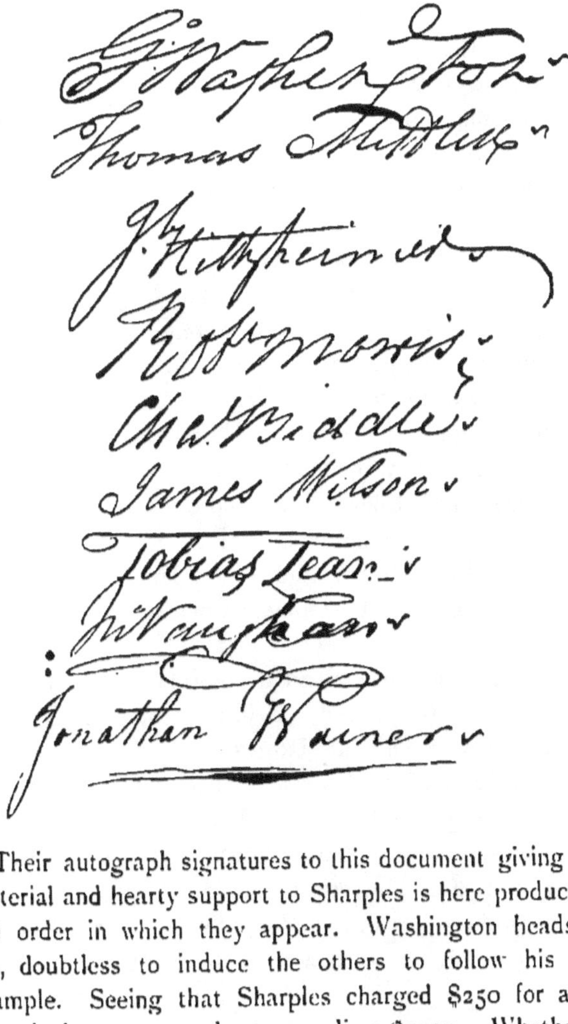

G. Washington
Thomas Mifflin
J. Hillhouse
Robt Morris
Cha Biddle
James Wilson
Tobias Lear
J. Vaughan
Jonathan Williams

Their autograph signatures to this document giving such material and hearty support to Sharples is here produced in the order in which they appear. Washington heads the list, doubtless to induce the others to follow his kind example. Seeing that Sharples charged $250 for an oil portrait, here were orders exceeding $2000. Whether he painted many of the worthies is not now known. He certainly painted Robert Morris, most probably for some public purpose. The fact of this portrait not being now traceable, goes to show how such often drop out of existence, even within the period of rather less than a century. Sharples' papers refer only to the known two oil paintings, the profile and full-face. The signature cannot refer to either of the two portraits known as the Sharples portraits sent to Robert Cary, as one of these was paid for by Mr. Cary, and the other was in all probability paid for anterior to Hamilton asking him to head a document purposing such support to "the artist from England." It has been suggested that the signatures were given as guarantees for payment for the portrait of the belles of the day, outlined in oils on canvases by Sharples, and, according to tradition, designed to hang in a Philadelphia ball-room. This could hardly have been the true solution of this guarantee document. Sharples was notoriously neglectful in the execution of commissions, proved by his having set off with De Witt Clinton and Van Ransalaer, on a long surveying expedition, at a moment when full of unexecuted commissions.

In connection with these signatures obtained by Hamilton, guaranteeing, as is believed, a defined support to Sharples, the following particulars are interesting :—

Thomas Mifflin was born at Philadelphia in 1744, of Quaker parentage; educated in Philadelphia College, and afterwards entered a counting-house. He visited Europe in 1765, and after his return entered into partnership with an elder brother. In 1772 and 1773 was elected a member of the Legislature; in 1774, a delegate to the first Congress. Appointed a major of one of the first regiments raised in Philadelphia, he accompanied Washington to Cambridge as aide-de-camp. In August was made Quartermaster-General; soon afterwards Adjutant-General; Brigadier-General in 1776, and Major-General in 1777. He commanded the covering party during the retreat from Long

Island, and was active in arousing the militia of Pennsylvania. He brought aid to Washington before the battles of Trenton and Princeton. After the battle of Germantown, he resigned his commission of Quartermaster-General on the ground of ill-health, and was immediately chosen a member of the new board of war. He was engaged in the Conway cabal against General Washington. He was elected a delegate to Congress in 1782, and was chosen President of Congress in 1783. He was a member and Speaker of the Legislature of Pennsylvania in 1785. In 1787 he was chosen a delegate to the Convention which formed the Constitution of the United States. He was President of the Supreme Executive Council of Pennsylvania from October, 1788, to October, 1790; was President of the Convention which formed the second Constitution of Pennsylvania, in 1790; Governor of Pennsylvania from 1791 to 1800; and was a member of the Legislature in 1800; in which year he died at Lancaster, Pennsylvania.

Jacob Hiltzeimer served as one of the representatives of the city of Philadelphia in the General Assembly of the Commonwealth, from the year 1786 until 1797, and resided in Seventh Street, below Market Street.

Robert Morris, a warm friend and patron of Sharples, was born at Liverpool, England, January 20th, 1733. He came to Philadelphia with his father when thirteen years of age, and entered the counting-house of Charles Willing, with whom he was in partnership from 1754 to 1793. He was supercargo on several voyages, during one of which he was taken prisoner by the French. He opposed the Stamp Act; and in signing the Non-Importation Agreement, in 1765, the house of Willing and Morris made a great sacrifice. From 1776 to 1778 he was a delegate to the Continental Congress, and voted against the Declaration of Independence, but afterwards signed it. He frequently exerted his personal credit to the utmost in support of the army, and raised a million and a half dollars to enable Washington to proceed to Yorktown, where Cornwallis was captured. He founded the Bank of North America, and from February, 1781, to November, 1784, he was its superintendent of finance. In 1786, he was a member of the Pennsylvania Legislature, and, in 1787, a member of the Convention which formed the Constitution of the United States. He was United States Senator from 1789 to 1795. He declined the office of Secretary of the Treasury, and recommended Alexander Hamilton for that office.

James Wilson was born near St. Andrew's, Scotland, about 1742. He studied at Glasgow, St. Andrew's, and Edinburgh. He came to Philadelphia, where he was first employed as tutor in the College and Academy; commenced the study of the law, and was admitted to the Bar in 1768. He practised at Reading, Carlisle, and Annapolis, and then returned to Philadelphia, which was his home during the remainder of his life. He wrote upon the controversy between the mother country and the Colonies. He was a member of the Conventions held in 1774 and 1775. In May, 1775, he took his seat in Congress, and voted in favour of the Declaration of Independence. He was a member of the Convention which formed the Constitution of the United States, and also of the Convention of Pennsylvania which met to consider the propriety of adopting that Constitution. His lectures on Law, delivered in the University of Pennsylvania, were published in 1804. He died at Edenton, North Carolina, on the 28th of August, 1798. He was father of Burd Wilson, a lawyer and judge in Pennsylvania, afterwards a clergyman of the Episcopal Church, and the biographer of Bishop White.

Charles Biddle was an active patriot during the American Revolution. Under the Pennsylvania Constitution of 1776, he was Vice-President of the Supreme Executive Council of the State, when Benjamin Franklin was President. One of his brothers was Commodore Nicholas Biddle, who was blown up in the *Randolph*, in a desperate and unequal conflict with a British ship of the line. In 1778, Charles Biddle married Miss Hannah Shepard, of North Carolina. Nicholas Biddle, for many years the President of the Bank of the United States, was one of their children.

John Vaughan, a native of England, and who resided in Philadelphia for half a century, was one of the truest philanthropists of the "City of Love." He was for many years the Librarian of the American Philosophical Society. The delight which most men take in making and hoarding dollars, he took in rendering services, in discharging benevolent offices, and serving his fellow-man for good. He would go from one end of the city to the other to obtain employment for an honest man. Would there were in our day more such blessed characters! He died on the 30th of December, 1841, at the close of his eighty-eighth year. Vaughan was a prominent member of the Unitarian Church in Locust Street, Philadelphia, and met his death through being knocked down by a runaway horse.

Tobias Lear was born at Portsmouth, New Hampshire, on the 19th September, 1762, and graduated at Harvard University in 1783. In 1785 he was General Washington's Private Secretary, and served him faithfully until his death, and was most liberally remembered by him in his will. Lear was frequently the medium of communication between Washington and Robert Cary. In 1801 he was made Consul-General at St. Domingo; and from 1804 to 1812 was Consul-General at Algiers, and Commissioner to conclude a peace with Tripoli. The latter duty he performed in 1805, much to the dissatisfaction of General Eaton, who was gaining important advantages over the Tripolitans.

Lear's conduct was approved by his Government, though much blamed by a portion of the public. He died at Washington City on the 10th of October, 1816, being at that time an accountant in the War Department.

It too frequently happens, and especially in America, that the noisy ones of the world alone are rendered prominent in its estimation. Tobias Lear was a man little heard of during his life, and afterwards known to but few, only as having been Washington's private secretary. He deserved more than this, for a more faithful, earnest man never served sovereign or people. Ever at his Chief's side in times of trouble as in hours of calm, and these latter were far less frequent than imagination would suggest, Tobias Lear's labours were rendered at times herculean. But for such a helper and friend, Washington must inevitably have succumbed to the weight of the terrible burden thrown upon his shoulders. The ordinary citizen of America has no pity for the public man, and no rest is permitted him. He must submit to unlimited importuning, and under endless forms. Lear was ever at hand, with a cheerfulness knowing no bound, to carry through the ceaseless labour devolving on him. He was in every sense a good, true, and faithful man. No matter how heavy the call on his time and attention, he never complained, nor did his habitual cheerfulness ever forsake him. He was not the mere secretary, his Chief highly valued his counsel, and his country owes him far more than it knows of. His judgment was of the highest order, and he had the happiness of securing his only coveted reward, the esteem of him he served. Washington appreciated and loved him.

During his residence in Philadelphia Sharples entertained Washington, Hamilton, and Tobias Lear at supper. Cary had an account of it from Sharples' pen. Despite all search it cannot be found.

CHAPTER VII.

Mary Washington—Existence of an authenticated Portrait by Middleton—Its mutilated condition—Letter of Washington stating its injuries, how occurring, and desiring repair—The portrait sent to England for restoration—Royal Academician Bird undertakes it—The widow Sharples medium of communicating with the Custis family as to restoration of the painting—Bird completes it—Cary eventually pays the cost—General Grant views the portrait—His letter to the owner, expressing great thankfulness for the privilege extended him.

MARY WASHINGTON! The very name is redolent of sweetness and goodness. Martha is grand, but somehow Mary is, if possible, more feminine and softer. How wide are the sympathies evoked where the trail of greatness is in the pathway! The mother of such a man as Washington must ever be an object of eager interest. The dark shadow of the grave, though enfolding her remains in its unbroken silence, has happily been prevented hiding from succeeding generations the features of her to whom the world owes so much.

It has been generally believed that no portrait of Washington's mother existed. The error is removed. Washington possessed a portrait of his mother, painted by an English officer named Middleton.

The painting was terribly mutilated during a journey to headquarters in Philadelphia, being reduced to such a condition as to prevent its being hung in any but a bedchamber. Sharples, when at Mount Vernon painting the great Chief and his wife, was consulted as to what could be done with it. A huge hole had been ground out of its centre, through abrasion of the posts of a bedstead carelessly placed in the waggon with the portrait, and its condition during many years was most woebegone. Several partially disjointed pieces of the canvas had been roughly glued on an improvised back, and although by this rude contrivance its more serious injuries were concealed, yet it was not presentable for mural decoration. Like a truly affectionate son, Washington ever retained it, worried and tattered as it was, in his bedroom, where it remained until sent to England—whether to Mr. Cary in Sharples' charge, when he returned after his first visit to America, is not known; but certain it is that Sharples and Cary were both concerned, not only in the means taken for its repair, but they went a step further, and after the paint had been transferred to a new canvas, its restoration, or, as termed in their memoranda, its "doing up," was confided to one of the ablest artists in portraiture then living, named Bird, who was a Royal Academician and portrait painter to the Princess Charlotte. Whether Sharples was alive and personally consulted Bird is not known. Sharples himself knew Bird, who appears to have been a personal friend of Robert Cary, Washington's agent, the man to whom America is indebted for the portraits of Washington and his wife.

> "Oh, that those lips had language! Life has passed
> With me but roughly since I heard thee last.
> Those lips are thine—thy own sweet smile I see,
> The same that oft in childhood solaced me;
> Voice only fails, eke how distinct they say,
> 'Grieve not, my child, chase all thy fears away!'
> The meek intelligence of those dear eyes
> (Blest be the art that can immortalize,—
> The art that baffles Time's tyrannic claim
> To quench it) here shines on me still the same."
>
> COWPER.

All doubt as to the portrait of Mary, Washington's mother, is prevented by a letter from Mount Vernon, bearing date 1792, several years before Sharples painted there, and which is addressed to Mr. Charles Carter, who married a niece of Washington. It is a communication in reply to one evidently on private matters. He had offered his services in getting the painting repaired, and which Washington declined. Washington's yearning to his mother's portrait evidences endearment and devoted affection. Mr. Carter would appear to have asked for an appointment in the War Office, failing this, an army commission for his son, and that he should be admitted as a resident member in the General's family. The General explains his utter inability to accede, and in his usual straightforward language explains his mode of dealing with such applications. As applicable to his mother's portrait, it is reproduced.

"Mount Vernon, May 19, 1792.

MY DEAR SIR,—Your letter of the 30th ult. was on its way to Philadelphia whilst I was on my journey to this place, owing to which I did not receive it until it reverberated; this must be my apology for not giving the receipt of it an earlier acknowledgment.

It is very good of you to offer to get the presumed needful done to my mother's portrait, painted by an Englishman named Middleton, who formerly held a commission in the British service, and who had been a professional artist in England. Robert Cary has frequently urged its being sent to London, that he might confide the repair of the hole and the completion of the picture itself—which, but for the face, is by most persons deemed imperfect—to one of the most eminent English painters; but I have been so long accustomed to look on the mutilation, as almost to disregard it. The portrait is identified with my whole life. My mother gave it me, and the large hole was thrust through it in course of waggon travel to Philadelphian quarters. Under the disfigurement, Mrs. Washington and myself ever afterwards preferred it hanging in my bedroom, where its wounded, unfinished, and apparently neglected condition escaped frequent unpleasant remark. Any change wrought in the picture beyond repairing the hole would be the reverse of improvement to my eye. I am happy above measure in having it, wounded and apparently neglected as it is, rather than incur the penalty of its absence.

It would give me pleasure to receive your son into my family if it could be made tolerably convenient to me, or if any advantage was likely to result from it to the young gentleman himself. I was in no real want even of Howell Lewis, but understanding that he was spending his time rather idly, and at the same time very slenderly provided for by his father, I thought for the few months which remained to be accomplished of my own servitude, by taking him under my care I might impress him with ideas and give him a turn to some pursuit or other that might be serviceable to him hereafter, but what that will be I am at present as much at a loss to decide as you would be; for as the heads of the different departments have by law the appointment of their own clerks—are responsible for the conduct of them, are surrounded always with applicants, and, I presume, have their own inclinations and friends to gratify—I never have in a single instance, and I am pretty sure I shall not now begin, recommended any one to either of them.

My family, now Howell is admitted into it, will be more than full, and in truth more than is convenient for the house—as Mr. Dandridge, a nephew of Mrs. Washington, is already one of it, and but one room for him, Howell, and another person to sleep in; all the others being appropriated to public or private uses (the words "purposes, although it is one of the largest houses in the city" followed here, but had been marked through by the General's pen).

If your son Charles is of age, and it should be your and his own inclination to pursue a military course, I would, if any vacancy should happen (at present there is none) in one of the regiments, endeavour to place him therein. You will perceive I have made age the condition—the reason is, it is established as a rule in the War Office to appoint none knowingly that are under it.

With love to Mrs. Carter.

Faithfully yours,
GEORGE WASHINGTON.

Charles Carter."

Nothing has been traced among Mr. Cary's letters or memoranda showing when or through whom the portrait of Mary Washington was sent to England for the necessary repair. Mrs. Sharples clearly had it in possession after her husband's death, and would appear to have held it for several years later. There would seem to have been a great deal done to it, according to a communication made by her to Mrs. Morgan, of Albany, to whom the widow had written, stating that she had twice addressed Mr. Custis, son of Lady Washington, on the matter, but had not received any reply. However wrecked its condition before voyaging to England, it is now the portrait of a very beautiful woman, and reflects the highest credit on Bird's restoration. True were Washington's words to Sharples as to his mother being the most beautiful woman he had ever seen. It would be sad to know that after Washington and his wife's death there should have been wanting, in those of his family left behind, heed for the portrait of his mother to which he had clung with such fond affection. It certainly does seem that with its disappearance from Mount Vernon, the poor maimed heirloom had ceased having any reverent guardian. This points to the conclusion that it had left there some time before his death. If Lady Washington had despatched it to England, more readiness would have been exhibited in having the repairs made, and there would have been greater probability of some instructions existing, but not a scrap has come to light. The most likely truth is that Sharples had it in charge to England on his first return there, and the reason of it remaining behind when he returned to America was that Bird had not finished it when Sharples embarked. Some think it arrived in England during the interval between Sharples' visits to America, and to have been sent to him in England direct from Mount Vernon, but there is nothing in proof of this. Probably communications had been addressed to Mr. Custis, and such definite instructions as must naturally, under the circumstances, have been desired, could not be obtained from him. The family would instruct minutely in accordance with his latest wishes, knowing as they did the love and veneration with which he regarded the portrait. Washington, Sharples said, had a manner of impressing his words such as he had never known in any other living man. He would, therefore, dwell on the remembrance of his conversations at Mount Vernon relative to the portrait, and Washington expressed wishes as to the repairs, or possibly any suggestions as to alterations he in conversation may have deemed prudent to urge as improving to it, although it is hardly probable he would himself venture on any great change, or intend much being done to it beyond mere repair of the hole. When at Mount Vernon, Sharples had explained that any patch made in the canvas would always be a desight, and had told him there were persons in London who could remove all the paint from the old canvas and transfer it on to a new canvas, which process was recommended for adoption. This would leave it open to any eminent painter to improve greatly its general character, although Middleton was no mean artist. The General could not be brought to believe in the safety of any such treatment, and naturally inquired why he, an artist, would not undertake it. It was needless endeavouring to explain that such work was mechanical, and did not fall within an artist's skill. But then it will be remembered that Sharples was a thorough mechanic. Eminent portrait painters, however, say that he would hardly be equal to such a task, or at any rate, it was one he would not have been justified in entering upon. The probability is that Sharples overcame Washington's scruples in regard to the poor tattered picture, and that he afterwards conveyed it to England for the needed repair.

All that is known is that the tattered picture was transferred to a new canvas, and that when this had been accomplished, it was placed in the hands of Bird, a Royal Academician, for him, as is presumed, to deal with as he deemed best. Bird was an eminent man, and we may be assured dealt with it in every way that was best calculated to render it what friends would desire it to be. He had, according to Mrs. Sharples' letters to Mrs. Morgan, "instructions from my husband to do all that could be done in improving the picture, every care being taken to preserve the likeness." This remark indicates Sharples' presence in London with the picture, and that he was a party to instruct the work, evidently something beyond repair: it was to be "improved." Sharples or Mr. Cary must have received some such orders as these when the portrait came from America. This order to Bird is certainly a very free commission, one that it would have been the height of imprudence to give in a general way; but Bird would hardly care for such a job, and we may be assured would not meddle with it in any way but for its improvement, and especially would he respect the painter's treatment of the face and features. Matters of detail he would very likely change so as to bring the subject more into harmony with his own views of what it should be, and it may safely be assumed that Middleton's portrait of Mary Washington came off Bird's easel in every way greatly improved. It is now unmistakably the work of a good painter, although a skilled examiner may say that more than one person had a hand in it. It is not an Opie or a Romney, but is, nevertheless, a thoroughly able work, and the whole world has cause of rejoicing that it fell into Bird's hands, and that a man of the sound judgment and discretion of Robert Cary had the selection of the artist to whom such a treasure should be entrusted.

The picture was allowed to remain in Mrs. Sharples' hands for some time after her husband's death, and it can only be assumed that she, in the first instance, paid Bird his charge, as Mrs. Morgan had corresponded thereon with Mr. Custis, but there was nothing to be found as to the sum paid; although from the fact of her transacting the business with a friend it would look as though she found difficulties in arranging it direct with Mr. Custis. Mrs. Sharples was not in straitened circumstances, she and her daughter had an income sufficient for their needs, and she clearly did not apply to Mr. Cary for the money paid Bird, and which would be about the same amount as he would have charged for painting a portrait, certainly not much short of a hundred pounds. In the first instance she paid it herself, though from the painting being afterwards found in Mr. Cary's possession, it would appear that he, as Washington's friend, had recouped her. There is nothing to show that Mr. Custis had ever made any application for the portrait to be returned to America, neither is there any evidence that Cary troubled himself about the money or sought to quit himself of the imposed possession. At the time of Sharples' return to America, the portrait of Washington's mother was left behind, and nothing more regarding it was traceable in any after communications. Mr. Cary reimbursed Mrs. Sharples her payment to Bird, and the picture seems never afterwards to have been claimed. It would be unjust to charge the portrait having been allowed to remain permanently in England as evidencing family indifference. It should be borne in mind that its disfigurement was such as rendered it utterly unpresentable. It had never been exhibited to visitors at Mount Vernon, or hung in any but a bedchamber. Moreover, it had been packed off in Washington's lifetime, and very probably had passed from recollection, an easy enough occurrence, consequent on delay with Bird, who always had his hands full and was notoriously heedless. At Washington and his wife's death there would be no remembrance of it with his executors, beyond an attic ragged old portrait, prized until damaged, but then considered worthless. Cary would be sensitive on the point of naming what he had paid Bird, and would be quite content to remain its possessor until some one applied for it. It was in Bird's hands for some years after Sharples' death; and when Cary passed away there was nobody who would appreciate it beyond the head of a very beautiful woman, said to be the mother of George Washington. It would appear clear, that but for Mrs. Sharples and Robert Cary, it might have shared the sad fate of thousands of other family portraits, in being carted away to a broker's shop as an article of mural furnishing. Even as such, Mary Washington would have held her own; she is, and ever will be, a beautiful woman;

and every beholder of her portrait, as restored by Bird, the Royal Academician, and who lived in her day, will admit Mary Washington's lovely face to be all the world would wish it, and must feel the truth of the remark of a New Englander who was present with General Grant on the occasion of his viewing the portrait, "Anybody would know she's somebody." The autotype reproduction given in this volume proves her to have been a truly beautiful woman.

During his last visit to England, General Grant saw the portrait of Washington's mother. Miss Edwardes, the owner, grand-niece of the Carys, having had his wish intimated to her, very graciously sent it to London, in order that he might be gratified without making a special journey into Northamptonshire. Grant thus feelingly acknowledged her kind attention :—

"General Grant presents his respectful compliments to Miss Edwardes, the envied owner of the Middleton painting of Mary Washington, and begs to tender her his hearty thanks for exceeding kindness in sending to London, for his convenience and gratification, this admirable and evidently 'to the life' portrait of Mary Washington, who, above all others, must be held in deepest affection and exalted remembrance by every American.

When mentioning at the Legation his desire to see the portrait, he had no wish, much less any intention, to put Miss Edwardes to the trouble of sending the treasure so long a distance; he therefore esteems more highly the honour conferred. He had seen the two portraits of General Washington, and that of Martha, his wife, by Sharples, owned by Mr. Robert Cary, who, he now learns, was great-uncle of Miss Edwardes. He fully realizes all that his countrymen have said regarding the excellence of these fine paintings, and their value, not alone to the people among whom should be their home, but to the whole world.

Of the many kindnesses shown him by friends in England, none is more deeply impressed. He has not removed the painting from the case, and has returned it in charge of a special messenger from the Legation. All endeavours to see Sharples' portrait of Robert Fulton, or to ascertain its owner, have been ineffectual. Should Miss Edwardes be enabled to help this object, his obligations would be further increased.

Whenever the day arrives for the return of these paintings to America, Congress will, he doubts not, unanimously do its duty in the matter. The painting of Mary Washington has especial claims as the only portrait of her known to exist. General Grant had hoped that Middleton's portrait was free for disposition, he hears therefore with regret that family arrangements prevent for a few years this desired accomplishment.

General Grant begs to repeat his becoming sense of the honour done him, as also to express his entire confidence that at the proper time Miss Edwardes' family will give due weight to his countrymen's natural wish to possess the gem, happily, for America, under her family control."

General Grant, from the moment of first seeing the Sharples Washingtons, unhesitatingly pronounced them as the portraits of future universal adoption. His words were, "They are the likenesses of the man, they tell us that man wrested our country from too high-handed rule, and anybody can see in that face all that we know him to have been." These words, so distinctively characteristic of Grant, are forcibly true of him regarding whom they were uttered. The people of the United States make history with remarkable rapidity. Grant frequently dwelt on the great national good Sharples portraits would serve, that the people needed a presentment more to its heart than any hitherto given them. Sharples had deep sympathies with the sect known as "Plymouth Brethren." Grant was aware of this, and stated to a gentleman at the American Legation in London, that he could read this in his treatment of the Washington subjects. He doubted not their power for good. "What we need," he remarked to the same friend, "is less sensation; we need what that face instructively conveys, the binding our people more closely in the bonds of a common brotherhood, the ensuring, under the blessing of a benign and merciful Providence, the unity of the country, and its future prosperity and peace! These portraits," he added, "will help mightily in working this change. I wish the originals could be seen in all our large communities; failing this, let the autotype reproductions get everywhere, but especially in the public schools." Grant, when thus giving expression to a cherished hope, was but repeating the words of Longfellow, who, just before his death, had so urgently named his hopeful wish they might be hung in all the public schools of the country.

Like Washington, Grant has passed away to his rest. Whatever his aspirations at one period of life may have been, its close would see no joys in the brilliant events of victorious armies. His heart hoped for a future for his country coming out of unity and peace and love. At the close of his life he believed that the change had not come "through observation," that it had not been brought about by any special efforts on the part of patriots, much less of politicians; that it was not the result of any visible movements on the part of the religious community, but that it came down upon the hearts of men like the dew from heaven, gently and silently.

While acknowledging this to be a benison from the God

of peace, it is not too much to say that, so far as any human cause or instrumentality is concerned, the influences which have brought it about centred in the sick-bed of one man, and that the change had its culmination in the funeral casket which was carried to its resting-place through an assemblage of more than two millions of people, gathered from the east and the west, the north and the south, to witness the burial of one whose greatest glory was not in the martial victories he had achieved, but in the motto and purpose of his later life, "Peace and Goodwill." As his painful and fatal illness progressed, it grew more and more apparent that he was the link prepared of God to bind the sundered sections of the nation together. A spirit of fraternity, a forgetfulness of past animosities, this was breathed in every feeble utterance that came from his lips; which, at the last, could be expressed only by the pencil in his hand, or by the grasp of that hand as he cordially greeted those who had once been his foes on the battle-field. With the brightened vision that often marks the last hours of the departing, he saw, as with prophetic eye, that the time was at hand when the long-cherished strifes of the early days of the Republic, which resulted at last in a fratricidal war, would be buried, and in the providence of God his was the tomb in which, we trust, they were buried.

The city sleeps, the mighty pageant's done;
   The radiant stars look out upon his grave
   Who marched and conquered, toiled and ruled, to save
The land from discord's bane, and keep her one.
What nobler service could a faithful son
   Perform, with all his heart, than that he gave
   To bind the Union fast, and free the slave?
These deeds will brighten as the ages run.
Lincoln and Grant, imperishable names,

> Henceforth with that of Washington entwined
> Above the hearth of each Columbian home!
> Ah, such a lustrous brotherhood proclaims
> That, in the New Atlantis, live the mind
> And quenchless fortitude of youthful Rome.

With reference to the portrait of Robert Fulton, the man who shares very largely the fame of first adapting the steam-engine to purposes of navigation, General Grant was not alone in his desire to get access to it. Like all others of Sharples' oil portraits, excepting the Washingtons, Fulton and his wife's portraits were left unfinished. They were purchased from Mrs. Sharples in that state. Romney or Bird finished the portrait of Fulton, Maclise that of his wife. Since their sale by Mrs. Sharples, two individuals only have owned them, both more than eccentric, the present possessor leading a secluded life, and declining to allow any visitors to his costly collection of paintings, mostly portraits of distinguished persons.

Fulton was an attached friend of Sharples. In his early years, as is well known, he worked and maintained himself as an artist. There are several portraits of his execution known in England. When in London he was one of Benjamin West's family household; he and Sharples being sympathizing friends, the latter desired to paint his portrait, seeing he was a very rising man in his newly-adopted profession as an engineer. This he did, and it undoubtedly exists in England. Sharples himself was a skilled mechanic, and speaks of Fulton as having greatly served him when in America. It is not a little remarkable that Fulton succeeded in building a steamer capable of propulsion under water. He accomplished this and much more, and he was the father of torpedoes. It was hoped to have included his portrait in this volume. The desire, consequent on eccentricity of the owner, has failed of accomplishment.

CHAPTER VIII.

Attractive nature of female excellences—their qualities illustrated in Mary Washington—Good Parson Baker's teachings—Mary Washington's family descent—Source of her religious inspiration—The home of her youth—Her sponsors at baptism—Armorial bearings of her family—Washington and Franklin families originally residents in same part of England—Washington assists in removal of his mother to Fredericksburg—Her example under bereavement—Washington relates the advantages she received from Parson Baker's instruction—Remarks on his mother's portrait—Her bearing as a widow, and watchful care of her children—Her example meet for general imitation.

WHAT princes are, what statesmen meditate, what heroes achieve, is rather an object of curiosity than of utility. They never can become examples to the bulk of mankind. It is when they have descended from their public eminence, when they have retired to their private and domestic station, when the potentate is lost in the man, that they become objects of attention, patterns for imitation, or beacons set up for admonition and caution.

The meek, the modest, the noiseless exhibition of female excellences occupy a smaller space in the annals of human nature than the noisy, bustling, forensic pursuits and employments of men. But when feminine worth is gently drawn out of the obscurity which it loves, and advantageously placed in the light which it naturally shuns, O how amiable, how irresistible, how attractive it is! A wise and good woman shines by not seeking to shine, she is most eloquent when she is silent, and she obtains all her will by yielding, by submission, by patience, by self-denial·

When religion is infused into those lovely forms, how the interest rises, how the frame is embellished, how the deportment is ennobled!

Loving her boy with a woman's love, Mary Washington desired not for him any world's fame, she was, in the true sense of the word, humble-minded, and yet she realized that the life of every man was of importance to himself, to his family, to his friends, to his country, and in the sight of God. Good Parson Baker had ever been at hand, aiding her in the conveying sound instruction, as in enforcing of every good precept, and by his example rendering the same doubly valuable. She knew that they were by no means the best men who have made most noise in the world, neither were those actions most deserving of praise which have obtained the greatest share of fame. Scenes of violence and blood, the workings of ambition, of pride, and of revenge compose the annals of men. Whatever her wishes were for her children, certain it is that for herself she desired that when death came, time should spread the veil of oblivion over her. The utmost she desired for the living ones given to her charge, was, that they might inherit piety and purity, temperance and humility, which are little noticed and soon forgotten of the world, knowing these to be held in everlasting remembrance before God. In her sight to be a child of God was more honourable than to be descended from kings, and that a Christian is a much higher character than a hero. This consideration influenced all she undertook, all she did. Her aim was to tread only in the quiet, narrow path, to impress her children's hearts with a knowledge that the eyes of God are ever upon us, to live as in His sight, knowing that every action as it is performed, that every word as it is spoken, and that every thought as it arises, is recorded in the book of God's remembrance, and must come into judgment. "Keep thy heart with all diligence," "set a watch on the door of thy lips," and "whether you eat or drink, or whatsoever you do, do all to the glory of God." Mary, we know, impressed on him, Let "Thou God seest me" be the leading commanding idea of thy life, in the city, and in the field, in society, and in solitude, by day and by night, and when you come to die you will find you have not far to go; to be "absent from the body" is to be "present with the Lord."

It has been too much the habit to say that nothing is known of the great patriot's mother, beyond the fact of her maiden name being Mary Ball, and that she was of a highly respectable family of English colonists. The arrival of the Sharples portraits in America, and the interest they naturally excited, has caused minute search into such of the Cary papers as were preserved at his death, and much information of deeply interesting character has in consequence been unearthed. So far from non-existence of records as to her family, or to the early life and conduct of this illustrious woman, it is from this new source made known that Washington from his own lips communicated to Sharples as much as suffices for an outline of the remarkable character she proved herself, leaving it to the world to fill the picture in. Studied rightly, it will be found to afford not a little instruction to future generations of women of all nations, who, it may be hoped, will strive to excel in those virtues, and imitate the example her life and character, so signally displayed, set before them.

Mary Ball, Washington's mother, was descended from an old English family of soldier breed, one of whom, Colonel William Ball, came out from England in the early part of the seventeenth century, and settled at the mouth of the river Corotoman, in Lancaster County, Virginia. Pioneer friends there would be, whose letters prepared the road.

Real or imagined slight on the part of friends in power had stirred the blood, and in this, as in many other cases of emigration before and since, caused the bidding good-bye to the "old country." Colonel Ball was a thorough soldier. He had married a young girl of English parentage, but whether prior to or after settling in Virginia, is not stated, although his wife's family were resident in the neighbourhood of the Balls at the time of Mary Washington's girlhood. Colonel Ball knew more of soldiership than farming, and there existed a tradition that he was more suited to command the district than to till it. He was a man of great physical power, a true gentleman, and died honoured, as he deserved to be. At his death, which occurred in 1650, he left two sons, William and Joseph, also one daughter named Hannah, who married with Daniel Fox, also of English parentage, though a Virginian by birth. William Ball, the eldest son of Colonel Ball, the original settler, left to his native State of Virginia a goodly legacy of eight sons and one daughter, five of the race leaving male issue. Colonel William Ball's second son Joseph's male issue had become extinct in 1779, though compensation for his planet setting was nobly yielded in answering before the world as the father of Mary, the mother of Washington.

All references to Mary Ball, from the earliest publications to the latest, assign much of her deeply religious character as having been inspired by the study of Sir Matthew Hale's "Moral and Divine Contemplations," a copy of which was in Augustine Washington's home, and bore on a fly-leaf the signatures of both his wives. Augustine's wiving had been happy in both efforts. Jane Butler we know, through Washington himself, was "fair to behold, and good as she was fair," and it is enough to learn from the same highest of all authority, "well educated." There cannot exist any desire to detract from the part until now assigned the worthy Sir Matthew Hale in laying the concrete foundation of Mary's beautiful character; by all means give him his full share, even under the new revelation that he was not her only study, and that she drank deeply at other streams of knowledge and thought. It was the happy province of both of Augustine Washington's wives to dwell only within the quiet precincts of domestic retirement; they were neither of them "strong-minded," in the modern sense, they were truly feminine, exemplifying that the life of a woman, almost in proportion as it is true to the loftiest impulses and purest principles by which she can be actuated, presents comparatively few incidents claiming circumstantial record or remembrance. Though the wife, or the mother of one who fills a large space in the world's eye, it is still usually hers to dwell only within the quiet precincts of domestic retirement. Margaret Conkling, in her admirable little work on Mary and Martha Washington, has eloquently written: "The hero, like a majestic river, that bears the wealth of cities on its ample waters, and diffuses benefits to thousands, speeds onward in his high career, his steps resounding in the ears of listening nations; while the mother, from whom, perchance, he derived the intellectual power that impels and sustains his lofty course, still, like a life-giving fountain whose sweet, bright waters diffuse beauty and health and happiness, lingers ever in the shade, revered in the protecting sanctity of *home*."

Jane Washington
and Mary Washington

The bold characters of the signatures of Jane Butler and

Mary Ball evidence that in both the fair ones distinctness and legibility had been well taught. These important characteristics were more in vogue in their days than in our own time of more scrambling manner.

The homestead occupied by Augustine Washington and his fair brides, and where Mary gave birth to George, was more humble in its character than would now be looked for in the home of persons in their position. It is not said the family were possessed of any store of wealth; had he been so endowed, Colonel William Ball would possibly have never wandered away to seek fortune in Virginia. Their home was unpretending, but they were content with it; once arriving at that happy state, its unprepossessing exterior would cease to be an eye-trouble. Mary was in her eight-and-twentieth year when she gave birth to George. William Gooch was Royal Governor of Virginia at the time, and Augustine Washington and his wife were frequent visitors as guests at his residence. Mary was then held and spoken of as the handsomest woman of her time, and held her personal charms much beyond the period usual with her sex. Middleton's portrait of Mary Washington was painted a few months before the birth of her son George.

DUTCH TILE IN CHIMNEY-PIECE OF THE OLD HOMESTEAD.

Washington's birth-place, we are told, was a four-roomed house, with a chimney at each end, perfectly plain outside and in. The only approach to ornament was a Dutch-tiled chimney-piece in the best room, covered with rude pictures of Scriptural scenes; but around the house there were thrift and abundance.

More than three hundred years have elapsed since Pope Gregory the Thirteenth ordained that ten days should be added to the tally of all times since the birth of the Saviour, in order to make up some fractional deficiencies in the calendar, and twenty-three years after this papal record was made, the British Government ordered the Gregorian Kalendar, or "new style," as it was called, to be adopted. The deficiency was then eleven days, and these were added. Accordingly we date the birth of Washington and celebrate its anniversary on the 22nd instead of the 11th of February.

This natal day of the Immortal is defined through an old family Bible of quarto form, dilapidated by use and age, and covered with Virginia striped cloth, and which record is in the handwriting of the patriot's father, in these words,

"George William, son to Augustine Washington, and Mary, his wife, was born ye eleventh day of February, 1731-2, about ten in the morning, and was baptized the 3rd April following, Mr. Bromley Whiting, and Captain Christopher Brooks godfathers, and Mrs. Mildred Gregory godmother."

All three of these were neighbours and friends. Mr. Bromley Whiting was a landowner residing close by, Captain Christopher Brooks also resided on his own property, his commission being in the local militia, and Mrs. Mildred Gregory, an attached friend of her who was then so unconscious of the future greatness of him to whom she had so recently given birth. She was a woman of sound religious principles, one that the mother knew had a right sense of sponsors' duties, and entered thereon with full resolve to support and aid her loved friend in the inculcation of principles conferring happiness in the world that is, and leading to bliss in the everlasting life beyond.

In the possession of an old Virginian family exists a roughly made picture, in which is represented a rampant lion, holding a globe in his paw, a helmet and shield, a vizor strong, and coat of mail, and other emblems of strength and courage, and for a motto the words of Ovid—

"Cœlumque Tueri."

At the back of the picture is written, "The coat of arms of William Ball, who came from England with his family about the year 1650, and settled at the mouth of Corotoma River, in Lancaster County, Virginia, and died in 1669, leaving two sons, William and Joseph, and one daughter, Hannah, who married Daniel Fox. William left eight sons (and one daughter), five of whom have (Anno Domini, 1779) male issue. Joseph's male issue is extinct. General

George Washington is his grandson, by his youngest daughter Mary."

THE BALL ARMS AS EXHIBITED IN THE AMERICAN HOMESTEAD.

In these early days all the names mentioned in connection with occurring events were zealous royalists, or what in England would be termed tories, and it is also a remarkable fact that the families of Washington and Franklin had been established in the same county of Northamptonshire in England, and within a few miles of each other, the Washingtons at Pulgrave, belonging to the landed gentry of the county, and in the great civil war had fought on the royal side; the Franklins at the village of Exton, living on the produce of a farm of thirty acres, and the earnings of their trade as blacksmiths, and espousing, some of them at least, and the father and uncle of Benjamin Franklin among the number, the principles of the Nonconformists. Their respective emigration, germs of great events in history, took place, that of John Washington, the great-grandfather of George, in 1657, to loyal Virginia; that of Josiah, the father of Benjamin Franklin, about the year 1685, to the metropolis of Puritan New England. There are now several families of

Washingtons claiming as belonging to the true and same stock. One especially in a small village called Meols, near the entrance of the river Mersey, close to Wallasey, Cheshire. These folk are small farmers and fishermen, but have through several generations steadfastly adhered to the story of their clanship.

The events of the disordered times immediately preceding the Revolution followed each other in startling and fitful succession, and finally resulting in the ever-memorable Declaration of Independence, Mrs. Washington suddenly beheld her son elevated to a position surrounded by dangers the most imminent, and comprehending responsibilities the most solemn and portentous that can devolve upon human agency. Resting her fears, her aspirations, and her faith upon that support which could alone sustain the spirit of so affectionate and so discerning a parent, amid trials peculiar and severe, we see this heroic woman resigning herself with the same tranquil submission and the same unaffected cheerfulness by which her life had hitherto been distinguished to the decrees of an overruling and inscrutable destiny.

Whatever be the dispositions, whatever the faculties of the child, whether earlier or later in life, the business neither of father nor masters can proceed wisely and well without the co-operation of the mother. Who knows so well as she the road to the understanding, the road to the heart? Who has skill like her to encourage the timid and to repress the bold? Who has power and address like a mother's to subdue the stubborn and confirm the irresolute? Who can with such exquisite art draw out, put in motion, and direct ordinary or superior powers? Who can so well place goodness in its fairest and most attractive light, and expose vice in its most hideous and forbidding form? Having been trained up, when a child, in the way wherein he should walk, " the man calls it to remembrance in old age, he approves it, he returns to it," and "departs from it" no more.

Before his departure from his native State, to assume the command of the patriots assembled at Cambridge, the Commander-in-Chief, ever mindful of his mother's comfort and happiness, even when most burdened by public cares and obligations, assisted in effecting her removal from her country residence in its vicinity to Fredericksburg.

Mrs. Washington was remunerated for thus renouncing a home hallowed by many tender and time-honoured associations, the peaceful asylum of her youthful family in the days of her early bereavement, the scene of their innocent sports, their juvenile education, and of her own strenuous exertions and self-sacrificing devotion during so many years of her life, by being placed in much nearer proximity to her friends and relatives, and in a position more secure from danger than any precaution could have rendered an isolated rural abode. Bestowing on him the more than ægis-shield of her blessing and her prayers, Mrs. Washington bade adieu to her son for a period, the duration and events of which no mortal vision could even faintly discern.

Long familiar with the most effectual means of escape from the dominion of too anxious thought, she hastened, after this painful parting, to busy herself with the arrangement and care of her new home, and sought in active usefulness and industry not only the solace of her own "private griefs" and apprehensions, but the high pleasure that springs from the consciousness of doing good. Ever possessed of far too much genuine self-respect and enlightenment to regard the necessity of homely toil as degrading or unfortunate, her practical ingenuity and personal efforts now supplied, in a good degree, the many deficiencies and deprivations arising from the pressing exigencies of the times, and materially assisted not only in providing for the wants of her own household, but in furnishing the means of that liberal charity which she had always exercised, notwithstanding her limited resources, and which was not remitted when increasing occasion had arisen for its continuance.

What an example under bereavement is seen in more than one deprivation suffered by Mary Washington in the course of her life! She set before her circle of friends that the most obvious and natural consolations of reason, under the loss of those dearly loved, as well as one of the most abundant consolations furnished by religion, is the belief that departed friends are at their death disposed of infinitely to their advantage. We weep and mourn while we reflect upon the deprivation of comfort which we have sustained, but we wipe the tears of sorrow from our eyes when we consider that our loss is their unspeakable gain. "Rachel, weeping for her children," refuses to be comforted so long as she thinks "they are not;" but her soul is tranquillized and comforted when her eyes in faith look within the veil, and behold them softly and securely reposing in the bosom of their Father and God.

The reconciliation of interrupted friendship, wrote Mary Washington to one who had been dear to her, but who, from causes of her own making, had for some years been estranged so far as she herself was concerned, "is one of the chief delights of human life. The pleasure of meeting again, after long absence, one whom we love, obliterates in a moment the pain caused by separation, and one hour of sweet communication compensates the languor, solicitude, and gloom of many years."

The innocent endearments of natural affection and the honest communications of private friendship are graciously intended to alleviate the cares of public life, and to strengthen the mind by diverting it from incessant and intense application to serious business. No man can always be a general, a statesman, or a king. And happy it is for those who occupy those exalted but troublesome stations that they are frequently permitted to sink the public in the private character, and to drop the hero, the senator, the judge, the sovereign, in the man.

Though long past the meridian of life, her equanimity, her healthful habits, and the systematic uniformity of her daily existence still gave Mrs. Washington the physical power essential for carrying into effect her plans of self-dependence and benevolent usefulness. It was at this time her almost daily custom, seated in an old-fashioned open chaise, to visit her little farm in the vicinity of the town, and while there to drive about the fields giving directions and personally superintending their execution.

In course of an earnest conversation with his English artist friend, when taking a before-breakfast morning walk at Mount Vernon, Washington spoke with fervour of his mother's sound education, and the great advantages she had enjoyed in the tuition for several years of the Rev. Thomas Baker, a man of refined education, and who had been brought up in one of the old grammar-schools of England, and was a sound classical scholar. Mr. Baker had followed the fortunes of an old college friend, coming to Virginia with him, and settling down quietly on the new soil to care for the souls of his friend and family and neighbours, though never swerving in love and devotion to the old country. The arrival of the mail was in those days the event in the lives of such as owed their birth away across the ocean. Its transit was confided to small sailing packets from Falmouth, commanded by officers of the Navy; bonny little craft they were, and occasionally making rapid passages to the Westward, so also it was no uncommon occurrence for them to take eight or nine weeks in getting out. The commanders of these vessels were great men in their little world; their names, as well as those of the marvels of naval architecture over which they were monarchs, were well known in every Virginian home, including that of the Rev. Thomas Baker especially, who received goodly stores of news by each, and whose life would have been an intolerable blank but for these Falmouth packets, whose arrivals were the golden events of his existence.

Thomas Baker availed of the Falmouth packets to keep up active correspondence with old University chums, and became a very fountain of European intelligence among the various English families who had turned their backs on the "old country," and adopted Virginia as their land of promise. He had extensive acquaintance with officers of the army, and received intelligence of the movements of the various regiments, and the promotions and varying fortunes of officers known to the families forming this small, but affectionately united Virginian circle. This gave eager interest to his budgets, not a little enhanced by communications from a sister, wife of an English member of Parliament, who supplied the Court gossip, served up in a manner that none but a woman's pen can uniquely supply. This lady of facile pen dilated fully on all great measures under discussion in Parliament, and gave fitting space to whatever was most worthy of attention in Church and other matters. The Baker despatches contained numerous excerpts from newspapers, such as prominent topics of news, speeches of public men, and other matters beyond the limit of even an unusually voluminous letter. The postage of such was no mean consideration, cents of our day were then incapable of much, a levy of shillings was the postal demand for each despatch to the Rev. Thomas Baker, and in every instance ungrudgingly yielded from his perhaps slender purse.

Augustine Washington had found a treasure in his college chum, clearly a man of far higher accomplishments than had been possessed by Williams, who later on became preceptor to his son George, and who is authoritatively quoted as "a capital hand at reading, spelling, English grammar, arithmetic, surveying, book-keeping, and geography." Justly, he boasted of having instilled these branches of erudition into the mind of his pupil, for there is ample proof that he mastered all. Thomas Baker, though doubtless in no way neglectful of the essential studies in which his successor in the Washington family had so thoroughly grounded his pupil, had clearly led his mother's mind to dwell earnestly and profitably on other and higher branches.

Washington is quoted by Sharples as using these words in regard to his revered mother's education, and the admirable manner in which it had for some years been directed by the spiritual friend who had cared for her with so great earnestness and devotion.

"Thomas Baker was a man of refined education, and devoted much of his leisure, of which he had a good deal, in grounding my mother in religious knowledge, which her mind was naturally inclined to receive, so also in directing her studies in such other branches of instruction as he deemed most fitting and likely to serve her in the education of children. He was in the habit of reading translations of portions of the best classic authors, and which he was very apt in making interesting by contrasts with modern writers. This most excellent man derived very real pleasure in these labours of love, and strove his utmost with, as he was pleased to speak of my mother, 'the most amiable, and yet the most impressional character I have ever known, a girl of great personal attractions, and yet utterly unconscious of their possession.'

"In addition to the instruction so earnestly imparted by this friend, from whom we were so early in life separated, my mother derived much advantage from the teaching of a French lady of Huguenot family, who resided with friends in her neighbourhood, a woman of marked attainments and studies of a higher class than those usually entered upon by young women. This lady deemed it in no way inconsistent with her Christian character and profession to impress rules for female deportment and the gracefully taking part in minuet dancing, in which my mother's tall and perfect figure specially adapted her to shine, as she did beyond most of the other youthful fair ones even of Virginia, in grace and elegance."

In his memoranda of daily life at Mount Vernon, transmitted to his wife in Philadelphia, Sharples alludes almost pathetically to the condition of the portrait of "the Chief's mother." "I would have liked to gratify him by putting it to rights; but apart from its maimed state, it needs more than I can properly manage, it should pass through the hands of one accustomed to such work. There is much in it needing to be painted out, and it has been cruelly injured through exposure to great fire heat. His reverence for the ill-used relic is extreme." Referring to it and his mother, he remarked, "Who can define the beginning of a mother's education of her children?" Following up the thought he further observed, "How few realize that the character of most men is formed and fixed before it is apprehended that they have, or can have, any character at all. Many fatally imagine that the few first years of life may be disposed of as we please; that a little neglect may easily be rectified. Never mind the morning; sleep it, trifle it away; a little closer application at noon will recover the loss. The spring returns, the flowers appear upon the earth, the time of the singing of birds is come. Sing with the birds, skip with the fawn, the diligence of a more advanced, more propitious season will bring everything round, and the year shall be crowned with the horn of plenty. Reason should detect and expose such absurdity, yet human conduct exhibits it in almost universal prevalence. Infancy and childhood are cast away; the morning is lost; the seed-time cast away, and with the natural consequences: a life full of confusion, an old age full of regret; a day of unnecessary toil, and a night of vexation; a hurried summer, a meagre autumn, a comfortless winter."

To the abiding effect of early maternal training, Mary Washington was largely indebted for her habits of unusual industry, economy, and regularity, as well as for the excellent constitution that gave vigour and practical usefulness to the operations of a naturally powerful intellect. To the ineffaceable impressions of infant years may also be ascribed the moral elevation and the exalted piety associated with her noble mind. Her affliction, in the premature death of her husband, which occurred April 13th, 1743, in their home at Fredericksburg, would with many have proved overwhelming. This almost sudden event left her with limited pecuniary resources the sole controller and guide of several children.

The having in early life the calamity of becoming a widow is a distressing, a delicate situation. It calls for every maxim of prudence, every council of friendship, every caution of experience, every support of piety. If a mourner indeed, she is guarded against affectation, and finds rational and certain relief in attending to and performing the duties of her station. She neither seeks a hasty cure of sorrow by plunging into the world, nor attempts an unnatural prolongation of it by affected retirement and sequestration. The tongue of Mary Washington uttered no rash vows, the pang of separation dictated no ensnaring resolutions, the indefatigable industry and ingenuity, whatever was necessary to the welfare and comfort of her family. Order, regularity, and occupation reigned supreme in her little world of home. She exacted implicit obedience from her children, and she tempered maternal tenderness with strict discipline; for we are told by Laurence Washington, of Chotank, who, as the companion of her son, occasionally shared her care and hospitality, that she was "indeed truly kind." He thus described his distinguished relative: "I was often there with George, his playmate, schoolmate, and young man's companion. Of the mother I was more afraid than of my own parents; she awed me in the midst of her kindness, for she was indeed truly kind, and even now, when time has whitened my locks, and I am the grandfather of a second generation, I could not behold that majestic woman without feelings it is impossible to describe." In that genuine and judicious kindness lies the secret of the power always maintained by this venerated mother over the minds of her offspring. If she assumed the right to direct the actions of others, her daily life exhibited such powers of self-control and self-denial as convinced her children, by more irresistible evidence than words could possibly convey, of the justice and disinterestedness by which she was habitually actuated.

That she rendered their home—simple, nay, even humble, though it might be—endearing to her children, is proved by the frequency and pleasure with which the happy band that once rejoiced in the comfort and security of her well-ordered abode, in after years revisited the maternal roof. An interdiction of the innocent amusements and relaxations, a taste for which is so natural to the young, formed no part of the system of juvenile training practised with such pre-eminent success by Mary Washington. She never rendered necessary restraint and discipline needlessly distasteful or repulsive by ascetic sternness or harsh compulsion. The power that sometimes gently coerced the subjects of her guidance was a *moral suasion*, far more effective and beneficial than influences such as those can ever exert.

Of all the mental qualities of this celebrated woman, perhaps none was more constantly illustrated in her life than her native *good sense,* the practical effects of which were infinitely more useful and precious to her children than she could possibly have rendered volumes of theoretical precept, however philosophical and profound. To her possession of this unpretending, but invaluable characteristic, emphatically, her illustrious son was indebted for the education that formed the basis of his greatness. This it was that taught the great Washington those habits of application, industry, and regularity that were of such essential service to him, alike in the camp and in the cabinet, and which so materially contributed to render his character a perfect model, bequeathed to successive ages. This it was, that, by inculcating and enforcing habitual temperance, exercise, and activity, strengthened and developed the wonderful physical powers that were rivalled only by the indomitable will and stupendous wisdom of her son.

To his mother Washington owed the high value he attached to "*the only possession of which all men are prodigal, and of which all men should be covetous:*" and from her early instructions he imbibed that *love of truth* for which he was remarkable, and which is so pleasingly and forcibly illustrated in some of the favourite anecdotes of our childhood.[1]

Trained to unvarying respect for the truths of revealed

---

[1] Juvenile readers can scarcely fail to be familiar with the stories of "The Little Hatchet," and of "The Sorrel Colt," almost the only authentic anecdotes of the childhood of the great patriot, and which also incidentally illustrate *more than one* of his youthful habits.

religion, in which she was herself a firm believer, and rigidly regardful of the dictates of an enlightened conscience, her gifted son was indebted to his mother for his quick moral sense, and the unflinching adhesion to principle that so strongly marked every act of his public and private life.

Mary Washington, we know, had all these things in her heart. It is the ordinance of Providence that the heaviest and most important part of education should devolve upon the mother. The fleety period which a son passes under the shadow of her wing should be a season sacred to wisdom and piety. If the mother lead not her son to the hallowed spring, if she fail to disclose to his eager eye and panting heart the loveliness of goodness, the excellency of religion; if she permit the luxuriant soil to be overrun with briars and thorns, in vain will she strive to redeem the lost opportunity by restraints and punishments, by precepts and masters, by schools and colleges, in a more advanced stage of life. The good or the mischief is done by the time that he comes out of her hands.

That Providence which imposes this employment on the feebler sex as a task, has contrived to render it the highest and most exquisite of female comforts; as in truth all impositions, nay, the very chastisements of Heaven are really blessings. Ask the good mother if there be any joy like the joy of hearing her child repeat the lessons which she taught him. Ask her if she recollects or regards her pain and anguish; her anxious days and sleepless nights. Ask her if all is not forgotten and lost in the progress which expanding faculties have made, and in the richer harvest which they promise. Ask her if she has not already received more than her reward. If this be just in its application to the mother of the world's true Patriot, then let it procure for mothers the respect and gratitude which every dutiful child finds highest gratification in rendering.

MRS. VAN RANSALAER.

CHAPTER IX.

Washington's pursuit in life directed by his mother—Mary Washington's life one of general privacy—Letter from Washington to his mother—Another letter assuring deference to her wishes—Mary's estimate of human greatness—Her interest deep though not over-sanguine of the triumph of America in the struggle—Her thankfulness at the success in passage of the Delaware—Her fervent gratitude in the surrender of Lord Cornwallis—Her meeting her son after this eventful occurrence—The ball at Fredericksburg—Declines relinquishing her independent home—Her home happiness and abstemious life—Lafayette's visit—Washington's last visit and general submission to his mother.

THE life of Mary Washington, for several years previous to the American Revolution, was passed almost in strict privacy. The incipient workings of the mighty spirit destined to achievements that should move the world, influenced, however, the youthful Washington, when only fourteen years of age, to form plans for his independent maintenance. He had actually taken the necessary steps preliminary to entering the English Navy, when the disapproval of his mother prevented the accomplishment of his design. Who shall say that the decisive interposition of his only parent did not save from a life of limited usefulness and comparative obscurity the embryo soldier and statesman?

A few years later, when he had reached early manhood, the young Virginian commenced his initiatory military career in the service of his native State.

In 1774 occurred, successively, the deaths of Mrs. Washington's two eldest sons, the younger of whom was soon followed to the grave by her husband's only child by his first wife. The influence of this rapid and mournful diminution of her family circle upon the wounded affections of Mary Washington must have been most saddening.

The only letters addressed to his mother, included in the published collection of General Washington's Correspondence, were written during the French War, in the earliest stages of which he served as adjutant of the northern division of Virginia militia, and as aide-de-camp to General Braddock. The first of these epistles was penned just after the memorable and disastrous battle of the Monongahela, at which nothing but the unconquerable determination, that not even severe illness could subdue, enabled the author to be present; and where, if he won some of his proudest laurels, he was perhaps exposed to greater personal danger than during any subsequent part of his military career.

This letter conveys an idea of the dignified and confidential intercourse that was uninterruptedly maintained between these distinguished correspondents:—

"To Mrs. Mary Washington, near Fredericksburg.

"Fort Cumberland, 18th July, 1755.

"Honoured Madam,—As I doubt not but you have heard of our defeat, and, perhaps, had it represented in a worse light, if possible, than it deserves, I have taken this earliest opportunity to give you some account of the engagement as it happened, within ten miles of the French Fort, on Wednesday, the 9th instant.

"We marched to that place, without any considerable loss, having only now and then a straggler picked up by the French and scouting Indians. When we came there, we were attacked by a party of French and Indians, whose number, I am persuaded, did not exceed three hundred men; while ours consisted of about one thousand three hundred well-armed troops, chiefly regular soldiers, who were struck with such a panic, that they behaved with more cowardice than it is possible to conceive. The officers behaved gallantly, in order to encourage their men, for which they suffered greatly, there being near sixty killed and wounded—a large portion of the number we had.

"The Virginia troops showed a good deal of bravery, and were nearly all killed; for I believe, out of three companies that were there, scarcely thirty men are left alive. Captain Peyrouny and all his officers, down to a corporal, were killed. Captain Polson had nearly as hard a fate, for only one of his was left. In short, the dastardly behaviour of those they call regulars exposed all others that were inclined to do their duty to almost certain death; and at last, in despite of all the efforts of the officers to the contrary, they ran, as sheep pursued by dogs, and it was impossible to rally them.

"The General was wounded, of which he died three days after. Sir Peter Halkes was killed in the field, where died many other brave officers. I luckily escaped without a wound, though I had four bullets through my coat, and two horses shot under me. Captains Orme and Morris, two of the aides-de-camp, were wounded early in the engagement, which rendered the duty harder upon me, as I was the only one then left to distribute the General's orders, which I was scarcely able to do, as I was not half recovered from a violent illness that had confined me to my bed and a waggon for ten days. I am still in a weak and feeble condition, which induces me to halt here two or three days, in the hope of recovering a little strength, to enable me to proceed homewards; from whence I fear I shall not be able to stir till towards September; so that I shall not have the pleasure of seeing you till then, unless it be in Fairfax. Please to give my love to Mr. Lewis and my sister; and compliments to Mr. Jackson, and all other friends that inquire after me.

"I am, most honoured Madam,
"Your most dutiful son."

From other sources it is known that the indisposition of which the writer so briefly speaks, in this epistle, was sufficiently serious to endanger his life. Nor can we believe his own intimation to have conveyed the first knowledge of this distressing intelligence to his mother. She had, however, the consolation to be, at the same time, informed of all that she could hope or even desire, in relation to his personal prowess and military skill.[1]

The remaining letter was written in anticipation of an event which occurred soon after the Battle of the Monongahela—the appointment of Colonel Washington to the chief command of the Virginia forces. His commission bears the same date as that of the letter, though the author was, as yet, uninformed of his promotion.

"TO MRS. MARY WASHINGTON.
"Mount Vernon, 14th August, 1755.

"HONOURED MADAM,—If it is in my power to avoid going to the Ohio again I shall, but if the command is pressed upon me, by the general voice of the country, and offered upon such terms as cannot be objected against, it

---

[1] It need scarcely be said that this was the celebrated engagement in which Colonel Washington gained so much honour, and the disastrous result of which was nearly averted by his daring courage, as it also might have been by his ready discernment and sagacious tactics, had General Braddock been guided by his advice in the incipient stages of the conflict.

would reflect dishonour upon me to refuse it. And that, I am sure, ought to give you greater uneasiness than my going in an honourable command. Upon no other terms will I accept of it. At present, I have no proposals made to me, nor have I any advice of such an intention, except from private hands.

" I am, &c."

The almost deprecatory tone that characterizes this epistle, the deference it indicates to the wishes and opinions of the parent to whom it was addressed, mark the character of the writer. It was apparently written in reply to a previous communication from his mother in relation to the same subject. Many practical objections to the acceptance of the post of Commander-in-Chief of the Virginian Frontier Army existed at this juncture; and we may infer that the sagacious and far-seeing maternal eye discerned these difficulties, and that Mrs. Washington counselled her son to avoid responsibilities that existing and uncontrollable circumstances might easily render not only objectionable, but for many reasons to be avoided.

Mary Washington had a right estimate of human greatness. She knew that the lives of most men, from the womb to the grave, pass away unobserved, unregarded, unknown. When their course is finished the whole history of it shrinks into two little articles; on such a day they were born, and after so many days they died. Of those who emerge out of the general obscurity, some begin their public career at an advanced period of life, and it consists of a few shining, interesting, important events, and is confined within the compass of a very few fleeting years, while the progress of a little selected band, whom an indulgent Providence has vouchsafed signally to nobilitate, and whom the historic pencil is fond to delineate, is distinguished from the cradle to the tomb by an uninterrupted series of splendid incidents, exemplary virtues, and brilliant actions. She had rendered prominent to her son in his earlier years only those exhibiting a mixture in which goodness predominates and finally prevails; in which virtue is seen wading through difficulties, struggling with temptation, recovering from error, gathering strength from weakness, learning wisdom from experience, sustaining itself by dependence upon God, seeking refuge from its own frailty and imperfection in Divine compassion. The fanciful representations from stories of fiction rarely amused—edify her they could not.

Daniel Webster, and since his day, Emerson, has confirmed the remark that the American people do not suffer from any over-reverence. It was a mild way of putting it, but certainly children of the New World do not, as a rule, make a great fuss when the old birds go to roost, and there is reason for thus accepting God's will with resignation. In the case of Mary Washington there is good reason for keeping her in mind; irrespective of her being the mother of the nation's great founder, she was a very remarkable character, though full of true feminine sweetness.

Mrs. Washington is said to have required from those about her a prompt and literal obedience, somewhat resembling that demanded by proper military subordination; a habit doubtless arising, in some degree, from a consciousness of the mental power that enabled her rightly to judge and wisely to direct. On one occasion, as we are told, she reproved an agent who, relying upon his own judgment, had disobeyed her orders, saying, " I command you,—there is nothing left for you but to obey!"

Thus, while occupied in her favourite pursuits, and preserved from all sense of loneliness by the frequent and interesting visits of her children and grandchildren, who were invariably most assiduous and affectionate in their endeavours to contribute to her happiness, several years rolled away. Nor, as may well be supposed, did Mrs. Washington in the meanwhile look with an unobservant or unsympathizing eye upon the changing and momentous aspect of public affairs. Her residence in Fredericksburg enabled her early to obtain the most important intelligence of the day, and we may believe the respectful attention of her son speedily and constantly supplied her with information denied to those possessing less claim upon his confidence and regard.

If not always as sanguine of the ultimate triumph of the American arms as more youthful and ardent spectators of the Revolutionary contest, she watched the progress of national affairs with patient and tranquil expectation. Frequently raising her thoughtful gaze from the painful contemplation of her country's struggles towards the Omnipotent Friend who aids the sacred cause of Liberty and Right, she gained a firm and hopeful constancy that shielded her noble spirit alike from unfounded enthusiasm and desponding distrust, and that rendered her an example worthy of all honour to those mothers who, like herself, had resigned their sons to their country in the hour of her greatest need.

When the glorious and heart-warming intelligence of the successful passage of the Delaware,[1] by Washington and his brave companions in arms, was communicated to his mother by the numerous friends who hastened to rejoice with and to felicitate her upon so auspicious and important an occurrence, she received the tidings with placid self-possession, and expressed her pleasure at the brightening prospects of her native land. But in relation to such portions of the despatches of her visitors as contained

[1] Dec. 1776.

eulogistic allusions to her son, she simply remarked that " George appeared to have deserved well of his country for such signal services," and added,—

" But, my good sirs, here is too much flattery ! still George will not forget the lessons I have taught him ; he will not forget *himself*, though he is the subject of so much praise."

And when, after the lapse of long, dark years of national gloom and suffering, Mrs. Washington was at last informed of the crowning event of the great conflict (it was to her son's thoughtful care she owed the *Express* previously despatched to her with the grateful news of the surrender of Lord Cornwallis), she raised her hands with profound reverence and gratitude towards Heaven and fervently exclaimed, " Thank God ! war will now be ended, and peace, independence, and happiness bless our country ! "

An interval of nearly seven perilous and adventurous years had passed, when Mrs. Washington enjoyed the happiness again to behold her victor-crowned and illustrious son.

Upon the return of the combined armies from Yorktown, the COMMANDER-IN-CHIEF repaired immediately to Fredericksburg, attended by a numerous and splendid suite, composed of the most distinguished European and American officers who had shared his protracted toils and his final triumph. No sooner had Washington dismounted than he sent a messenger to apprise his mother of his arrival, with a request to be informed when it would be her pleasure to receive him. Then, dismissing for a time the attributes and attendants of greatness, he repaired unaccompanied, and on foot, to the modest mansion where his venerable parent awaited his coming.

Mrs. Washington was alone, and occupied in some

ordinary domestic avocation, when the gladdening intelligence of her son's approaching visit was communicated to her. She met him on the threshold with a cordial embrace, her face beaming with unmingled pleasure, and welcomed him by the endearing and well-remembered appellation associated with the pleasing memories of early years. The quick eye of maternal tenderness readily discerned the furrowed traces of the ceaseless and wearing responsibilities that had for years been the burthen of his thoughts, and in the unforgotten tones, and with the simple affectionateness of other days, Mrs. Washington immediately and earnestly adverted to the subject of her son's health.

At length, turning the conversation to scenes and themes hallowed to each by the most cherished remembrances, these devotedly attached and happily re-united mother and son talked long of mutual friends and former times. But to the peerless fame of the Commander-in-Chief of the Armies of America *there was not the most remote allusion!*

If there be pure and perfect joy upon earth, it is that which fills the heart of a parent when hearing of the wisdom, the virtue, and the prosperity of a darling child. How great a share fell to the lot of Mary Washington! If there be sorrow which admits not of consolation, it is the sorrow of a father for the vice or folly of an ungracious, thankless son, and for the misery into which he has plunged himself. The patriarch Jacob felt both these in the extreme. It was her happy lot to experience only the happy contrast.

We may rest assured that as the immortal SAVIOUR OF HIS COUNTRY gazed upon the beloved and expressive countenance of his mother turned approvingly and affectionately upon him, his happiness was unalloyed and exalted as earth can bestow.

The unexpected arrival of WASHINGTON and his suite

created the most enthusiastic delight among the citizens of Fredericksburg. Not only the inhabitants of the town, but numbers of gentlemen from its vicinity hastened to welcome the deliverers of their country with every demonstration of respect and hospitality; happiness irradiated every face, and all were soon engrossed by eager preparations for festive pleasure. It was determined to celebrate the joyful occasion by a splendid ball. Mrs. WASHINGTON received a special invitation. She answered that, "although her dancing days were *pretty well over*, she should feel happy in contributing to the general festivity." The company assembled at a much earlier hour than modern fashion would sanction. Gay belles and dignified matrons graced the occasion arrayed in rich laces and bright brocades,— the well-preserved relics of scenes when neither national misfortune nor private calamity forbade their use.

Numerous foreign officers were present, in the brilliant uniforms of their respective corps, glittering with the dazzling insignia of royal favour and successful courage. Thither came veteran heroes, the blessed and honoured of after times, whose war-scathed visages bespoke the unflinching bravery and persevering devotion with which they had served their country through long years of hardship and danger. There, too, now swayed only by the light breath of pleasure, waved in billowy folds the dear-won banners of the "tented field." Music poured its spirit-stirring strains upon the soldier's ear, not to summon him to deeds of arms; but by its gentler influences to inspire the chivalrous gallantly that well became the hour,—the gleesome jest, the merry laugh,

"Nods, and becks, and wreathed smiles!"

But despite the soul-soothing charm of music, the fascinations of female loveliness, and the flattering devotion of the gallant brave, all was eager suspense anb expectation, until there entered, unannounced and unattended, the MOTHER OF WASHINGTON, leaning on the arm of her SON. Was there ever more thrilling scene than this majestic man and woman on this more than eventful occasion?

Hushed was each noisy tone, subdued each whispered word, as with quiet dignity and unaffected grace they slowly advanced. Nature had stamped upon the brow of both the unmistakable signet of nobility, and

"The vision and the faculty divine"

spoke in the imposing countenance of each, and directed every movement of the majestic pair.

All hastened to approach the august presence; the European officers to be presented to the parent of their beloved commander, and old friends, neighbours, and acquaintances to tender the compliments and congratulations appropriate to the occasion.

Mrs. Washington received these peculiar demonstrations of respect and friendship with perfect self-possession and unassuming courtesy. She wore the simple, but becoming and appropriate costume of the Virginia ladies of the olden time, and even

"The cynosure of beauty's sheen"

was for a time forgotten, while all eyes and all hearts were irresistibly attracted by the winning address and unpretending appearance of the venerable lady.

The European strangers gazed long in wondering amazement upon this sublime and touching spectacle. Accustomed to the meretricious display of European courts, they regarded with astonishment her unadorned attire, and the mingled simplicity and majesty for which the language and manners of the MOTHER OF WASHINGTON were so remarkable.

Having for some time regarded with serene benignity the brilliant and festive scene which she had so amiably consented to honour by her presence, Mrs. Washington expressed the cordial hope that the happiness of all might continue undiminished until the hour of general separation should arrive, and quietly adding that "it was time for old people to be at home," retired as she had entered, leaning on the arm of the Commander-in-Chief.

It will interest to know that the immortal WASHINGTON danced on this occasion for the last time; in the stately minuet, so well adapted to the advantageous display of his graceful air, and elegant and imposing form. He is also described as having been inspired with great cheerfulness and animation, while thus momentarily courting the aerial graces. His mother took part in a minuet with all her grace of earlier years. The French gentlemen present declared that Paris itself could boast nothing more perfect than the dancing of the fair and the gallant Americans assembled at this celebrated ball.

Re-established at Mount Vernon, it was the earnest desire of Washington that his mother should thenceforth reside under his roof. He had frequently before urged the same request, and his sister (Mrs. Fletcher Lewis, of Fredericksburg, the only sister of Washington, whom she so closely resembled, that when she was arrayed in his usual head-dress, her features were undistinguishable from his), who was always most assiduous in fulfilling the duties imposed by nature and affection, had repeatedly endeavoured to persuade her aged parent to live apart from her no longer. But the venerable matron, notwithstanding 'the affectionate entreaties of her children, continued to conduct a separate establishment, with the same indefatigable industry and judicious management which she had earlier exhibited. She still obeyed—

"The breezy call of incense-breathing morn"

with as much alacrity as of yore, and still gave her attention to the most minute details of domestic affairs.

In this tranquil retreat she long continued to receive the frequent and fondly-respectful visits of her many old and attached friends, as well as of her children,[2] and her children's children, blest in her happy and honoured age by the soothing consciousness of a virtuous and well-spent life.

To the urgent and oft-repeated requests of her children, that she would make with them the home of her age, Mrs. Washington replied,—

"I thank you for your dutiful and affectionate offers, but my wants are few in this life, and I feel perfectly competent to take care of myself." And when her son-in-law, Colonel Lewis, proposed to her to assume the general superintendence of her affairs, she resolutely answered,—

"Do you, Fielding, keep my books in order, for your eyesight is better than mine, but leave the executive management to me."

Mary Washington's practical sense was the seat of her mental power; her sound judgment judged safely upon all

---

[2] We find many proofs in the published correspondence of Washington, of the affectionate devotion with which he paid this tribute of respect to his mother. Thus he assigns his absence on a visit to her as a reason for not previously replying to a letter from the Secretary of Congress; and afterwards again, in a letter to Major-General Knox, he offers the same explanation of a similar delay. When his mother was ill, we perceive that he pleads this honourable errand without reserve, as presenting claims superior to any public obligation. In an epistle written towards the close of the year 1788, there are allusions to a prolonged sojourn under the maternal roof, &c., &c.

subjects to the extent of her knowledge; and her knowledge upon all practical subjects pertaining to the duties of a true mother was extensive. Her matronly dignity of manner was very marked, and she commanded universal respect by universally respecting her commands.

Mrs. Washington lived an advanced and abstemious life, and she lived thus long, too, mainly because she lived upon the bounties of temperance. She aspired to the wealth of goodness rather than of gold, and to the fame of great sense rather than great station; she attained both, retained both, and enjoyed both until death. She drew forth the love of friends, and her company was as widely sought for as her character was widely imitated; her individual attractiveness in society was great; she is described unlike what most women are, yet just what all women should have been. She enjoyed more than most, because she was a lady in all her enjoyments, and in all things the lines of prudence were to her precious as life. Her life should be read to be followed, and followed because it leads aright. Mrs. Washington was slow to adopt inadaptive customs, she preferred taste to style, or rather the style of true taste, comfortable dress, though fashion denounced the device, and convenience art to what was artfully common. Her simplicity of life, like its lasting solidity, was attained by simple observation and solid reflection. What she thought was thought with sincerity, and her every thought was truth; what she said was said with sensibleness, and her every saying was sacred; what she did was done in simplicity, and her every deed was a duty.

Mrs. Washington's home happiness was great; she there superintended a family, which has since become more famous than faulty sovereigns; she there likewise gave birth to a child, which has given birth to a republic. Her connubial, like her maternal love was constant; she had been careful in bestowing her affections, yet when bestowed her bliss was to cultivate the soil in which she had planted the purest seed of her soul. Her kindness of spirit towards her kindred and race was less the spirit of passion than that of supreme sense. She possessed that virtue of virtues, a practical system in everything she performed, from the earliest to the latest years of her life. Remarkable for possessing so numerous and such vitally important characteristics, she added yet that of a felicitating cheerfulness.

She drew largely upon the future for her present happiness. If she could not at first succeed in her designs, she struggled designedly on until she succeeded, at least in seeing a way worthy her striving. She hoped for the best in all things, even though in most things she should enjoy, at the best, only her hopes. She exhibited the possession of the faculty of firmness to an extraordinary degree for her sex.

Mrs. Washington was gifted with an energy of thought and action, becomingly befitting the American matron, her motives were exalted, exalting, too, the ideas of all within her influence; her servants obeyed her bidding energetically because her energy served to transfuse through them the spirit of their chieftess; she never feared the storms of natural fatigues and death, but she wisely secluded herself from the booming blasts of unnatural sorrows and an early death. She prayed for length of life, not because she feared death, but from fear that death would seize her before she had accomplished life's delightful works.

Mrs. Washington's age was passed in recalling, with unwearied pleasure, the uncommon events of her past eventful existence with a goblet filled with the steel-bright and life-blessing waters of death before her, and a cluster of long-ripening Christian deeds behind her, and looking upward beheld a better life.

x

Previous to his departure for France, after the termination of the Revolutionary War, the Marquis de La Fayette visited Fredericksburg expressly for the purpose of making his personal adieus to the mother of his beloved hero-friend and that he might solemnly invoke her blessing. This amiable visitor, who had frequently before enjoyed the happiness of conversing with her, repaired to the unobtrusive abode of Mrs. Washington, accompanied by one of her grandsons. As they approached the house they observed an aged lady working in the adjoining garden. The materials composing her dress were of home-manufacture, and she wore over her time-silvered hair a plain straw bonnet. "There, sir," said the younger gentleman, "is my grandmother."

Mrs. Washington received her distinguished guest with great cordiality, and with her usual frank simplicity of address.

"Ah, Marquis!" she exclaimed, "you see an old woman. But come, I can make you welcome to my poor dwelling, without the parade of changing my dress."

The conversation of this interesting group soon turned, as was most natural, upon the brightening prospects of the young Republic.

The marquis spoke of the deep interest he cherished in all that related to the prosperity of the land of his adoption, and poured forth the fond and glowing encomiums of a full heart at each allusion to his former Chief—his friend, his Mentor, his "hero."

To the praises thus enthusiastically lavished upon her son by the noble Frenchman, his hostess only replied, "*I am not surprised at what George has done, for he was always a good boy.*"

Thus did the true greatness of this extraordinary woman often manifest itself. It was her pleasure frequently to revert to the early days of her august son, and to express her approbation of his dutiful and upright conduct; but she never appeared in the slightest degree elated by the honours that were showered "thick and fast" upon his glorious name. With unaffected piety she referred each and every occurrence of life to the great First Cause, and when the notes of jubilant praise swelled high, even above the din of battle and the wailings of a nation's despair, it was her earnest maternal aspiration that the "good boy" of her early care might never "*forget himself!*"

Mrs. Washington was always remarkable for that unequivocal proof of superiority, the powerful influence she exerted over the minds of others. Her ideas of the respect due to her as a parent remained unchanged either by the lapse of time, or by the development of mighty events with which her wonderful son was so closely identified. Ever his trusted counsellor and friend, to her he was always the same in relative position. To her he owed his existence; to her the early discipline of his extraordinary intellect, and of his high moral nature; and to her he was indebted for the sage advice and prudent guidance of maturer years.

Nor did her son manifest the slightest dissent from this sentiment. His adopted grandson tells us that "to the last moments of his venerable parent he yielded to her will the most implicit obedience and felt for her person and character the highest respect and the most enthusiastic attachment."

Perhaps the life of this celebrated lady afforded no more convincing proof of the genuine nobleness of her character than was evinced by the constancy with which she maintained the peculiar sentiments and principles of her youth. We may believe that a mind less perfectly balanced would have rendered, at least, an unconscious homage to the power of circumstances so novel and so imposing as those in which she was placed.

It was Mrs. Washington's habit, during the latter years of her life, to repair daily to a secluded spot near her dwelling, formed by overhanging rocks and trees. There, isolated from worldly thoughts and objects, she sought in devout prayer and meditation, most appropriate preparation for the great change which she was admonished by her advanced age might nearly await her.

But one of the many weaknesses that usually characterize humanity was manifested by this heroic woman. Upon the approach of a thunderstorm she invariably retired to her own apartment and remained there until calmness was restored to the elements. This almost constitutional timidity was occasioned by a singularly distressing incident of her youth—the instant death, from the effects of lightning, of a young friend, who was, at the moment when the accident occurred, sitting close beside her.

Before Washington's departure for the seat of government, to assume the duties of President of the United States, he went to Fredericksburg to pay his parting respects to his aged mother. Her health had become so infirm as to impress her with the conviction that she beheld for the last time the crowning blessing of her declining age.

Forgetting all else in the same mournful belief, the calm self-possession that no calamity had for years been able to shake, yielded to the claims of nature, and, overpowered by painful emotion, the mighty chieftain wept long, with bowed head, over the wasted form of his revered and much-loved parent.

Sustained, even in this trying hour, by her native strength of mind, the heroic mother fervently invoked the blessing of Heaven upon her sorrowing son, and solemnly bestowing her own, bade him pursue the path in which public duty summoned him to depart.

Mrs. Washington retained unimpaired possession of her

mental faculties to her latest moments, but during the last three years of her life her physical powers were much diminished by the effects of a distressing malady with which she was long afflicted.

This most painful of all diseases, cancer in the breast, terminated her earthly existence in her eighty-third year. Her death occurred on the 25th of August, 1789. She had been forty-six years a widow.

A favourite lesson inculcated by Mary Washington in her children's minds, was the right use of money. She would tell them that of all the evil propensities to which human nature is subject, none is so general, so insinuating, so corruptive, and so obstinate as the love of money. It begins to operate early, and it continues to the end of life. One of the first lessons which children learn, and one which old men never forget, is the value of money. Of all passions it is best able to justify itself by reason, and is the last to yield to the force of reason. "Ambition and pride," she would say, "those powerful motives of human conduct, are but ministering servants to avarice. Age, which blunts all our other appetites, only whets this; and after the heart is dead to every other joy, it lives to the dear, the inextinguishable delight of saving and hoarding. Philosophy combats, satire exposes, religion condemns it in vain: it yields neither to argument, nor to ridicule, nor to conscience. Like the lean kine in Pharaoh's house, it devours all that comes near it, and yet continues as hungry and meagre as ever."

We listen with peculiar attention to those lips which are to speak to us no more, and the man and the words which we neglected while there was a prospect of their continuing longer with us we prize, we cleave to, and wish to retain when they are about to be taken away from us. We discover the value of nothing until we are threatened with or feel the want of it, and we awake to a sense of the happiness which we have possessed by the bitter reflection that it is gone from us for ever.

It is well to trace important events up to their sources, to mark the gradual progress of human affairs; to observe the same persons at different periods of their existence and in different situations; to discover on what delicate hinges their fortunes have turned; and to see the goodness of God improving the effects from the slightest and most unlikely causes. When revolutions in private families and in empires are pursued up to the springs from whence they flow, they are often found to commence in some little error, inadvertency or folly, which at the time might have been despised or neglected! just as mighty rivers begin their course in some paltry obscure stream which the peasant could dry up with the sole of his foot. The past is infinitely less perspicuous to the eye of human understanding than the future is to divine intelligence; God "seeth the end from the beginning, saying, My counsel shall stand, and I will fulfil all My pleasure." The periods which make the most brilliant figure in the page of history were periods of anxiety and trouble to the men and the nations who then figured on the scene. A life of many incidents, we may be assured, is a life of much distress. When the writer has got a great deal to relate, the person whose life is recorded has had a great deal to suffer.

We have only to read the words of King Lemuel, the prophecy which his mother taught him, Proverbs xxxi. 1—9, and judge how a mother may be an useful "help" in instructing a son, a grown son, and that son a prince. The mother's influence over the child, as it begins earlier, so it is of much longer duration than the father's. In Washington's case the father had been removed at such early period as to have caused the loss of all remembrance of him, and he had, as it were, double parentage in his mother. How general is it that a son, as he becomes a man, or approaching that state, feels uneasy under the restraint of paternal austerity; he longs to shake the yoke from off his neck; he pants for independence—he must obtain it.

George Washington never felt his mother's yoke galling, or longed for emancipation from the silken fetters in which her gentle fingers had entangled his soul. He submitted himself even in the choice of a profession. His early desire was to have entered the navy; her own views inclined otherwise; no reasons ever passed between mother and son beyond the expression that it should be otherwise. What an example for the youth, not only of America, but of the world! In the perfection of understanding, in the plenitude of power, in the self-gratulation of independence, to her milder reason he submits, her unassuming sway he readily acknowledges, and, independent on all things else, he feels that he cannot do without the smiles of maternal approbation, the admonitions of maternal solicitude, the reproofs of maternal tenderness and integrity.

The highest pleasure experienced by the writer of these memorials is in having been the instrument, however unworthy, in laying before the world such information regarding Mary Washington as shall for ever remove the wrong impressions resulting from erroneous statements of American biographers that "little is known regarding her." Among the Cary papers has been found a copy of what is designated through a memorandum docketing them, as the "Religious thoughts and experiences of Mary Washington, given to her son George, and which, in an hour of thankfulness to the Almighty for the nation's deliverance from great peril, is transmitted to Robert Cary as a thank-offering for earnest, cordial help."

No further explanation is traceable, nor indeed in the mind of the writer is any needed, regarding these fervent, heartfelt expressions, sought by an earnestly religious mother to be impressed on her son.

The early loss of husband and children was a trial such as poor frail humanity could not have borne without the special grace of God the Comforter. True it is that our greatest griefs spring from our holiest and best joys. God bestowed on Mary Washington the highest of all earthly good things, in her family affections. Her, as her son's, highest pleasures were found in duty. Let none who read these her "thoughts and experiences" deem her other than the wonderfully cheerful spirit she in truth was. To her all life was happy, and one marked feature in her beautiful character was that she thoroughly enjoyed life, largely traceable to her having found enjoyment in every duty which she had to perform. Let none henceforth say of this grand woman (whose personal charms, through Middleton's portrait, this volume is privileged to present to the world) that "little is known of her." It may more truthfully be said, "Of whom know we so much?"

Sent to George Washington by his mother after the surrender of Lord Cornwallis:—

"Truly does this event proclaim that the Great Sovereign of heaven and earth governs the world. There are no accidents of fortune. Things are not left to the wills of men, to blind chance, to their own contingency, but are all inspected, guided, and ordered by Him. *He* is still the same, and will order all things well. No snares, intrigues, or difficulties puzzle or prevent the ways and purposes of God. Whatsoever contrivances and confusions be amongst men, He still keeps His throne, never lets loose the reins of His government of the world, though the instruments of His over-ruling power may be guilty of violence and injustice. *If thou seest the oppression of the poor, and violent perverting of judgment and justice in a province, marvel not at the matter, for He that is higher than the highest, regardeth; and there be higher than they.* The tragical rents and revolutions of states and kingdoms, the disappointment of councils, the defeats of armies long flushed with success, the dissolving of majesty, the pulling asunder the thrones of mighty empires, the numerous accidents and traverses of human life,—all depend upon the disposing will and pleasure of God.

They who continually make God their defence, that trust to His protection, rely and cast themselves upon Him for safety, shall find Him a sure safeguard: they are His particular care and charge, under His special providence and defence, secure from all hurt and danger: he that dwelleth in the secret places of the Most High, shall abide under the shadow of the Almighty. He shall cover thee with His feathers, and under His wings shalt thou trust. He loves us better than we love ourselves, and better knows what is fit for our interest, our universal welfare, which is lodged more intimately in His heart than it can be in ours. Although our sins deserve Thy wrath, and nothing that we can do deserves Thy favour, yet *godliness hath the promise of the life which is to come.* It was Thy errand into the world to save us from perishing. Thou art effectively the Saviour of the body. And shall we not trust Thee in what Thou hast undertaken, who trust man if we judge him faithful?"

In an hour of national despondency his mother had sent him the following:—

"O Merciful Saviour, how have I been blessed by Thee in the enjoyment of calmness and resignation during times of trouble and perplexity, arising through the prospects and prognostics of approaching miseries; when men's hearts were failing them for fear, and for looking after those things they feared to be coming upon them. Thou gavest me inward *peace* and *rest*, which *they* can never possess, who entertain *evil tidings* with dismayed minds, and have nothing to trust to, or rest upon, but what may be damaged or taken from them. *Fear* of *future trouble* is the great disturber of human life, molests our quiet hours with dismal apprehensions; prevents not, nor eases, an expected calamity; torments us before it comes, more than the calamity itself."

"External comforts or crosses should make little accession to, or diminution from the satisfaction and serenity of our spirits. It is far better not to *need*, to be above, than to *enjoy abundance*. *All* is well so long as it is well *within*. When *Simeon* had the *Infant Saviour* in his arms, and *Zaccheus Christ* in his house, how little were they taken with, or concerned for, other things. It is not *abundance* men need, but *satisfied minds*. For wealth, none are nearer happiness nor further from the grave. In the twinkling of an eye all are turned out of the world, as naked as they came into it. A few fleet moments make but a little difference. God is too *just* to do us wrong, too *good* to do us hurt, and too *wise* not to know what will do us good or hurt."

"O merciful Saviour, comfort the hearts of all whom Thou honourest to suffer for their country's sake in these days of peril and uncertainty. Open our hearts to share their sorrows, and be it our privilege to make sacrifices for their sakes. Considering our great *examples of suffering and patience*, how can we be *impatient sufferers?* Who can be troubled at want, that worships a God willing to live and die in sorrow? Undervalued, traduced, envied, reproached, betrayed, abandoned, put to death by His countrymen. His tribute paid by a fish; His triumphs solemnized by another age's colt; born among beasts, lived among publicans, died among thieves; His birth without a cradle;

His burial without a rag or grave of His own; and the price of His blood buys a burial-place for strangers. Why wouldst Thou be thus homely, but that by contemning worldly glory, Thou mightest teach us to do so, and sanctify *poverty* unto them, whom Thou callest unto *want;* since Thou, who hadst the choice of all earthly conditions, wouldst be born poor, and live despised? Who can murmur and repine under the harshest usages, that considers Thou (who knew all from the beginning) chosedst uncivil men to crowd Thee with the horse and the ass in a public stable; to have contempt thrown upon Thy poverty? He that hath *many mansions* for others in His Father's house hath no privacy in an inn, and complains not, repines not at it. He that would have given his churlish host an eternal house in heaven for the asking for, could not have the least part of his here, because his parents seem poor. Oh, ye suffering ones in this world, none will have cause to complain of coarse robes, hard bed, thin table, who call to mind how it was with the Great King! Let us try to realize that those *idols* of the world's esteem (riches and honour) are so far from making us *truly happy*, they cannot even be numbered among *good things.*"

" We must not expect that all God's Providence in governing the world should centre in our particular conveniency and happiness! Human events and several persons' interests are so interwoven by Him that they have a mutual dependence among themselves; and their meetings, which we think *casual*, are *twice* necessary, as His decree, and for many ends. We must consider ourselves as pieces of the universe, and engines which that great work, man, sets going for executing His ends; which being all good, all means tending to them must be so also. We must therefore bear our crosses, not only with patience, but joy and thankfulness, as accounting ourselves happy we are instruments in His hand to do His work and advance His glory; which must needs please Him, doing that willingly which others do out of constraint. How great an evil is discontent with our allotment! By desiring to have our will in such a particular, we should perhaps cross God in a thousand He hath to bring about; because it is possible a thousand things may depend upon that one thing we would have to be otherwise than it is. I will be henceforth willing to be crossed in some few things, that His work may go on in all, and His end attained or furthered in *many* things by the *one thing* I am crossed in."

" We forget that we are all servants to the same Master, who disposes all the concerns of men by an unerring wisdom, and is alone to determine the place we shall serve Him in. We think that Providence, which governs others, should only serve us; and distribute to us not what it, but ourselves think good. The common Father of mankind disposes things for the public advantage of this great family; and there cannot be a greater contempt of His wisdom than to dispute His choice. Men look upon themselves as single persons, without reference to the community whereof they are members. God hath placed none of us in so barren a soil, so forlorn a state, but there is something in it which may afford us comfort; if we husband *that* to the utmost, it is scarce imaginable what improvement even he that appears the most miserable may make of his condition."

" This *world* is a *state* of *probation*, we live *in it* on no other terms than to be liable to all the hazards and troubles, changes and vicissitudes that attend *mortality*. *Vanity* and *vexation* are the essence of all earthly things, incorporated into the mass of this visible creation. *In the world we shall have tribulation*, the ordinary lot of all those, the Captain of whose salvation was made perfect through sufferings. To be *offended* at *them*, is to be *offended* that we are *men* or *Christians*. If you be without chastisement, whereof all are partakers, then you are not sons. It is the character and brand of the wicked that *they are not in trouble as other men*. Every true Israelite expects his father *Jacob's legacy*. *The archers have sorely grieved him, and shot at him and hated him*. And to find his days as his, not only *few* but *evil*. Heaven's highest favourites have no work of privilege, but the unspeakable advantage of making them easy and useful by considerate, submissive, contented minds. Patience lessens pain and suffering; trouble aggravates every sad accident; contentment makes it none at all. If we *will*, it cannot harm us; if we give way to it we wound ourselves, and join with it to make us miserable, and a single mischief a great many; but if we quietly sit still, and *in patience possess our souls*, we are what we were before the evil came, only our souls have the addition of the greatest joy and pleasure by the victory we have obtained over it and ourselves. The greatest of our *misfortunes* is our *impatience*. Discontent is worse than any evil we feel; contentment is better than any comfort we want or desire. How pleasant is it to a Christian to find himself willing to be without that which he most desired; and to suffer that to which he was most averse, far sweeter than the obtaining and enjoying of that he longed for."

"Impatience is our greatest misery. He that is ever *content* with what he is, makes himself happy without a fortune, and when others judge him most unfortunate. While we *neglect* our *duty*, we cannot but be troublesome to ourselves; while we secure *that*, we cannot be much distressed in any calamity. This, were there nothing else, is abundantly sufficient to recommend and endear religion to us; that the sincere observance of it not only prevents *many troubles*, but affords support under *all*. We can justly complain of nothing that separates us not from the love of God, who is perpetually concerned for human affairs, and particularly intends their *happiness* who place it only in *Him*. In a turbulent world, in unsettled times, amidst the straits and difficulties we are liable to pass through, nothing can be more desirable than to be above misfortunes, to be free from molestation and anxious thoughts, to meet all vicissitudes and events with constant equal tempers, to undergo all crosses with becoming, contented minds, to entertain the harshest accidents with equanimity and acquiescence of soul, wholly submitted unto, and fully satisfied with, the divine disposal."

"How great an impostor is this world unto us! In the diversity of reports and opinions, in the eager pursuit of worldly greatness, in the hungry hunt after carnal pleasures, in the heats of passion, in the cries of the poor, in the oppression of the rich, in the throng of business, in the remission of idleness, in the diversion of friends, in the spite of enemies, in the hopes and fears, joys and sorrows of this evil world, how few find rest and content! How great is the excellency of divine contentment! How necessary and profitable, pleasant and comfortable, beautiful and amiable; how it makes us rich and happy, in despite of the world; fits us to do and receive good!"

"This world hath six parts of our time allowed her by God, yet still cries, 'Give, give: how violently hath she urged me to encroach on the Sabbath by sitting too late the night before, or rising too early on the day after!' Alas, my soul! is this world six times more precious than Jesus, than Jehovah, that I should rob Him of His seventh part of my time for her sake? Blessed Redeemer, come up higher in my heart, and ye worldly concerns, get you down, and sit below His footstool. Lord, why should earthly cares trouble me on Thy day. Vain thoughts are sin's advocates and Thy adversaries. O, forgive their wickedness: and as fire melts away, so let them perish at the rebuke of Thy countenance. How long shall vain thoughts lodge within me? How long shall the august, the everlasting state of things be to my soul as a dark shadow, as the image of a dream. On this sacred morning why do I not live as just entering into eternity? as if beholding the glorious appearance of the great God my Saviour? Are not eternal things as certain now as they will be hereafter? Why then live I not alway in the believing view, and under the deep impression of the heavens vanishing, the elements melting, the earth flaming, the angels everywhere dispersed, to gather the elect from the four winds of heaven, and of their ascending to meet the Lord in the air, and be for ever with Him! What a trifle will the pleasures, honour, or wealth of this world—nay, of a thousand worlds—be to me then."

"Reason informs me that men being made for eternity, their time should be partly sequestrated to the contemplation of eternal things; that, being of a social nature, they ought to associate in their principal business the worship of their God; and that to avoid distraction, it is proper there should be one fixed season of public devotion common to all. What a mercy for man is the Sabbath! What weary pilgrims, wandering in pathless deserts, were we but for this pledge of immortality, whereon from inexhausted stores God pours down His spiritual blessings on us, and whereon we sit basking in the rays of His countenance, forget things below, and with angels and saints converse with Him, are warmed with love to Him, live on Him, and in Him, and express our joy in songs of grateful praise! But how transcendent their felicity who celebrate the everlasting Sabbath above! who, being far removed from weariness and pain, and rid of every evil thought, enjoy God and the Lamb to the utmost strength of their boundless wishes."

"Awake, my soul, the wings of the morning have begun their rapid course; the early sun, the warbling birds sing their Creator's praise. Almighty Father, all things Thy name resound, Thou Eternal Cause, Supporter, End of All, wake up my soul, and join the choir; thy Maker's praise proclaim. But soft! a Maker's praise is not the half thou owest. Praise thy Redeemer—praise. On this blessed day thy Jesus rose—rose early for thy good. On this great day He finished the purchase of thy bliss; then early burst the bonds of death. Wake, wake my soul, praise thy righteous, thy risen, thy exalted Lord!"

"*When we gave up* ourselves to Thee, Thou becamest ours; and we did it on that condition, that Thou shouldest receive and save us. I expect, O my Saviour, but the performance of Thy covenant, and the discharge of Thy undertaken office. As Thou hast caused me to believe in Thee, to love Thee, to serve Thee, to perform the condition Thou hast laid upon me, though with many sinful failings, which Thou hast pardoned, so now Thou wilt let my soul, which hath trusted in Thee, have the full experience of Thy fidelity; and take me to Thyself, according to Thy covenant, and remember the word unto Thy servant, upon which Thou hast caused me to hope. How many promises hast Thou left us, that we shall not be forsaken by Thee, but that we shall be with Thee where Thou art, that we may behold Thy glory."

No mention is made in the Cary papers as to any occasions of these meditations of Mary Washington, beyond those called forth by Lord Cornwallis' surrender.

THE DAUGHTER OF PATRICK HENRY.

CHAPTER X.

Washington's distrust of the French Revolution—His personal sacrifices during his terms of Presidency, 1789 to 1796—Imminent danger of the country during his second Presidency—Avails of the horrors excited by the French Revolution for praiseworthy purposes—Sharples' devotion to Washington—Washington's genius evidenced in his conduct at time of the Declaration of Independence, retrieves the desperate condition of the country's affairs—The intrigues of Genet—Washington's message of December, 1793, on the country's foreign relations—Great excitement everywhere—Washington dignified and unswerving—Robert Cary tracks the designs and doings of Genet and other enemies in America—Pinckney's despatches make known England's desire for peace—Cary's great love and devotion to Washington.

SHARPLES names how deeply his heart had entered into the intense anxieties through which the great Chief had passed during his chief magistracy, events which had convulsed the whole political world, and which had tried most severely his moderation and prudence. The French Revolution had taken place. Sharples had learned from Washington that from the beginning of that revolution he had no great confidence in its beneficial operation. He must have desired the abolition of despotism; but he is not to be called the enemy of liberty, because he dreaded the substitution of a more oppressive yoke. It is more than probable that his wary and practical understanding, instructed by the experience of popular commotions, augured little good from the daring speculations of inexperienced visionaries. The progress of the revolution was not adapted to cure his distrust, and when, in 1793, France, then groaning under the most intolerable and hideous tyranny, became engaged in war with almost all the governments of the civilized world, it was matter of deliberation with Washington whether the republican envoy or the agent of the French princes should be received in America as the diplomatic representative of France. Whatever may have been his private feelings of repugnance and horror, his public conduct was influenced only by his public duties. As a virtuous man he must have abhorred the system of crimes which was established in France. But as the first magistrate of the American Commonwealth, he was bound only to consider how far the interest and safety of the people whom he governed were affected by the conduct of France. He saw that it was wise and necessary for America to preserve a good understanding and a beneficial intercourse with that country, in whatever manner she was governed, so long as she abstained from committing an injury against America. Guided by this just and simple principle, uninfluenced by the abhorrence of crimes which he felt, he received Genet, the minister of the French Republic, and was soon shocked by the outrages which that minister committed, or instigated, or countenanced against the American Government. The conduct of Washington was a model of firm and disciplined moderation. Insults were offered to his authority in official papers, in anonymous libels, by incendiary declaimers, and by tumultuous meetings. The law of nations was trampled under foot. His confidential ministers were seduced to betray him, and the deluded populace were so inflamed by the arts of enemies that they broke out into insurrection. No vexation, however galling, could disturb the tranquillity of his mind, or make him deviate from the policy which his situation prescribed. With a more confirmed authority, and at the head of a longer established government, he might perhaps have thought greater vigour justifiable. But in his circumstances, he was sensible that the nerves of authority were not strong enough to bear being strained. Persuasion, always the most desirable instrument of government, was in his case the safest; yet he never overpassed the line which separates concession from meanness. He reached the utmost limits of moderation, without in the least being betrayed into pusillanimity. He preserved external and internal peace by a system of mildness, without any of those virtual confessions of weakness, which so much dishonour and enfeeble supreme authority. During the whole of that arduous struggle, his personal character gave that strength to a new magistracy which in other countries arises from ancient habits of obedience and respect. The authority of his virtue was more efficacious for the preservation of America than the legal powers of his office.

It was during this turbulent period that he was re-elected to the office of President of the United States, which he held from 1789 till September, 1796. No magistrate of any commonwealth, ancient or modern, ever occupied a seat so painful and perilous. Certainly no man was ever called upon so often to sacrifice his virtuous feelings—and he had no other sacrifices to make—to his public duty. In the spring of 1794 he sent an ambassador to Paris, with credentials addressed to his "dear friends, the citizens composing the Committee of Public Safety of the French Republic," whom he prays God "to take under His holy protection." Fortunately, the American ambassador was spared the humiliation of presenting his credentials to those bloody tyrants. Their power was subverted, and a few of them had suffered the punishment of their crimes, which no punishment could expiate, before his arrival at Paris.

Washington had another struggle of feeling and duty to encounter when he was compelled to suppress the insurrection in the western counties of Pennsylvania by force of arms. But there he had a consolation, in the exercise of mercy, for the necessity of having recourse to arms. Never was there a revolt quelled with so little shedding of blood. Scarcely ever was the basest dastard so tender of his own life as was this virtuous man of the lives of his fellow-citizens. The value of his clemency is enhanced by recollecting that he was neither without provocations to severity, nor without pretexts for its exercise. His character and his office had been reviled in a manner almost unexampled among civilized nations. His authority had been insulted. His safety had been threatened. Of his personal and political enemies, some might, perhaps, have been suspected of having instigated the insurrection; a greater number were thought to wish well to it; and a very few showed much zeal to suppress it. But neither resentment nor fear, nor even policy itself, could extinguish the humanity of Washington. This seems to have been the only sacrifice which he was incapable of making to the interest of his country.

Would that the enemy could show the like moderation under circumstances of even greater provocation, ofttimes endured by Washington, and which were never allowed to swell into revenge;—when incensed at Lisle's treachery, Lord Cornwallis, for instance, had recourse to most severe orders in return. The penalty of death was denounced against all militiamen who, after serving with the English, went off to the insurgents. Several of the prisoners in the battle of Camden, men taken with arms in their hands and with British protections in their pockets, were hanged. A proclamation was issued, sequestering the estates of those who had been the most forward to oppose the establishment of the royal authority within the province. These and even more severe measures exceeded the bounds of justice, certainly they did those of policy. This was shown by the fatal event, when on the overthrow of the royalist cause in South Carolina, the measures of Lord Cornwallis became the plea for other executions, and for every act of oppression that resentment could devise. Within the limited sphere of his own command, Lord Rawdon had recourse to some measures still severer and far less to be justified. In a letter to one of his officers, which was intercepted, he wrote: "I will give the inhabitants ten guineas for the head of any deserter, belonging to the volunteers of Ireland; and five guineas only, if they bring him in alive." No amount of provocation or of precedent in his enemies, no degree of youthful ardour in himself, could excuse these blamable words. When, however, called upon to vindicate them, Lord Rawdon declared that many of his threats were meant only "to act on the fears and prejudices of the vulgar," and by no means to be carried into practical effect.

Throughout the whole course of Washington's second presidency, the danger of America was great and imminent beyond example. The spirit of change seemed to have shaken all nations. But in other countries it had to encounter ancient and solidly established power. It had to tear up by the roots long habits of attachment in some nations for their government, of awe in others, of acquiescence and submission in all. But in America the Government was new and weak. The people had scarce time to recover from the ideas and feelings of a recent civil war. In other countries the volcanic force must be of power to blow up the mountains, and to convulse the continents that hold it down, before it could escape from the deep cavern in which it was imprisoned; in America, it was covered only by the ashes of a late convulsion, or at most by a little thin soil, the produce of a few years quiet. The Government of America had none of those salutary prejudices to employ which in every other country were used with success to open the eyes of the people to the enormities of the French Revolution. It had, on the contrary, to contend with the prejudices of the people in the most moderate precautions against internal confusion, in the most measured and guarded resistance to the unparalleled insults and enormous encroachments of France. Without zealous support from the people, the American Government was impotent. It required a considerable time, and it cost an arduous and dubious struggle, to direct the popular spirit against a sister republic, established among a people to whose aid the Americans ascribed the establishment of their independence. It is probable, indeed, that no policy could have produced this effect, unless it had been powerfully aided by the crimes of the French Government, which proved the strongest allies of all established governments; which produced such a general disposition to submit to any known tyranny, rather than rush into all the unknown and undefinable evils of civil confusion, with the horrible train of new and monstrous tyrannies of which it is usually the forerunner. Of these circumstances Washington availed himself with remarkable address. He used the horror excited by the atrocities of the French Revolution for the most honest and praiseworthy purposes: to preserve the internal quiet of his country; to assert the dignity and to maintain the rights of the commonwealth which he governed against foreign enemies. He avoided war without incurring the charge of pusillanimity; he cherished the detestation of Americans for anarchy without weakening the spirit of civil liberty; and he maintained, and even consolidated, the authority of government without abridging the privileges of the people.

Sharples, be it rememberd, reached America at a time when the great Chief was suffering deeply through the designs of men jealous of his power, greatness, and influence.

Cary was a relied-on friend. It is seen by confidential correspondence that he was in the great Chief's confidence, and finding the newly-arrived artist commended very warmly by him, and that on acquaintance he proved to be an English gentleman of mark, and worthy of confidence, he opened his heart to him in a degree such as fell to but few. Sharples appreciated this, proved by a letter to Mr. Cary, in which he wrote :—

"I would have walked barefoot the mileage of the wide Atlantic Ocean for the great, the inexpressible honour, even of having had if it were but one sitting from him, the greatest of all men."

Washington's resignation, in 1796, must have occurred just prior to Sharples painting his portraits. It was, perhaps, a measure of prudence, but it may be doubted whether it was beneficial for his country in the then unsettled state of public affairs. In his valedictory address at this time, as in that given before to his countrymen on the occasion of quitting the command of the army, his whole heart and soul is laid bare. Other State papers have, perhaps, shown more spirit, more eloquence, greater force of genius, and a more enlarged comprehension of mind; but none ever displayed more simplicity and ingenuousness, more moderation and sobriety, more good sense, more prudence, more honesty, more earnest affection for his country and for mankind, more profound reverence for virtue and religion, more ardent wishes for the happiness of his fellow-creatures, and more just and rational views of the means which alone can effectually promote that happiness.

At our now distance of time, it is possible to look dispassionately at the events of the American War, so as to arrive at a correct judgment, such as could not have been the case with such momentous events during the period of their occurrence. It may be said, generally, that within a very short period after the Declaration of Independence, the affairs of America were in a condition so desperate, that perhaps nothing but the peculiar character of Washington's genius could have retrieved them. Activity is the policy of invaders, and in the field of battle the superiority of a disciplined army is displayed. But delay was the wisdom of a country defended by undisciplined soldiers against an enemy who must be more exhausted by time than he could be weakened by defeat. It required the consummate prudence, the calm wisdom, the inflexible firmness, the moderate and well-balanced temper of Washington, to embrace such a plan of policy, and to persevere in it; to resist the temptations of enterprise; to fix the confidence of his soldiers without the attraction of victory; to support the spirit of the army and the people amidst those slow and cautious plans of defensive warfare which are more dispiriting than defeat itself; to contain his own ambition and the impetuosity of his troops; to endure temporary obscurity for the salvation of his country, and for the attainment of solid and immortal glory; and to suffer even temporary reproach and obloquy, supported by the approbation of his own conscience and the applause of that small number of wise men whose praise is an earnest of the admiration and gratitude of posterity. Victorious generals easily acquire the confidence of their army. Theirs, however, is a confidence in the *fortune* of their general; that of Washington's army was a confidence in his *wisdom*. Victory gives spirit to cowards, and even the agitation of defeat sometimes imparts a courage of despair. Courage is ofttimes inspired by success, and it may be stimulated to desperate exertion even by calamity, but it is generally palsied by inactivity. A system of cautious defence is the severest trial of human fortitude. By this test the firmness of Washington was tried.

Mount Vernon's peaceful retreat opened its welcome gate to its illustrious owner at the conclusion of the war; but it was only for a little while that he was permitted to return to its domestic scenes, from which nothing but a paramount sense of duty had the power to withdraw him. He was not allowed long to enjoy the blessed privacy in which the artist Sharples had enjoyed his society. The Supreme Government of America, hastily thrown up, in a moment of turbulence and danger, as a fortification against anarchy, proved inadequate to the preservation of general tranquillity and permanent security. The confusions of civil war had given a taint to the morality of a portion of the people, which rendered the restraints of a just and vigorous government more indispensably necessary. Confiscation and paper money, two great schools of rapacity and dishonesty, had widely spread their poison. In this state of things, which threatened the dissolution of morality and government, good men saw the necessity of concentrating and invigorating the supreme authority. Under the influence of this conviction it was that the Convention of Delegates assembled at Philadelphia, which strengthened the hands of the federal union, and bestowed on Congress those powers which were necessary for the purposes of good government. Washington was decreed by Providence to be elected the President of this Convention, as he, three years after, was elected President of the United States of America, under what was called "The New Constitution;" though it would have been more correctly styled a reform of the Republican Government, as that Republican Government itself was only a reform of the ancient Colonial Constitution under the British Crown. None of these changes extended so far as an attempt to new model the whole social and political system.

Looking back hispassionately on the great events of that

war, it is seen that the whole efforts of Washington and his great ally and friend, Hamilton, in the Government, from the conclusion of the War in 1783, to the retirement of that able man from public life in 1796,—the year during which the artist Sharples saw so much of both,—were devoted to tempering the democratic ardour which had broken out with such vehemence in their country after the declaration of its independence, and laying the foundation of a lasting pacific intercourse with England. Yet so strongly were the sympathies of the people enlisted on the side of France and revolution, that it required all his immense popularity, and all the wisdom of his wise counsellor, Hamilton, to counteract, in 1793, the loudly expressed wish of the decided majority of the American citizens to declare war against Great Britain. So vehement was the clamour that on more than one occasion at that period, it was apparent that the federalist party, to which he belonged, had lost the majority in the Chamber of Representatives; and such was the fury of the public journals, that he was openly accused of aspiring to the monarchy, and of being "like the traitor Arnold, a spy sold to the English." But the godlike Washington, unmoved, pursued steadily his pacific policy.

The horrors of the French Revolution cooled the ardour of many of its ardent supporters in America, and one of the last acts of the Immortal was to carry, by his influence in Congress, which, as we learn on the authority of Chief Justice Marshall, had procured its passing there only by the casting vote of the President, a Commercial Treaty with Great Britain.

It is only after the lapse of nearly a century, and following the long continuance of more amicable relations between the two countries, which nothing short of demoniacal inspiration should ever disturb, that the consummate wisdom of Washington is realized in his successful avoidance of further collisions with the mother country. The intrigues of Genet, and the more than ill-advised measures of the English Government, had brought the neutrality so zealously guarded by Washington into imminent hazard. American seamen were being constantly, at that time, impressed, a wrong to which they were specially exposed from national similarity; and in addition to this frequently occurring fretful annoyance, England persistently adhered to asserted rights in holding the ports to the south of the lakes, which, according to treaty stipulations, ought unquestionably to have been given up. Washington did not feel himself in a position to press American rights under the treaty with the vigorous hand that some would urge; questions having risen in some of the State courts, to obstruct the fulfilment of the American part of such treaty, which regarded the payment of British debts contracted before the war. In addition to these causes of anxiety, there had existed such a scarcity in France, consequent on the failure of the crops, that a famine was apprehended. England, availing herself of her naval ascendency, determined, if possible, to cut off French supplies from abroad. In June, 1793, all British cruisers were instructed to detain all vessels bound to France with cargoes of corn, flour, or meal, take them into port, unload them, purchase the cargoes, make a proper allowance for the freight, and then release the vessels; or to allow the masters of them, on a stipulated security, to dispose of their cargoes in a port in amity with England. The provisions laid down for observance in carrying out this determination, though seemingly simple, were in practice most difficult, and eminently calculated to add to the already existing bad feeling. It is impossible to over-estimate the difficulties encountered by Washington in his efforts to avoid collision with England through these burning questions. A large party in the country advocated immediate seizure of the lake forts; others urged a more determined course in regard to the impressment of seamen found on board American ships; while there was not wanting a noisy multitude who clamoured for a determined stand against any meddling with the United States' vessels occupied in transport of provisions to any destination. Either one of these questions might easily have involved the country in war. He alone realized that any renewal of war at such a moment was to imperil all that had at such heavy cost been won. Among the many unworthy and pretended reasons set up by his enemies for his prudent and conscientious conduct in all these various dangerous matters, and which in no feature went beyond the bounds of right and strict justice, yet his action was cited by partisan writers as indicative of his preference of England to "our ancient ally, France." Despite the various machinations against him, the Head of the State held his own against all his many enemies, and his speech at the opening of the Congress on the 2nd December, 1793, closed with words impressing on members the magnitude of their task, the important interests confided to them, and the conscientiousness that should reign over their deliberations. "Without an unprejudiced coolness, the welfare of the Government may be hazarded; without harmony, as far as consists with freedom of sentiment, its dignity may be lost. But, as the legislative proceedings of the United States will never, I trust, be reproached for the want of temper or candour, so shall not the public happiness languish from the want of my strenuous and warmest co-operation."

A few days later, the 5th December, 1793, in a message to both Houses concerning foreign relations, he spoke feelingly with regard to those with the representative and executive bodies of France:—

"It is with extreme concern I have to inform you that the proceedings of the person whom they have unfortunately appointed their minister plenipotentiary here, have breathed nothing of the friendly spirit of the nation which sent him; their tendency, on the contrary, has been to involve us in war abroad, and discord and anarchy at home. So far as his acts, or those of his agents, have threatened our immediate commitment in the war, or flagrant insult to the authority of the laws, their effect has been counteracted by the ordinary cognizance of the laws, and by an exertion of the powers confided to me. Where their danger was not imminent, they have been borne with from sentiments of regard for his nation; from a sense of firm friendship towards us; from a conviction that they would not suffer us to remain long exposed to the action of a person who has so little respected our mutual dispositions; and, I will add, from a reliance on the firmness of my fellow-citizens in their principles of peace and order."

There was great excitement throughout America, as well as much questioning in France, and not a little in England, when this message became known. Fiery spirits in France pretended to see insult in its every word. Its truthfulness and justice were generally admitted in England. John Adams, speaking of it, said: "The President has given Genet a bolt of thunder." He questioned, however, whether Washington would be supported in it by the two Houses. "Although he stands at present as high in the admiration and confidence of the people as ever he did, I expect he will find many bitter and desperate enemies arise in consequence of his just judgment against Genet."

The truth of Adams' remark was soon exemplified in the choice of Speaker being determined by a majority of ten against the administration, in the House of Representatives; yet it was manifest from the affectionate answer on the 6th, of the two Houses, to Washington's speech, and the satisfaction expressed at his re-election, that he was not included in the opposition which, from this act, appeared to await his political system. The House did justice to the purity and patriotism of the motives which had prompted him again to obey the voice of his country, when called by it to the Presidential chair:—

"It is to virtues which have commanded long and universal reverence, and services from which have flowed great and lasting benefits, that the tribute of praise may be paid, without the reproach of flattery; and it is from the same sources that the fairest anticipations may be derived in favour of the public happiness."

This public recognition went far to condone the insults under which he had suffered. Notwithstanding the popular ferment in favour of France, both Houses may be said to have approved the course observed by Washington in regard to that country; and so far as his proclamation of neutrality went, while the House approved of it in guarded terms, the Senate pronounced it a "measure well-timed and wise; manifesting a watchful solicitude for the welfare of the nation, and calculated to promote it." These were healthful, comforting words to a spirit sorely tried, and in a letter to Robert Cary he speaks of them as "all I would wish inflicted on my maligners." These few, but truly Christian words, written unreservedly to an English gentleman, his trusty friend, far removed from the arena of strife, thoroughly exemplify his noble, forgiving spirit, and will pass down through time as a golden example to others under far less irritation and trial.

The public rebukes administered to Genet by Washington bore no seeming effect. Not content with compromising the neutrality of the United States at sea, he attempted to endanger it on land. From documents received, it appeared that in November, 1793, he had sent emissaries to Kentucky, to enrol American citizens in an expedition against New Orleans and the Spanish possessions; furnishing them with blank commissions for the purpose.[1] It was an enterprise in which the adventurous people of that State were ready enough to embark, through enthusiasm for the French nation, and impatience at the delay of Spain to open the navigation of the Mississippi. Another expedition was to proceed against the Floridas; men for the purpose to be enlisted in the South, to rendezvous in Georgia, and to be aided by a body of Indians and by a French fleet, should one arrive on the coast.

It is not intended, or even desired, to conceal in any way the character of the friendship subsisting between Washington and Robert Cary in London. Originating in business acts as his agent in sale of the tobaccos grown on his Virginia estates, correspondence, and the occurring historical events attending and arising out of the separation of the countries, had created a bond of sympathy between them; and on more than one occasion Robert Cary had strenuously exerted himself to bring about a friendly understanding between the Governments of the old and new country. Cary was a man of position, of integrity, and weight, for he never stirred save in an upright, truthful cause. So great had this become, that at the time (June, 1793) when England issued such orders to her cruisers as could hardly fail of mischief, the wisest men in the country regarded affairs as very critical. On the 6th of the following month of November, the British Government had given them additional instructions to detain all vessels laden with the produce of any colony belonging to France, or carrying supplies to any such colony, and to bring them

[1] American State Papers, ii. 36.

with their cargoes, to British ports, for adjudication in the British Courts of Admiralty. Numerous captures of American vessels had occurred in pursuance of these orders, and the public feeling had naturally been greatly irritated thereby.

Congress shared and participated in the popular excitement. Measures of high-handed character were discussed, and some such passed. It had, not without good reason, regarded the captures of American vessels as a measure little short of an open intention, if not amounting to a declaration of war. An embargo was laid, prohibiting all trade from the United States to any foreign place for the space of thirty days, and vigorous preparations for defence were adopted with but little opposition.

The high-handed resolutions to the effect that all debts due to British subjects be sequestered and paid into the treasury, as a fund to indemnify citizens of the United States for depredations sustained from British cruisers, and that all intercourse with Great Britain be interdicted until she had made compensation for those injuries, and until she should make surrender of the western ports, had thrown to the winds all moderate feeling. The popular excitement was at fever heat. Meetings were held on the subject of British spoliation.

Irving tells us that peace or war was the absorbing question. The partisans of France were now in the ascendant. It was scouted as pusillanimous any longer to hold terms with England. "No doubt," said they, "she despises the proclamation of neutrality, as an evidence of timidity; every motive of self-respect calls on the people of the United States to show a proper spirit." It was suggested that those who were in favour of resisting British aggressions should mount the tricoloured cockade, and forthwith it was mounted by many; while a Democratic

Society was formed to correspond with the one in Philadelphia, and aid in giving effect to their popular sentiments.

In the midst of this tumult, when passion endangered peace, Washington's trusty friend Robert Cary, as an advocate of peace and goodwill, moved about from pillar to post among public men in London, rendering signal service in gaining over indirectly the minds of leading statesmen, first to side with moderation, through his earnest appeal to justice and truth, followed by a more becoming sense of what was due to their own immediate kinsmen, brothers in blood, in thought, as in language and purpose. In forcible language he reminded the head of the English Government of the great Chief's integrity, truthfulness, and purity of heart. "Has he in the smallest act ever deceived the nation from which he sprang?" Further he reminded the then ruler of Britain of the great labours Washington had endured in carrying the new government to its acknowledged successful point, pictured the treachery of France, and urged that strict justice alone should direct all acts and dealings between the countries.

There was an eventful pause; the efforts of a plain, simple-hearted, right intending man, such as Robert Cary, took effect, as they have done in more recent critical moments of England, and right and good sense prevailed. While the public mind was in this inflammable state, Washington received advices from Mr. Pinckney, the American Minister in London, informing him that the British Minister had issued instructions to the commanders of armed vessels revoking those of the 6th of November, 1793. Lord Grenville also, in conversation with Mr. Pinckney, had explained the real motives for that order, showing that, however oppressive in its execution, it had not been intended for the special vexation of American commerce.

Washington laid Pinckney's letter before Congress on the 4th of April, 1794. It had its effect on all parties, and there was a generally evident solicitude to avoid a rupture. Jefferson, though as he said, "groaning under the insults of Great Britain, yet I hope some means will turn up of reconciling our faith and honour with peace, for I have seen enough of one war never to wish to see another." It was an hour which drew from Hamilton: "'Tis as great an error for a nation to overrate as to underrate itself. Presumption is as great a fault as timidity. 'Tis our error to overrate ourselves and underrate Great Britain; we forget how little we can annoy, how much we may be annoyed."

Robert Cary, the plain London merchant, who obtained for his fellow-men in England and America true presentations of his ideal Washington, and who silently, and as it were unknown, exerted himself in quieting the elements disturbant of peace, was no common man. His love and admiration of Washington was intense, and although in the early history of the events leading to the separation of the countries he was a loyalist, yet the same force impelling Washington had like effect on him. He entered heart and soul into all his trials and struggles. Robert Cary, like his ideal, had been soundly educated; his was a granite foundation laid in one of England's old-fashioned public grammar schools. He knew enough of classic lore to cause his mind to realize that the world could, in times of need, produce men of higher stuff than the mere worshipper of dollars. He had read of Leonidas and his Spartan band, and could realize that the world in his own day held at least one heart as rightly patriotic as were those whose deeds stand out as an example of patriotism overtopping in its stature, and outshining in its lustre, all the heroisms of doing and enduring for country's sake which the intervening ages can present. He felt it towered over all subsequent histories of the world as such an illustration, and perhaps none will be recorded in those still to be written, that will excite so great and universal admiration. And, what adds to its lustre, the Spartan band went to their death to produce an example. Their fate was not an accident, like a thousand heroic deaths on the battle-field. The gorge in the mountains gave remarkable power to a few against a host of armed men, and it enabled the few to deal death and destruction to many times their number of the enemy. But when they planted themselves in the narrow and tortuous pass, they did not expect to hold it. They did not look to arrest the huge invasion longer than an hour or two at most. It was not for their practical value as a defence that they sold their lives, but to do a deed that should live in the longest memories of the Grecian nation and language; that should burn a vestal flame on the altar of patriotism for ever, and fire every man, woman, and child of the commonwealth with new love and devotion to their country. They did not overrate the influence of their example. They had Greece only in their hearts when they performed the deed; but it overspread nations and ages then unborn, and filled their histories with its inspiration.

There are diversities even in patriotism. Robert Cary saw in Washington's sufferings for country, and in his purity and rectitude of heart and action, an example greatly needed in modern times, one that he felt would shed lustre on the future life of the great New World then starting into life, and his hopes have not been unfulfilled. He saw in Patriotism one of the greatest facts in the character and history of human nature, and that in one essential characteristic it parallels, on a lower level, the great central doctrine of the Christian religion, and that it finds its best inspiration and expression in suffering—the suffering of the one or the few for the many, for the commonwealth, for the nation. Cary knew Washington's heart, and had shared his anxieties and sorrows. The fact of his somewhat deserted state at critical moments excited his deepest sympathies. He was on terms of intimacy with Edmund Burke, who chummed with men on higher grounds than notoriety, worldly position, or even mental power. His estimate was that of real worth, which alone was the key to his great heart. Burke had early seen Washington's greatness, that he was to be the bright star of the Modern Firmament, and a Cary's urging helped to stay the force in England's Parliament acting against him. Burke felt the existence of a class of sufferings which do for nations, as a society, what individual experiences do to the particular country in which they transpire, sufferings which educate peoples, who in antecedent times have been mutual enemies to feel for and with each other in some event, bringing to one of their number a great affliction. It is this class which produce the flower of that slow-growing plant, international sympathy and benevolence. Burke thoroughly realized the grand generality of Paul, uttered to the cynical casuists of Athens in the midst of Mars Hill, "God hath made of one blood all nations of men."

It was the wisdom of Burke that laid down the axiom that to judge any living American by an European standard would generally result in error. He also foreshadowed and drew attention to the circumstance connected with the race of cultivators in America as altogether unparalleled in any other age or country of the world, and which has since been so eloquently expressed by the historian Alison. In every nation that has hitherto appeared, the enjoyment of property and engrossing of mankind in the cases of agriculture, have been found to be attended with the strongest possible attachment by the owner of the soil to the whole freeholds which they cultivate; and nothing short of the greatest disasters in life has been able to tear them from the seats of their childhood, and the spots on which their own industry and that of their fathers has been exerted. Mungo Park has told us how strong this feeling is in the heart of Africa among the poor negroes: "To him no water is sweet but that which is drawn from his own well, and no shade refreshing but the tabba-tree of his native dwelling. When carried into captivity by a neighbouring tribe, he never ceases to languish during his exile, seizes the first opportunity to escape, rebuilds with haste his fallen walls, and exults to see the smoke ascend from his native village. In Ceylon, Bishop Heber tells us, the attachment of cultivators to their little property is such, that it is not unusual to see a man the proprietor of the hundred and fiftieth part of a single tree. In France, the same principle has always been strongly felt, and Arthur Young long ago remarked, that it continues with undiminished strength, though the freehold is reduced to the fraction of a tree; while in Canada, local attachment operates among the *habitant* of French descent with such force, that in place of extending into the surrounding wilds, the cultivators divide and subdivide among their children the freeholds they have already acquired; population multiplies *inwards*, not *outwards*, and instead of spreading over and fertilizing the desert, it leads, as in old France, to an infinite subdivision among the inhabitants of the land already cultivated.

In America, on the other hand, for the first time in the history of mankind, this strong and general feeling seems to be entirely obliterated. Though the labourers have probably derived greater advantages from the cultivator of the soil than any other people that ever existed, yet they have no sort of attachment either to the land which they had acquired, or to that which they may have inherited from their fathers. Not only is real property generally sold and divided at the death of the head of a family, but even during his lifetime, immigration from one spot to another is so frequent, that it may be considered the grand social characteristic of the American people. To turn money into land, and take root in the soil, and leave his descendants there, is the great object of ambition in the Old World; to turn land into money and leave his children afloat, but affluent in society is the universal advice in the New. This peculiarity is so remarkable and so totally at variance with what had previously ever been observed in nations engaged in the cultivation of the soil, that it may be considered, in a social point of view, as the grand characteristic of society in the United States of America.

The great problem of the overflow of nations on the lands of the New World is shown by memoranda left by Sharples to have been the subject of an earnest conversation between himself and Washington during his stay at Mount Vernon. Up to that period no great multitude had crossed the ocean to the new paradise prepared for them by the great benefactor whose wisdom and humanity in providing homes for countless millions were on a par with his patriotism. The Chief said, "At no distant future, the despotically misgoverned and those forced out from over populated or less fertile countries will here seek an asylum. God grant our country may ever extend a welcome hand to the oppressed and needy of the whole world, then will America be fulfilling the great and providential destiny which my heart tells me the Almighty has willed to be hers." Beneficent words worthy of the heart of the Founder.

Nearly a century of years has rolled by since Washington gave utterance to this dream of his great heart. It is a fitting subject to take a retrospect of the earlier features of this gathering of multitudes. Its progress in more recent times evidences the correctness of his far-seeing mind and judgment.

When European enterprise first sought successfully permanent colonization on the shores of America, the spirit of adventure was not confined to those who were bound together by similar opinions, or the same habits of life. Diversity of motive led to the hazardous undertaking of emigration. The men who seated themselves on the pleasant waters of Virginia, impelled mostly by the hope of better fortunes, were sent forth and led out on their pilgrimage by the fast friends of the crown and staunch adherents to the religious establishment of England. Next in order were the amphibious Hollanders, who brought with them their phlegmatic coolness, their untiring patience, calm courage, and indomitable industry; they had fought at home a hard battle with the ocean and conquered; and having snatched there a domain from the sea, they came to build up a domain on a land uncivilized, but they brought with them reverence for God, and held fast to the principles of the Synod of Dort.

Next made his way to the iron-bound shores of New England, the stern old Puritan. He was brave, and his courage was sustained by enthusiasm; he sought to establish not merely a colony, but a *religion* also. He might be right or he might be wrong in his opinions—many of his children have since abandoned these; but he was honest and knew no fear of man. Heroic, indeed, were those brave men who faced the horrors of the awful winter of 1630. These, in a touching memorial, preserved by their own historian, when they were bidding a long, and, to some, an everlasting farewell to the homes of their childhood, called the Church of England their "dear mother," ever acknowledging " that such hope and part as they had obtained in the common salvation, they had received in her bosom and sucked from her breasts." Yet, they were not in America conformists to the Church of England? Their religious system approached nearer in its ceremonials to the Reformed Churches of France.

And now the hardy Scandinavian from Sweden comes; and prepared to cope alike with the rigours and the perilous labours of subduing a wilderness in which there lurked a savage foe; he holds to the faith taught by the great German reformer, and calls himself a Lutheran.

Presently appears Cecil Calvert, Lord Baltimore, within the limits of what is now Maryland, planting his colony of Romanists at old St. Mary's. And to his honour be it said, he offered religious freedom to all.

Next in the train is Penn, the leader of a pacific yet industrious and honest sect, who came to teach that human hearts might be won by kindness more easily than savage courage could be conquered by arms.

The persecuted French Huguenot next found his way, seeking an escape from death and the privilege of worshipping God in peace, and finds a friendly asylum in more than one spot on the American continent. The names of this persecuted body of men still live among their descendants in Massachusetts, New York, Virginia, and both the Carolinas.

The brave mountaineer of Switzerland, too, was not wanting. His undying love of home is attested by the names bestowed on some Southern towns, and the forests of the Carolinas resounded in early times with the songs in which the expatriated Swiss poured forth his fond remembrance of the mountains and the valleys of his dear fatherland. His devotions were the prayers of a French Protestant.

And last of all, in this enumeration, comes the German

Moravian, who penetrates the wilderness and plants his settlement, not for the sake of worldly gain, not to gratify earthly ambition, but that, in the noble spirit which has ever marked his brotherhood, he may, in the midst of peril and at every personal sacrifice, preach to the heathen the unsearchable riches of Christ.

How varied the mass! Different in religion, different in social feelings and manners, different in language; agreeing in but the single fact that all are exiles from a fatherland, here God in His providence brought together on the American continent, the Englishman and the Hollander, the Swede and the Swiss, the German and the Frenchman. All brought with them the principle of religion; all acknowledge the name of Christ, each in his own way; and from many different spots in the land go up, to the same God, the prayers of the Protestant Episcopalian, and the Episcopalian of the Church of Rome, of the Reformed Dutch and the Lutheran, of the Moravian and the Huguenot. And this was the beginning of a great and free people.

Now how shall this heterogeneous mass be fused into one great, consolidated nationality? With but limited intercourse in the beginning, owing allegiance, in some instances to different sovereignties in different parts of Europe, and with different speech; the difficulties in the way of such a fusion seem, to mere human enterprise, insurmountable— but that God who led forth all those wanderers from many lands, and who, from the beginning, in His wise providence, meant that there should be fusion, and that there should rise up here a powerful, united, and happy nation, as an instrument for the accomplishment of his purposes on this earth; that God so orders events that gradually these disjointed materials shall assume something like the form of unity. The God that had made him a *man* implanted in him all the elements which go to the making of man who will brook no insolent invasion of his rights as a man. Finally, the silent course of events in the lapse of time brought all the colonies under *one* sovereignty, that when the " hour and the man " should come, all should feel that they had *one*, and but one common enemy.

The hour and the man did come. The hour was when the first blood was shed at Lexington; the man was George Washington. And thus God had brought these early settlers their first sense of the indispensable necessity of consolidation; but the light as yet was very feeble—they caught but a glimpse of the nationality; they were very far from having reached it. The pressure from without, and that alone, created all the union they had; they had not had time, nor were they ready yet to find enduring, God-created links of union *within;* that was yet to come, for God's providences moved gradually. At length, against fearful odds, and by evident interposition of God Himself, as the brave old fathers piously acknowledged (for they were not ashamed to pray), they were recognized before the world as a free and independent people.

But was it thereby made *one nation*, prepared, as the youngest in the sisterhood of nations, to take its place on earth? Far from it; the achievement of independence merely did not make it *one nation :* it only gave it the right and the power to make it so if so determined. But the importance of nationality did not appear to be felt; but God saw fit to teach it them by *experience* that might not be forgotten. It formed the old articles of confederation, the grand feature of which was simply a mutual pledge to stand by each other in resisting aggression; for then, having long lived as separate colonies, and having known no other advantage of combination but that of opposing consolidated strength to the assault of a common foe, the federated land saw no need of *nationality*. It was for the moment content to be simply a league of petty and independent sovereignties.

The wise and the good of all parties saw that some better bond of *unity* was necessary; and it was this that under God gave birth to the CONSTITUTION OF THE UNITED STATES.

The principles embodied in that instrument became the people's sovereign, because they made it so. To that loyalty and allegiance are due. What matters it whether supreme authority be placed in a charter or a prince? It must reside somewhere. Let those who prefer it place it in a human being as the exponent and representative of certain unwritten principles, which they call a constitution. Americans embody the principles themselves, with no intervention of a human representative or exponent; they have written them down, that they may be plainly read and understood of all the people, who, by themselves, or others chosen by themselves, made them the supreme principles, which, in government, should control all others. And in the instrument care was taken to avoid the collisions and bloodshed which sometimes flow from the ambition of human aspirants to a throne; provision it was hoped was made for a peaceful mode of securing from the supreme power justice to all rights; for, if in the lapse of time and altered state of society, the new relations created should call for modifications or alterations in these principles, the people, who made the parchment monarch, quietly and by fixed rules, can introduce such changes as the majority may declare necessary. Alas! it proved insufficient to prevent war with the South, although the Constitution triumphed in the end. But, changed or unchanged, it stands a monument of the patriotism and wisdom of the good old fathers, who shed their blood to purchase the power and the right to put it there. There it stands, rightfully demanding the love, the loyalty, the obedience of every true American heart.

CHAPTER XI.

Mount Vernon Washington's goal of happiness—His visits there when a child—Lawrence Washington's marriage with Anne Fairfax—Their residence at Mount Vernon built by him—George as a boy visiting there—Joseph Ball's letter to Mary Washington, discouraging the sending George to sea—Early susceptibility to female attractions—Appointed public surveyor to Culpepper County—Excels as an athlete—Introduced to Martha Custis—Courtship, marriage, and early married life—Domestic habits—George Mason his neighbour and friend—The churches in which he worshipped, and their ministers—Martha Washington's children—Her daughter's death—Destroys her husband's letters—Lawrence at Mount Vernon—Sharples assists in improving the grounds—Washington and Lafayette—Able summary of Washington's character from Hunt's Merchant's Magazine.

MOUNT VERNON was Washington's pictured goal of earthly happiness, and yet how few and comparatively short were the opportunities permitted him to enjoy there the hoped-for rest. It is pleasant to know the real enjoyment vouchsafed to him on occasions of his heart being open to receive sunny impressions when really at rest in his Virginia home, and which are happily thus recorded:—

"Strange as it may seem," wrote he to General Knox, on an occasion when revelling in peaceful enjoyment of his simple home life, "it is nevertheless true, that it was not until very lately that I could get the better of my usual custom of ruminating, as soon as I waked in the morning, on the business of the ensuing day; and of my surprise at finding, after revolving many things in my mind, that I was no longer a public man, nor had anything to do with public transactions. I feel now, however, as I conceive a weary traveller must do, who, after treading many a weary

ANGELICA PEALE.

Daughter of the Artist, who placed the Crown of Laurel on Washington at Valley Forge...

Reproduced by the Autotype Company.

step with a heavy burden on his shoulders, is eased of the latter, having reached the haven to which all the former were directed, and from his housetop is looking back, and tracing, with an eager eye, the meanders by which he escaped the quicksands and mires which lay in his way, and into which none but the all-powerful Guide and Dispenser of human events could have prevented his falling."

Later on we see him as the worn and wearied soldier sighing for respite from ceaseless mental and bodily labour, and when feeling the effects of a more than physically overtaxed constitution. In a letter to Lafayette when deriving benefit from repose this same year, he writes,—"Free from the bustle of a camp and the busy scenes of public life, I am solacing myself with those tranquil enjoyments of which the soldier, who is ever in pursuit of fame; the statesman, whose watchful days and sleepless nights are spent in devising schemes to promote the welfare of his own, perhaps the ruin of other countries—as if this globe was insufficient for us all; and the courtier, who is always watching the countenance of his prince in hopes of catching a gracious smile, can have very little conception. I have not only retired from all public employments, but I am retiring within myself, and shall be able to view the solitary walk, and tread the paths of private life, with heartfelt satisfaction. Envious of none, I am determined to be pleased with all; and this, my dear friend, being the order of my march, I will move gently down the stream of life until I sleep with my fathers."

Augustine Washington died in the spring of 1743, when his son George was eleven years of age, and by his last will and testament bequeathed his estate of Hunting Creek, upon a bay and stream of that name, near Alexandria, to Lawrence Washington, a son by his first wife,

Jane Butler. It was a noble domain of many hundred acres, stretching for miles along the Potomac, and bordering the estates of the Fairfaxes, Masons, and other distinguished families.

Lawrence, who seems to have inherited the military spirit of his family, had lately been to the wars. Admiral Vernon, Commander-in-chief of England's navy in the West Indies, had lately chastised the Spaniards for their depredations upon British commerce by capturing Porto Bello, on the isthmus of Darien. The Spaniards prepared to strike an avenging blow, and the French determined to help them. England and her colonies were aroused. Four regiments, for service in the West Indies, were to be raised in the American colonies; and from Massachusetts to the Carolinas the fife and drum of the recruiting-sergeant were heard. Lawrence, then a spirited young man of twenty-two, was among the thousands who caught the infection, and, obtaining a captain's commission, he embarked for the West Indies in 1741 with between 3000 and 4000 men, under General Wentworth. That officer and Admiral Vernon commanded a joint expedition against Carthagena, in South America, which resulted in disaster. According to the best authorities not less than 20,000 British soldiers and seamen perished, chiefly from a fatal sickness that prevailed, especially among the troops, who were commanded by General Wentworth. To that scourge, Thompson, in his "Summer," thus touchingly alludes:—

"You, gallant Vernon, saw
The miserable scene; you, pitying, saw
To infant weakness sunk the warrior's arm,
Saw the deep-racking pang, the ghastly form,
The lip pale, quivering, and the beamless eye
No more with ardour bright; you heard the groans

Of agonizing ships, from shore to shore,
Heard, nightly plunged amid the sullen waves,
The frequent corse; while on each other fixed
In sad presage, the blank assistants seemed
Silent, to ask, whom fate would next demand."

In the midst of that terrible pestilence the system of Lawrence Washington received those seeds of fatal disease against whose growth it struggled manfully for ten years, and then yielded.

Lawrence returned home in the autumn of 1742, the provincial army, in which he had served, having been disbanded, and Admiral Vernon and General Wentworth recalled to England. He had acquired the friendship and confidence of both these officers. For several years he kept up a correspondence with the former, and received from him a copy of a medal struck in commemoration of the capture of Porto Bello by Admiral Vernon. This was preserved at Mount Vernon until Washington's death.

Lawrence intended to go to England, join the regular army, and seek preferment therein; but love changed his resolution and the current of his life, for

"Love rules the court, the camp, the grove,
And man below, and saints above."

Beautiful Anne, the eldest daughter of the Honourable William Fairfax, of Fairfax County, became the object of his warm attachment, and they were betrothed. Their nuptials were about to be celebrated in the spring of 1743, when a sudden attack of gout in the stomach deprived Lawrence of his father. But the marriage took place in July. All thoughts of military life as a profession passed from the mind of Lawrence, and, taking possession of his Hunting Creek estate, he erected a plain substantial mansion upon the highest eminence along the Potomac front of his domain, and named the spot MOUNT VERNON, in honour of the gallant admiral.

WESTERN FRONT OF MOUNT VERNON AS IT APPEARED IN 1858.

In this mansion Lawrence resided until his death, and but little change was made in its appearance from the time when it came into the possession of his brother George by inheritance until the close of the old War for Independence. It has been described as a house of the first class then occupied by thrifty Virginia planters; two stories in height, with a porch in front, and a chimney built inside, at each end, contrary to the prevailing style. It stood upon a most lovely spot, on the brow of a gentle slope, which ended at a thickly-wooded precipitous river-bank, its summit nearly 100 feet above the water. Before it swept the Potomac with a magnificent curve, its broad bosom swarming with the graceful swan, the gull, the wild duck, and smaller water-fowl; and beyond lay the green fields and shadowy forests of Maryland.

When Lawrence was fairly settled with his bride in this new and pleasant home, little George was a frequent and much-petted visitor at Mount Vernon. His half-brother loved him tenderly, and, after their father's death, he took a paternal interest in all his concerns. The social influences to which he was subjected were of the highest order. The Fairfaxes held the first rank in wealth and social position, both in England and in Virginia; and the father-in-law of Lawrence, who occupied a beautiful country seat, not far from Mount Vernon, called Belvoir, was a man of distinction, having served as an officer of the British army in the East and West Indies, and officiated as Governor of New Providence, one of the Bermudas. He now managed an immense landed estate belonging to his cousin, Lord Fairfax, a tall, gaunt, raw-boned, near-sighted man, upon whom had fallen the snows of sixty winters, and who, made shy and eccentric by disappointed love in early life, was now in Virginia and living at Belvoir, but secretly resolving to go over the Blue Mountains of the West, and make his home in the deep wilderness, away from the haunts of men. Thither he went a few years later, and in the great valley of Virginia took up his abode in a lodge at a spot where he resolved to build a manor-house, in the midst of 10,000 acres of arable and grazing land, call it Greenway Court, and live a solitary lord over a vast domain. But the mansion was never built, and in that lodge the lord of the manor lived during all the stormy days of the French and Indian war, and as a staunch loyalist throughout the struggles of the Americans for independence, until the news came one day that his young friend Washington had captured Cornwallis and all his army. Then, says tradition, he called to his servant and said,—

"Come, Joe, carry me to my bed, for
I'm sure it's high time for me to die!"

> "Then up rose Joe, all at the word,
>   And took his master's arm,
>   And to his bed he softly led
>   The lord of Greenway farm.
>   Then thrice he called on Britain's name,
>   And thrice he wept full sore,
>   Then sighed—'O Lord, Thy will be done!'
>   And word spake never more."

It was early in 1785, at the age of ninety-two years, that Lord Fairfax died at Greenway Court, loved by many for his generosity and benevolence.

Lawrence Washington was also distinguished for his wealth and intelligence. He was adjutant-general of his district, with the rank and pay of major, and at this time was a popular member of the Virginia House of Burgesses. At Mount Vernon and at Belvoir the sprightly boy George, who was a favourite everywhere, became accustomed to the refinements and amenities of English social life in its best phases, and this had a marked influence upon his future character.

There were other influences there which made a deep impression upon the mind of the thoughtful boy. Sometimes the companions-in-arms of his brother, or officers from some naval vessel that came into the Potomac, would be guests at Mount Vernon, and perils by field and flood would be related. In these narratives Sir William Fairfax often joined, and related his experience in the far-off Indies, in marches, battles, sieges, and retreats. These fired the soul of young Washington with longings for adventure, and accordingly we find him, at the age of fourteen years, preparing to enter the English navy as a midshipman, a warrant having been procured. His brother and Mr. Fairfax encouraged his inclination, and his mother's reluctant consent was obtained. A vessel of war was lying in the Potomac, and the lad's luggage was on board, when his mother received the following letter from her uncle in England, dated Stratford-by-Bow, 19th May, 1747:—

"I understand that you are advised and have some thoughts of putting your son George to sea. I think he had better be put apprentice to a tinker, for a common sailor before the mast has by no means the common liberty of the subject; for they will press him from a ship where he has fifty shillings a month and make him take twenty-three, and cut, and slash, and use him like a negro, or rather, like a dog. And as to any considerable preferment in the navy, it is not to be expected, as there are always so many gaping for it here who have interest, and he has none. And if he should get to be master of a Virginia ship (which it is very difficult to do), a planter that has three or four hundred acres of land and three or four slaves, if he be industrious, may live more comfortably, and leave his family in better bread, than such a master of a ship can. . . . He must not be too hasty to be rich, but go on gently and with patience, as things will naturally go. This method, without aiming at being a fine gentleman before his time, will carry a man more comfortably and surely through the world than going to sea, unless it be a great chance indeed. I pray God keep you and yours.

"Your loving brother,
"JOSEPH BALL."

Joseph Ball, you were a brother indeed when you sent this good advice to your loving niece Mary. Many uncles forget young relatives after marrying, and especially do they cease corresponding with them if their lot is cast in far-off lands. Most probably you knew her virtues and goodness, and, above all, may not the Great Almighty have directed your heart to manifest this interest in that boy? You never ceased your interest through distance. Mary had the same good sense in acting on your good advice, as her son evidenced in yielding to his mother's judgment and wishes by following the same. What strange outcomes may be seen by such as watch and observe thoughtfully! These lines, for instance, are penned close to that very Stratford-le-Bow, in England, where John Ball lived when he wrote that letter to his brother's child, Mary, and which determined the future liberties of a world. The portrait of Mary, by Middleton, as those of her son George and his wife Martha, by Sharples, have been destined to get back to England, hallowing a residence a few miles only from that same spot. How true it is, that the realities of life are more remarkable than the conjurings of fiction!

This letter, without doubt, made the mother decide to act according to the desire of her heart, for already a friend had written to Lawrence: "I am afraid Mrs. Washington will not keep up to her first resolution. . . . I find that one word against his going has more weight than ten for it." She could not expose her son to the hardships and perils of the British navy, so vividly portrayed by his uncle. Her consent was withdrawn, and George Washington, with disappointed ambition, returned to school, fell desperately in love with a "lowland beauty" (who reciprocated not his passion, but became the mother of General Henry Lee), indited sentimental verses, as young lovers are apt to do, sighed for a time in great unhappiness, and then went to live with his brother at Mount Vernon, in partial forgetfulness that he had once dreamed that—

"She was his life,
The ocean to the river of his thoughts,
Which terminated all."

Now it was that young Washington's real intimacy with the Fairfax family commenced, and an attachment was formed between himself and George William Fairfax, his senior by six or seven years, who had just brought his bride and her sister to Belvoir.

Young Washington's heart was tender and susceptible, and that bride's beautiful sister tried its constancy to his first love very sorely. To his young friend "Robin" he wrote: "My residence is at present at his lordship's, where I might, was my heart disengaged, pass my time very pleasantly, as there is a very agreeable young lady lives in the same house (Colonel George Fairfax's wife's sister); but as that is only adding fuel to fire, it makes me the more uneasy, for by often and unavoidably being in company with her, revives my former passion for 'your Lowland Beauty,' whereas, was I to live more retired from young women, I might in some measure alleviate my sorrows by burying that chaste and troublesome passion in the grave of oblivion." Thus wrote George Washington before he was sixteen years of age.

He was soon taken from these temptations. He was a tall, finely-formed, athletic youth, and Lord Fairfax, who was a passionate fox-hunter, though old in years, invited him one day to join him in the chase. His lordship was so charmed with his young friend's boldness in the saddle, and enthusiastic pursuit of the hounds and game, that he took him to his bosom as a companion; and many a hard day's ride this young and old man had together after that in the forests of Virginia.

But a more noble, because a more useful pursuit than the mere pleasures of the chase, now offered its attractions to the lad. Master Williams had taught him the mysteries of surveying, and the old Lord Fairfax, having observed his practice of the art at Mount Vernon, and his extreme care and accuracy, proposed to him to go to his broad possessions beyond the Blue Ridge, where lawless intruders were seated, and prepare his domain for settlement, by running boundary lines between large sections. The lad gladly acceded to the proposition, and just a month from the time he was sixteen years of age he set off upon the arduous and responsible enterprise.

In the wilderness around the south branch of the Potomac the future leader received those lessons in woodcraft, that personal knowledge of the country and its dusky inhabitants, and, above all, that spirit of self-reliance which was ever a most marked and important trait in his character—which fitted him for the great duties of a commander.

So satisfactory were young Washington's services on the occasion, that he received, soon after his return, the appointment of public surveyor, and upon the records of Culpepper county may be read, under date of July 30th, 1749 (O. S.) that "GEORGE WASHINGTON, Gent., produced a commission from the President and Master of William and Mary College, appointing him to be surveyor of this county, which was read, and thereupon he took the usual oaths to his Majesty's person and government, and took and subscribed the abjuration oath and test, and then took the oath of a surveyor, according to law." Part of each year he was beyond the Alleghaines with no other instruments than compass and chain, acquiring strength of limb and purpose for future great achievements, and putting money in his purse at the rate of a doubloon and sometimes six pistoles a day. These expeditions he always remembered as the greatest pleasures of his youth.

An admirable article published some forty years ago in *Putnam's Magazine* thus stated the family occurrences at the time :—

"The good father was cut off by a sudden illness before

he had reached his fiftieth year, and George, with a large family of brothers and sisters, was left to the care of his mother. Each child had an estate, for the father was rich in lands; but the proceeds of all were placed wholly within the widow's control during the minority of the children, a circumstance which speaks plainly enough the husband's confidence in her judgment and kindness. Two sons of the first marriage were young men at the time of their father's decease, but Mrs. Washington had five children of her own, of whom George, at that time about eleven, was the oldest. He was absent, Mr. Weems says, when his father was so suddenly summoned, and arrived at home only to find him speechless, and to witness his final departure. The family seems to have been very much united, and George and his half-brothers were ever firm friends. After his father's death he lived for a while with the younger of them, Augustine, in Westmoreland, the place of his nativity, which had been bequeathed to the second son. Here he went to school, to a Mr. Williams, who, Mr. Weems says, "knew as little of Latin, perhaps, as Balaam's ass," but who was able to give him the elements of common school knowledge, which were happily enough in this case. We need not doubt the report that he was very soon the natural head of the school, not so particularly by means of scholarship as through certain other qualities so amply exhibited in after-life. He was the umpire in all little school quarrels, the boys having implicit faith in his justice; he was easily the leader in all athletic sports, through life his delight; and by some strange, prophetic instinct—prophecy often works its own fulfilment—it was his pride to form his schoolmates into military companies, with corn-stalks for muskets and calabashes for drums, and these he drilled and exercised, as well as commanded and led to mimic battle. He is said to have been famous for hindering quarrels, however, and perhaps his early developed taste for military manœuvres was only an accidental form of that love of mathematical combination and extreme regularity and order of every kind which characterized him through life. But there was a political bias, too, for the boy-army was arrayed in two bands, one of them personating the French, always an antagonistic idea to the English; the former commanded by a lad named William Bustle, the latter always by George Washington. It is rather remarkable that so exciting a sport did not end in quarrels, if not in lasting enmity, for the temperament of Washington was impetuous, and his passions were fiery, though we are little accustomed to think so, from our habit of contemplating only his after-life, so marked by self-control. He was, nevertheless, known as a peacemaker, even thus early, and we have every reason to believe that peace continued to be his darling idea through all the struggles which duty led him to engage in.

He was also noted for running and wrestling, pitching the bar, and leaping with a pole. Whatever stirred his blood and brought into exercise the stalwart limbs and muscles with which nature had endowed him, was his delight. His young lady cousins complained that George cared nothing for their company, but would always be out of doors. And an old gentleman, a neighbour, is quoted as saying, "Egad! he ran wonderfully! We had nobody, hereabouts, that could come near him. There was young Langhorne Dade, of Westmoreland, a confounded clean-made tight young fellow, and a mighty swift runner too, but he was no match for George."

Colonel Lewis Willis, his playmate and kinsman, had "often seen him throw a stone across the Rappahannock, at the lower ferry of Fredericksburg," a feat, it seems, not very likely to be equalled in our degenerate days. This great strength was inherited from his father, whose fowling-piece—still extant, it is believed—is of extraordinary weight, confirming the tradition of the old planter's muscular powers.

That his efforts to live up to his own notions of right began very early we must conclude from the interest that he inspired in his half-brothers—not the most likely persons, as the world goes, to overrate him—and they seem to have been ever his warmest friends. The eldest brother having been an officer in the war against the French, and served also at the siege of Carthagena and in the West Indies, under General Wentworth and Admiral Vernon. He was residing on the property left him by his father—that farm, for ever famous, which he had called Mount Vernon, in compliment to the gallant admiral; and here George went to live with him, soon after leaving school.

This was in his sixteenth year. Before this time he had shown a decided predilection for geometry, trigonometry, and surveying, which, as the profession of a surveyor was at that time particularly profitable, his friends had encouraged, and he had pursued the requisite studies with characteristic earnestness. The last two years of his school-life were chiefly given to the theory and practice of the art which laid the foundation of his fortune, not only by the opportunity it gave him of purchasing new lands advantageously, but by the habits he then acquired of calculation, accuracy, and neatness, so conspicuously useful to him through all the important affairs which devolved upon him in after-life. When, by way of practice, he surveyed the little domain around the school-house, the plots and measurements were entered in his book with all the care and precision of the most important business; and if an erasion was required, it was done with a penknife, and with such care that scarce the trace of the error can be perceived.

"Nor was his skill," says Mr. Sparks, "confined to the more simple processes of the art. He used logarithms, and proved the accuracy of his work by different methods. The manuscripts fill several quires of paper, and are remarkable for the care with which they were kept, the neatness and uniformity of the handwriting, the beauty of the diagrams, and a precise method and arrangement in copying out tables and columns of figures. These particulars will not be thought too trivial to be mentioned, when it is known that he retained similar habits through life. His business papers, day-books, ledgers, and letter-books, in which, before the Revolution, no one wrote but himself, exhibit specimens of the same studious care and exactness. Every fact occupies a clear and distinct place. The constructing of tables, diagrams, and other figures relating to numbers or classification was an exercise in which he seems at all times to have taken much delight."

Washington had but two teachers, one, an old fellow named Hobby, one of his father's tenants, sexton as well as schoolmaster of the neighbourhood, who used to boast, after he was superannuated and somewhat addicted to strong potations, especially on the general's birthdays, that it was he who, between his knees, had laid the foundation of George Washington's greatness by teaching him his letters; and the other the Mr. Williams already mentioned, who was, according to Mr. Weems, "a capital hand" at reading, spelling, English grammar, arithmetic, surveying, bookkeeping, and geography, and often boasted that he had made George Washington as great a scholar as himself. Doubtless to Weems' thoroughness in teaching what he did know, his great pupil owed much of his acquired power; a good foundation in a few things is the best beginning for a boy of ability; his mother's instruction, however, proved the more important.

Among the influences that conspired to mature the mind and refine the manners of Washington, we must account his intimacy with the Fairfax family, sensible as well as well-bred people, and living on a large fortune in the exercise of liberal hospitality. Lord Fairfax, besides the social advantages which resulted from his rank, had had a University education, when such culture was a distinction, and he seems, moreover, to have been a person of independent ways of thinking, and a discernment and practical sagacity not always found in high places. His nephew, William Fairfax, was wealthy, and held a high position in the colony. The family was, altogether, the first in the district where they lived, and one such family inevitably does much towards raising the general standard of manners and ideas in its neighbourhood. A young man must be dull indeed if the society of gentlemen and elegant women has no inspiration for him. When we read George Washington's " Rules of Civility and decent Behaviour in Company and Conversation," we need no assurance that no grace of manner, refinement of expression, or conventional improvement that came under his observation at Mr. Fairfax's passed unnoted. The exquisite propriety of address and conduct, so often mentioned as having distinguished him, may not improbably have owed no little of its finish to these early opportunities; to suppose so much elegance the natural product of innate refinement, in spite of plain farmer's living in early youth, and the rough career of a practical surveyor afterwards, might be more complimentary, but scarcely so rational. Lord Fairfax was not a courtier, any more than his American planter-nephew; and Washington never became one; but only in all circumstances a gentleman. This is as evident in the early journal from which we have just quoted a few passages, as in the letters written in after-life to ladies and the most distinguished men. Self-respect ever regulates and limits his complimentary expressions, as it had in early life afforded the standard by which he judged so unerringly the dispositions of others towards himself, and decided on the fitness of the circumstances in which he was placed. He had an exquisite sense of personal respect, and as he never forgot, or was mistaken about the amount of it due to others, so he never hazarded his own claims by requiring more than he knew himself entitled to, and able to exact. In reading his correspondence, so voluminous and various, as well as so remarkable in other respects, this propriety is ever most striking.

It is most interesting to observe, in studying the career of Washington from the very beginning, how entirely he was a man of peace, though so much of his life was passed in making war, and that with an iron will and unflinching thoroughness. He seems to have done his duty in the character of a soldier just as coolly and regularly as he did in that of a surveyor. He knew his work, and he set about it with all his powers of mind and body; but we never feel for a moment that it was work that he loved. He loved rural life, the occupations of the farm, the sports of the field, the enjoyments of the fireside. Much has been said of his reserve, as if it were exclusiveness; but his letters and his constant home practice show conclusively that no man depended more upon friendship, or found society more necessary to his enjoyment. He kept only his cares to himself, and those only when to impart them would have been injurious or unprofitable. As he grew older, weighty business made him more grave and silent; but we should always carry with us, in attempting to appreciate his character as a man, the idea of him that we gather from the record of his earlier days; the kindliness, the sociability, the generous confidence, the courageous candour that marked him then, and evidently formed part of the very structure of his being. Whoever can read his journals and early letters without imbibing an affection, as well as reverence for him, must have sat down to the task with enormous prepossessions, derived from the accounts of his later life.

Washington's first interview with Mrs. Custis, afterwards his wife, is thus delightfully narrated in a memoir of Martha Washington, in Longacre's American Portrait Gallery, by Sparks attributed to the pen of G. W. P. Custis.

"It was in 1758 that an officer, attired in a military undress, and attended by a body servant, tall and *militaire* as his chief, crossed the ferry called Williams', over the Pamunkey, a branch of the York river. On the boat touching the southern or New Kent side, the soldier's progress was arrested by one of those personages who give the *beau idéal* of the Virginia gentleman of the old régime, the very soul of kindliness and hospitality. It was in vain that the soldier urged his business at Williamsburg, important communications to the Governor, &c. Mr. Chamberlayne, on whose domain the *militaire* had just landed, would hear of no excuse. Colonel Washington was a name and character so dear to all the Virginians, that his passing by one of the old castles of Virginia without calling and partaking of the hospitalities of the host was entirely out of the question. The colonel, however, did not surrender at discretion, but stoutly maintained his ground, till Chamberlayne, bringing up his reserve in the intimation that he would introduce his friend to a young and charming widow then beneath his roof, the soldier capitulated on condition that he should dine—only dine—and then, by pressing his charger and borrowing of the night, he would reach Williamsburg before his Excellency could shake off his morning slumbers. Orders were accordingly issued to Bishop, the colonel's body-servant and faithful follower, who, together with a fine English charger, had been bequeathed by the dying Braddock to Major Washington on the famed and fatal field of the Monongahela. Bishop, bred in the school of European discipline, raised his hand to his cap, as much as to say, 'Your honour's orders shall be obeyed.'

"The colonel now proceeded to the mansion, and was introduced to various guests (for when was a Virginian domicile of the olden time without guests?), and, above all, to the charming widow. Tradition relates that they were mutually pleased on this their first interview; nor is it remarkable. They were of an age when impressions are strongest. The lady was fair to behold, of fascinating manners, and splendidly endowed with worldly benefits; the hero, fresh from his early fields, redolent of fame, and with a form on which 'every god did seem to set his seal to give the world assurance of a man.'

"The morning passed pleasantly; evening came, with Bishop, true to his orders and firm at his post, holding the favourite charger with one hand, while the other was waiting to offer the ready stirrup. The sun sank in the horizon, and yet the colonel appeared not; and then the old soldier marvelled at his chief's delay. ' 'Twas strange, 'twas passing strange;' surely he was not wont to be a single moment behind his appointments, for he was the most punctual of all punctual men. Meantime the host enjoyed the scene of the veteran on duty at the gate, while the colonel was so agreeably employed in the parlour; and proclaiming that no guest ever left his house after sunset, his military visitor was without much difficulty persuaded to order Bishop to put up the horses for the night. The sun rode high in the heavens the next day when the enamoured soldier pressed with his spur his charger's side and speeded on his way to the seat of government, where, having despatched his public business, he retraced his steps, and at the White House the engagement took place, with preparations for the marriage.

"And much hath the biographer heard of that marriage from grey-haired domestics, who waited at the board where love made the feast and Washington was the guest. And rare and high was the revelry at that palmy period of Virginia's festal age, for many were gathered to that marriage of the good, the great, the gifted, and the gay, while Virginia, with joyous acclamation, hailed in her youthful hero a prosperous and happy bridegroom.

"'And so you remember when Colonel Washington came a-courting of your mistress?' said the biographer to old Cully, in his hundredth year.

"'Ay, master, that I do,' replied the ancient family servant, who had lived to see five generations; 'great times, sir, great times; shall never see the like again.'

"'And Washington looked something like a man, a proper man—hey, Culley?'

"'Never seed the like, sir; never the likes of him, though I have seen many in my day: so tall, so straight—and then he sat a horse and rode with such an air! Ah! sir, he was like no one else. Many of the grandest gentlemen in their gold lace were at the wedding, but none looked like the man himself.'

"Strong, indeed, must have been the impressions which the person and manner of Washington made upon the rude, 'untutored mind' of this poor negro, since the lapse of three-quarters of a century had not sufficed to efface them.

"The precise date of the marriage cannot be discovered among the records of the vestry of St. Peter's Church, New Kent, of which the reverend Mr. Mossom, a Cambridge scholar, was the rector, and performed the ceremony, it is believed, about 1759. A short time after their marriage, Colonel and LADY WASHINGTON removed to Mount Vernon, on the Potomac, and permanently settled there."

Like other gentlemen living near the Potomac, Washington was fond of aquatic sports. He kept a handsome barge which, on special occasions, was manned by black oarsmen in livery. Pleasant sailing-boats were frequently seen sweeping along the surface of the river, freighted with ladies and gentlemen going from mansion to mansion on its banks—Mount Vernon, Gunston Hall, Belvoir, and other places—on social visits.

Washington and his wife frequently visited Annapolis and Williamsburg, the respective capitals of Maryland and Virginia. For fifteen consecutive years he was a member of the Virginia House of Burgesses, and Mrs. Washington spent much of her time with him at Williamsburg during the sessions. Both fond of amusements, they frequently attended the theatrical representations there and at Annapolis, that entertainment being then a recent importation from England, the first company of actors, under the direction of Lewis Hallam, having first performed in the Maryland capital in 1752. They also attended balls and parties given by the fashionable people of Williamsburg and Annapolis, and frequently joined in the dance. But after the Revolution, Washington was never known to dance, his last performance being in a minuet, of which he was very fond, on the occasion of a ball given at Fredericksburg in honour of the French and American officers then there, on their way north, after the capture of Cornwallis towards the close of 1781.

But it must not be supposed that during these years of his earlier married life Washington's time was wholly or even chiefly occupied in the pleasures of the chase and of social intercourse. Far from it. He was a man of great industry and method, and managed his large estates with signal industry and ability. He did not leave his farms to the entire care of his overseers. He was very active, and continually, even when absent on public business, exercised a general supervision of his affairs, requiring a carefully-prepared report of all operations to be transmitted to him weekly for his inspection and suggestions.

He was very abstemious, and while his table always furnished his guests with ample and varied supplies for their appetites, he never indulged in the least excess, either in eating or drinking. He was an early riser, and might be found in his library from one to two hours before daylight in winter, and at dawn in summer. His toilet, plain and simple, was soon made. A single servant prepared his clothes, and laid them in a proper place at night for use in the morning. He also combed and tied his master's hair.

Washington always dressed and shaved himself. Though neat in his dress and appearance, he never wasted precious moments upon his toilet, for he always regarded time, not as a gift but as a loan, for which he must account to the Great Master.

Washington kept his own accounts most carefully and methodically, in handwriting remarkable for its extreme neatness and uniformity of stroke. This was produced by the constant use of a *gold pen*. One of these, with a silver case, used by Washington during a part of the old war for independence, he presented to his warm personal friend, General Anthony Walton White, of New Jersey, one of the most distinguished and patriotic of the cavalry officers of that war in the southern campaigns. It is now in the possession of Mrs. Eliza M. Evans, near Brunswick, New Jersey, the only surviving child of General White. In one end of the silver pen-case is a sliding tube for a common black-lead pencil, the convenient "ever-pointed" pencil being unknown in Washington's time. That was invented by Isaac Hawkins, and patented by him in London in 1802.

From his youth Washington kept a diary. For many years these records of his daily experience were made on the blank leaves of the "Virginia Almanac." This man of mighty labours kept such records, from day to day, for more than forty years; and he frequently noted therein minute particulars concerning his agricultural operations.

Thus minutely journalizing his agricultural proceedings, keeping his own accounts, making all his own surveys, and even before the Revolution, having an extensive correspondence, Washington found much daily employment for his pen. The labours in his library, and a visit to his stables, usually occupied the hours before breakfast. After making a frugal meal of Indian cakes, honey, and tea or coffee, he would mount his horse, and visit every part of his estate where the current operations seemed to require his presence, leaving his guests to enjoy themselves with books and papers, or otherwise, according to their choice. He rode upon his farms entirely unattended, opening the gates, pulling down and putting up the fences, and inspecting, with a careful eye, every agricultural operation, and personally directing the manner in which many should be performed. Sometimes the tour of his farms in the course of the morning might average, in distance, twelve or fifteen miles; and on these occasions his appearance was exceedingly plain. Mr. Custis, his adopted son, has left on record a description of him on one of these occasions, in the latter years of his life, which he gave to a gentleman who was out in search of Washington.

"You will meet, sir," said young Custis to the inquirer, "with an old gentleman riding alone, in plain drab clothes, a broad-brimmed white hat, a hickory switch in his hand, and carrying an umbrella with a long staff, which is attached to his saddle-bow—that person, sir, is General Washington." The umbrella was used to shelter him from the sun, for his skin was tender and easily affected by its rays.

His breakfast-hour was seven o'clock in summer and eight in winter, and he dined at three. He always ate heartily, but was no epicure. His usual beverage was small beer or cider, and Madeira wine. Of the latter he often drank several small glasses at a sitting. He took tea and toast, or a little well-baked bread, early in the evening, conversed with or read to his family when there were no guests, and usually, whether there was company or not, retired for the night at about nine o'clock.

So carefully did Washington manage his farms, that they became very productive. His chief crops were wheat and tobacco, and these were very large—so large that vessels that came up the Potomac took the tobacco and flour directly from his own wharf, a little below his deer-park, in front of his mansion, and carried them to England or the West Indies. So noted were these products for their quality, and so faithfully were they put up, that any barrel of flour bearing the brand of "GEORGE WASHINGTON, MOUNT VERNON," was exempted from the customary inspection in the British West India ports.

Upon the spot where that old wharf once stood, at the foot of a shaded ravine scooped from the high bank of the Potomac, through which flows a clear stream from a spring, is a rickety modern structure, placed there for the accommodation of visitors to Mount Vernon, who are conveyed thither by a steamboat twice a week. There may be seen the same ravine, the same broad river, the same pleasant shores of Maryland beyond; but, instead of the barrels of flour, the quintals of fish and the hogsheads of tobacco which appeared there in Washington's time, well-dressed men and women—true pilgrims to a hallowed shrine, or mere idle gazers upon the burial-place of a great man—throng that wharf as they arrive and depart on their errands of patriotism or of curiosity.

MOUNT VERNON LANDING-WHARF.

Among those who came to Mount Vernon to consult with Washington respecting public affairs, was his neighbour and friend of Gunston Hall, George Mason. He was six years older than Washington, of large, sinewy frame, an active step and gait, locks of raven blackness, a dark complexion, and a grave countenance, which was lighted up by a black eye, whose glance was felt with power by those upon whom it chanced to fall. He was one of the most methodical of men, and most extensive of the Virginia planters at that time; and, like Washington from Mount Vernon, shipped his crops from his own wharf, near his elegant mansion of Gunston Hall. He was proud, yet extremely courteous; and while no man could be a warmer and more faithful friend than he, his bearing was such as to excite admiration rather than love. His strong mind was thoroughly cultivated, and he was conversant with the minute particulars of English general history, and especially with the political history of the English Empire. His mind was quick to perceive, his judgment equally quick to analyze and arrange; and these qualities made him a most skilful statesman. In council he was eminently wise; in debate he was distinguished for extraordinary ability; and as a political writer, he was without a peer in his country, when the rising dispute with Great Britain was occupying the thoughts of men in both hemispheres. Such was the man with whom, at Mount Vernon and at Gunston Hall, Washington held close conference for many years, while the flame of the Revolution was slowly kindling.

The storm of the Stamp Act season passed by, but it was succeeded by many others. In the intervals Washington was engaged in agricultural pursuits at Mount Vernon, and the pleasures of social life. In all the public affairs of his neighbourhood he was an active participant; and as early as 1765, the year when the Stamp Act became a law, he was a vestryman of both Truro and Fairfax parishes, in which Pohick in the country, and Christ Church in Alexandria, were the respective places of worship. In that year his name is appended to a declaration, with others, that he would " be conformable to the Doctrines and Discipline of the Church of England, as by law established." With his name appear those of George Mason, George William Fairfax, Edward Payne, Captain Charles Broadwater, and more than twenty others.

During the earlier years of his married life, Washington

attended Pohick Church, seven miles from Mount Vernon, more frequently than any other. The first church of that name was a frame building, and stood on the south side of Pohick Creek, about two miles from the present edifice. About the year 1764 it became so dilapidated as to be no longer fit for use. The parishioners were called together to consult upon the erection of a new one. Among those assembled was Washington, and the father of George Mason, then advanced in years and greatly respected. When the question of the location of the new church came up for consideration, there was a difference of opinion. Mr. Mason was in favour of the old site, and Washington was opposed to it. Mr. Mason made a pathetic appeal in favour of the old site, pleading that there was the spot where their fathers had worshipped, and it was consecrated by their graves which surrounded it. Washington and others took the ground that the spot was far less convenient for the parish than a more central one. The subject took a shape that required more reflection, and a second meeting was called. Meanwhile Washington made a careful survey of the whole neighbourhood, marking the place of every house and the relative distances on a distinct map. When the second meeting was held, Mason again appealed to the sympathies of the people, when Washington appealed to their common sense, by simply presenting his map, and explaining it in a few words. His almost mute argument prevailed, and the site of the present church was selected.

Preparations were now made for the erection of the new church, but it was not completed until the year 1773. Washington drew the ground-plan and elevation of the building for the use of the architect. They are very neatly sketched with China ink upon good drawing-paper, and occupy a space thirteen by fifteen inches square.

Of the ministers who officiated at Pohick, there were

none more beloved than the Rev. Lee Massey. He was the companion of Washington from his youth; at his solicitation, and that of Mason, Fairfax, M'Carty, Chichester, and others of that parish, he was induced to relinquish the profession of the law, study divinity, and become their pastor. His speech becoming impaired by the loss of his front teeth, he left the pulpit, and studied medicine as a means of affording relief to the poor.

Another clergyman who officiated occasionally at Pohick church, after the regular stated services of the Church of England had ceased there, was the eccentric Mason L. Weems, the earliest biographer of Washington. The style of that biography was so attractive to the uncultivated readers of his day, that it passed through some forty editions, and even now it finds a sale. His character appears to have been a curious compound of seriousness and levity, truthfulness and exaggeration, reverence and profanity. He was an itinerant in every sense of the word. He was a man of considerable attainments as a scholar, physician, and divine; and his benevolence was unbounded. When a boy of fourteen years, he was found at night teaching half-clad, half-fed children, who gathered eagerly around him; and all through life he was ready to share a crust with the unfortunate. He used wit and humour freely on all occasions. "Whether in private or public, in prayers or preaching," says Bishop Meade, " it was impossible that either the young or old, the grave or the gay, could keep their risible faculties from violent agitation." He would pray with the negro servants at night, and fiddle for them by the roadside by day. For many years he was a travelling bookseller, preaching when invited, haranguing the people at courts, fairs, and other public gatherings, and selling the Bible out of one hand and Paine's "Age of Reason" out of the other, alleging, as an excuse for the latter performance, that he always carried the antidote with the poison.[1] His fund of anecdote was inexhaustible; and after giving a promiscuous audience the highest entertainment of fun, he found them in good mood to purchase his books. At Mount Vernon he was always a welcome guest, for Washington loved his goodness of heart, and overlooked his foibles. Mr. Weems died at Beaufort, South Carolina, in May, 1825, at an advanced age.

Benson Lossing, in his admirable volume on "Mount Vernon and its Associations," thus describes the country churches in which Washington habitually worshipped when in the neighbourhood:—

"After the Revolution, for reasons not clearly seen, Washington attended Christ Church at Alexandria (of which he was a vestryman) instead of Pohick, others of the latter parish followed, and after a while regular services ceased in that part of the country. Washington owned a pew in Christ Church from the establishment in 1764, and occupied it constantly after 1873, until his death. Some of his name have held possession of it ever since. Judge Bushrod Washington[2] succeeded the general in its occupancy; then his nephew, John A. Washington, the father of the late proprietor of Mount

CHRIST CHURCH, ALEXANDRIA.

---

[1] "Portrait of Mason L. Weems," p. 76.   [2] "Christ Church, Alexandria," p. 77.

Vernon; and lastly that proprietor himself. Christ Church, at Alexandria, was finished in 1773, and Washington paid the highest price for a pew in it.

I visited Pohick Church a few years ago, and found it falling rapidly into decay. It stands upon an eminence north of Pohick Creek, on the border of a forest that extends almost uninterruptedly to Mount Vernon. Around it are the ancient oaks of the primæval woods, interspersed with chestnuts and pines. It was just at twilight when I reached the old fane, and after making a sketch of it I

POHICK CHURCH IN 1858.

passed on to seek lodgings for the night. The next day was the Sabbath, and being informed that a Methodist meeting was to be held in the church, I repaired thither at the usual hour, and took a seat in Washington's pew, near the pulpit. There I awaited the slow gathering of the little auditory. When all had assembled, men and women and children, white and black, the whole congregation numbered only twenty-one persons. I could not refrain from drawing a parallel with the scenes of other days under that venerated

G g

roof, when some of the noblest of Virginia's aristocracy worshipped there, while clergymen, in surplice and gown, performed the solemn and impressive ritual of the Church of England. Now, a young man, with nothing to distinguish him from other men but a white cravat, stood as teacher within the old chancel by the side of the ancient communion table. He talked sweetly of Christian charity:

> "Oh, the rarity
> Of Christian charity,"

and asked the little company to join with him in singing the hymn—

> "Come, Holy Spirit! Heavenly Dove!"

When the service was over, I made note with pen and pencil of all within. It was a melancholy task, for decay with its busy fingers was at work all around me, making sure prophecies of the speedy desolation of a building

PULPIT IN POHICK CHURCH.

hallowed by association with the beloved Washington. Upon the wall, back of the chancel, were still inscribed the Law, the Creed, and the Lord's Prayer, upon which the eyes of Washington and his friends had rested a thousand times. A large proportion of the panes of glass were broken from the windows, admitting freely the wind and the rain, the bats and the birds. The elaborately wrought pulpit, placed by itself on one side of the church, was sadly marred by desecrating hands. Under its sounding-board a swallow had built her nest, and upon the bookledge the fowls of the air had evidently perched. These things brought to memory the words of the "sweet singer of Israel "—" Yea, the sparrow has found a home, and the swallow a nest for herself, where she may lay her young, even Thine altar, O Lord of Hosts!"

Field had a pleasant countenance and fine portly figure. He was, on the whole, rather fat, and loved his ease. "When at Centreville, on the eastern shore of Maryland, in 1798," says Rembrandt Peale in a letter to a friend, "Field and I took a walk into the country, after a rain. A wide puddle of water covered the road beyond the fence on both sides. I climbed the fence and walked round, but Field, fat and lazy, in good humour paid an old negro to carry him on his shoulders over the water. In the middle of it, Field became so convulsed with laughter that he nearly shook himself off the old man's back."

Field went to Canada, studied theology a little, was ordained a priest of the Established Church, and became a bishop.

A shadow fell upon Mount Vernon in the spring of 1773. No child had blessed the union of Washington and his wife, and her two children received the most tender parental care and solicitude from their step-father. He appeared to love them as his own. Martha was a sweet girl of gentle temper, graceful form, winning ways, and so much a brunette that she was called "the dark lady." Just as she was blooming into womanhood, pulmonary consumption laid its withering hand upon her. For several months her strength had been failing, and letters filled with expressions of anxiety went frequently from her mother to Washington, who was engaged in his duties in the House of Burgesses at Williamsburg. At length a most alarming letter reached him. He had just made arrangements to accompany Lord Dunmore, the Governor, on a long tour of observation west of the mountains, but he hastened to Mount Vernon. He found the dear child in the last moments of earthly life.

His manly spirit was bowed with grief, and with deep feeling he knelt at the side of her bed and prayed most earnestly for her recovery. Upon the wings of that holy prayer her spirit ascended, and when he arose and looked upon her pale and placid face, death had set its seal there. She expired on the 19th of June, when in the seventeenth year of her age. Her departure left a great void in the heart of the mother, and Washington remained for some time at Mount Vernon, in seclusion, to console his afflicted wife, instead of taking the contemplated journey with the Governor.

Darker and darker grew the clouds of war; and during more than seven years Washington visited his pleasant home upon the Potomac but once, and then only for three days and nights. Mrs. Washington spent the winter in camp with her husband, and many are the traditions concerning her beauty, gentleness, simplicity, and industry, which yet linger around the winter-quarters of the venerated commander-in-chief of the armies of the Revolution. For many long years she was remembered with affection by the dwellers at Cambridge, Morristown, Valley Forge, Newburgh, and New Windsor. When, on each returning spring, she departed for her home on the Potomac, the blessings of thousands—soldiers and citizens—went with her, for she was truly loved by all.

Pleasant would it be to read the scores of letters written by Washington to his charming wife during all that campaigning period and his subsequent services in civil life. That pleasure can never be enjoyed. Only one letter to her—the message informing her of his appointment to the command of the army—is known to be in existence, and that, with one to her son on the same subject, written on the following day, had prior to the war with the South, been carefully preserved at Arlington House. Mrs.

Washington, in obedience to his wish, destroyed all his other letters to herself shortly before her death.

There are few anecdotes of his private life. We know little of him in those hours when he threw off the cares of state or generalship, and talked and acted as other men. We have caught impressions of him from his grave countenance in pictures, and from the ponderous tomes that tell of plans and battles, and sieges and marches, until there are many into whose minds it never entered that he could smile and have his hours of sportive gaiety.

The want of more detail of Washington's life is especially lamentable; this deficiency, however, corresponds with other of the world's greatest men The private life of that glorious man was as free from stain as his public life was surpassingly admirable. They who cherish the memory of greatness that had no alliance with goodness may well be rejoiced that nothing remains of it but the record of the actions that have won for it its name. They may well rejoice at the silence of history, fearful that its further story, had it one to tell, would mar the fascinating and deceptive illusion. But the lovers of Washington could gain from every event of his life only fresh evidences of his exalted purity, his ennobling sense of right, his disinterested self-sacrifice. And how eagerly every little anecdote of his boyhood or manly relaxation has been seized upon and treasured up! How many children have been stimulated to inflexible truth, in the face of suffering, by the story that is told of him in his youth—every one knows it—when he injured with his hatchet one of his father's favourite trees; yet told the truth about it in the face of expected punishment. What a bearing this little anecdote has exerted over many minds, giving a colouring to the impressions of his whole after and remarkable life!

There was a sentiment about Mount Vernon from the

beginning. Lawrence Washington, when he purchased the estate, chose to name it after Admiral Vernon, under whom he had served at Carthagena—a significant fancy, corresponding well with a certain vein which one discovers early in the study of Washington's turn of mind, as displayed in letters and journals written long before he became famous. The Washingtons were, in those dim, distant days, people of thought, feeling, and a high sense of honour. It was not without purpose that Mrs. Washington, while her gallant sons yet stood boys at her knee, imbued them with the calm and noble sentiments of Sir Matthew Hale. Their entrance into active life was guarded on all sides by worthy and patriotic thoughts, planted by that wise mother as sentinels against all insidious approaches of evil. Mount Vernon became to Lawrence the memorial of a gallant sailor who had been a hero to him, both by public conduct and private kindness; and George, then a boy, and a frequent inmate of his brother's family, had thus a domestic example, both kindly and dignified, in his elder brother's respect and love for his old commander. When he afterwards, as a direct consequence of his affectionate care, excellent judgment, and already matured integrity, before he was of age, received this very Mount Vernon as a legacy from his brother, who died early, he thought not of changing the name first bestowed by peculiar and individual feeling, but set himself about adorning the place, adding to its area by gradual purchases, and bringing up the whole towards his own ideal of what a rural property ought to be. From that day to the day of his death his choicest pleasure was the care of those acres—1300 in number ultimately—of which the more personal and interesting 200, including those on which stand the mansion and offices, and those made priceless by the presence of sacred dust never to be disturbed, have through a public subscription become the property of the nation.

George Washington Parke Custis, the last survivor of Washington's family, died at Arlington, Va, Saturday morning, October 10th, 1857. He was born April 30th, 1781. His father, Colonel John Parke Custis (a son of Mrs. Washington by her first husband), dying when Mr. Custis was quite young, he was brought up at Mount Vernon in the family of General Washington.

At the time of his death it was said of him that the whole country knew him, and his patriotism will long be remembered. Closely allied to the Washington family, fond of calling himself the child of Mount Vernon, he was never so much in his element as when he was talking or writing of the Great Chief and the men and times of the Revolution. As he said of himself once, 'His was the destiny of no common man,' for he had been fondled on the knee of the father of his country, and received from him the kindness of a parent. He repaid that care and affection with filial devotion, and to the day of his death all the recollections of his life centred around, or radiated from, the time when he was one of Washington's family. He lived to a good old age, retaining his mental faculties to the last. Though Mr. Custis was never in public life, he was, in his younger days, an eloquent and effective speaker, and had a fondness for oratory as long as he was able to gratify those who constantly called on him to make public addresses.

Sharples appears to have been taken into counsel at Mount Vernon as to some details of tree and shrub planting, some alterations in the laying out done during the period of Washington's occupation in the camp being deemed advisable. It seems that he had delighted the General by a plan he had drawn of the immediate surroundings of the house, showing the roads and paths as laid out, and with lines marking suggested changes. All of these were approved, and orders went forth for an immediate conformity thereto, not, however, without much opposition from a veteran coloured gentleman, who, during his master's absence, had usurped a good deal of power, and which he had in some degree retained, and was therefore not inclined to resign without a struggle. Every innovation was opposed: one path was "too close to the steep," and "would be washed away first heavy rain;" another would lay bare the roots of favourite trees; while the stopping existing paths and laying same down to grass was not to be endured, seeing the trouble they had cost in the making. The veteran darkey had a great notion that everything should be straight as an arrow—curves were abominations. Sharples suggested a series of terraces leading down to the landing-stage on the river's edge as a substitute for a continuous steep path. This, however, was an outrage on his every notion of landscape-gardening, and for quietude sake had to be abandoned. For several years the General had been gradually withdrawing from the culture of tobacco, which as owner he saw would pauperize land unless some system of manuring could at reasonable cost be introduced to stay the exhaustion. His friend Cary's agency, so far as it depended on tobacco, had become a sorry affair, and Indian corn had not then been exported in any but small quantities. He, however, busied himself in substituting it and wheat, and introducing the then new method of crop rotation.

In their daily walks on the estate, Washington dwelt with evident delight on the happy time passed there with La Fayette, than whom a truer republican never existed. As Washington expressed himself: "He indeed was gold from the mine, and the head of Liberty was on the ingot, without passing through the mint of circumstances. He had the common-sense 'democracy'—the true zeal for the equality of men—the supremacy of the laws and the happiness of the people." It was thus in his youth, when he was among the most cherished and welcomed of all that the Old World sent out. He learned the value of republicanism by being the friend of Washington, that man who never trusted a theory for its gloss, but tried it by its truth. Washington is said to have never really loved but one man—such was his caution and reserve—and that man was La Fayette. This is an unjust saying. He was gratefully attached to his friend Robert Cary, and it is not too much to say that Sharples, as his accredited representative, had deservedly engaged his affection. He is known to have been a man of much culture. The historian Dunlap tells us this, as also that his gift of conversation was remarkable. We have from his own written account how the Chief revelled in their relation. The artist did not sleep in the house at Mount Vernon, which was very limited in accommodation. On arrival there he had been "billeted," as the Chief termed it, at a cottage of one of the house servants near at hand, a coloured man, who had a wife and four little darkies. This cottage would appear to have been generally availed of on occasions of overflow, not unfrequent. The room dedicated was "remarkably clean, but very hot when the sun's rays poured upon it;" and "I ascertained from my sable hostess that Lady Washington had made frequent visits to see that all was in order and nicely kept. I take all my meals with the Chief at Mount Vernon; they are most elegantly served, but without the least profusion, and the attendance is of military precision. I observed that we never partook of food without the General offering grace to the Giver, so also at the close of every repast."

La Fayette was no less the child of France than of America. He was with his own country in all her vicissitudes, ever practical and right—deserting no principle, but yielding always the shadow when by such concession the substance could be gained—struggling, and striving, and combating by voice and sword, and best of all, by example, for the life of republicanism in France. This he never deserted, and though suspected and denounced, he never while he lived, ceased to be the republican.

It was forcibly stated, in an article published in Hunt's Merchant's Magazine in 1847, that by every variety of commentary has almost every fibre of the character of General George Washington been illustrated. His military talent has, in all its phases, been brought to the notice of the world—weighed, analyzed, reviewed—until it has come out of the fierce ordeal, established as of the very first order of judgment, energy, bravery. His reputation as a statesman has been blazoned abroad with a vigour derived alike from the truth and its forcible use. Men have honoured themselves by giving the power of their intellect to the history of his devotion to his country. All his movements in war, all his acts in the Cabinet, are on record; and he is one of the very few men that ever trod the earth of whose reputation it is safe that the knowledge of it should be thorough.

But George Washington was a great man in other departments of life than those blended with the army and the State; and it is to a feature in his character, less prominently before the world, but one of the most valuable, of which we should speak in this article. It is the order, regularity, method, punctuality, and above all the rectitude—the unsullied and unchangeable devotion to his engagements, which distinguished him, and which, combined, are the very qualities that make up the merchant. In all these the example of Washington may fittingly be urged upon the consideration of the merchants of the Union. The old merchants of the colonies were the very men who perilled the most in arraying themselves on the side of a separation from England. Theirs was no cheap patriotism—no offering of words, but the severing of a profitable mercantile connection—the riving asunder of relations that involved sacrifices alike keen and costly. From among those merchants some of the most valued and useful of the officers and soldiers of the Revolution were taken, and they proved themselves as active in the trade of war, as they had ever been vigilant in the war of trade.

The education of Washington was purely a practical one. All that he added to this was the result of efforts in maturer life, generally made as events demonstrated the particular necessity of the study. This was a business foundation early laid; and though at a time of life when boyhood is usually in its recklessness, the various parts of a business education were thoroughly built up in his character.

At the age of thirteen he studied the intricate forms of business with an ardour which showed what was in him— with a method which demonstrated how that was to be developed. He copied out bills of exchange, notes of hand, bills of sale receipts, and all the varieties of the class, which he denominated " Forms of Writing," and these are remarkable for the precision and the elegance with which they are copied. His manuscripts even then were of the utmost neatness and uniformity, the diagrams always beautiful, the columns and tables of figures exact, and in unstained and unblotted order. Old Tim Linkinwater would have looked most approvingly over his work, and admitted "George" to the awful books of "Cheeryble Brothers." His excellent historian, Mr. Sparks, who has given us that rarest of all books, a reliable biography, remarks that these excellent habits of method and order thus early formed continued through life. His business papers, ledgers, daybooks, in which none wrote but himself, were models of exactness. The description of them might apply to those of the most careful bookkeeper in our metropolis. Every fact had its place, and was recorded in a plain, clear handwriting, and there was neither interlineation, blot, or blemish. Frank Osbaldistone's father could have asked no more. Is it any wonder that with such ideas of what the methods of a business man should be, we should find as one of his " Rules of Behaviour "—a code of laws drawn up for his own government, when at the immature age to which we have already referred, and wonderful in their fitness—the following :—

"12th. Let your discourse with men of business be short and comprehensive."

In the 46th, "Undertake not what you cannot perform, but be careful to keep your promise."

These rules—this manifestation of a " business talent "—were not merely the development of some temporary purpose, but firmly fastened rules of life, which were made to mould his life, and their value to him soon became manifest. He left school at the age of sixteen; and such was his reputation for probity and habits of business—for diligence and habits of despatch—that several eminent Virginia gentlemen were anxious to secure his services; and he soon became busied in laborious duties, the cares of which found an agreeable relief by the society of his cherished brother Lawrence, at Mount Vernon—a name whose associations were thereafter to be rendered so glorious. With that brother, in 1751, he left the soil of his country for the first and last time, and made a visit of four months to the West Indies. Throughout all this tour the traits of character of which this article is particularly designed to speak were constantly manifesting themselves. He daily copied the log-book, noted everything, looked at everything, and was never idle. When at Barbadoes, the commerce of the island was one of the subjects concerning which he made investigation, and about which he made appropriate records in his journal.

The time soon came for him to be the actor in the greater scenes of life, and were it within the design of this article to follow his steady advance from one station of usefulness and honour to another, it would only be to point to the same unchanging rectitude and fidelity to every engagement—the same precise order—the same undeviating exactness. The boy who had with such care collated and prepared the details of an exercise at school, brought into like order the statistics necessary to be studied before a campaign could be wisely commenced. Everything that could illustrate the duty of the soldier—the province of the commander—the plan of attack or defence—the topography of the field of battle—was, by his indomitable industry, his steadfast method, brought into a condensed form, that it might be easily grasped by the mind—that "the business" of the war might be well done.

Nor was it in war alone that the man of order developed himself. We quote in full what Mr. Sparks says upon the subject of his conduct in this respect when President of the United States :—

"During the Presidency it was likewise his custom to subject the treasury reports and accompanying documents to the process of titular condensation with a vast expenditure of labour and patience; but it enabled him to grasp and retain in their order a series of isolated facts, and the results of a complicated mass of figures, which could never have been mastered so effectually by any other mode of approaching them."

From 1759 to 1764 Washington was, in some measure, an acting merchant; for in that calmest period of his life—after the brief, but brilliant episode of the Braddock campaign, most honourable to himself, however disastrous to one whose name was more prominent, and before the great drama of the Revolution—he regularly exported to London the product of his large estate on the Potomac. The shipments were made in his own name, and to his correspondents in Bristol and Liverpool, to which places his tobacco was consigned. Are there none of these precious bills of lading yet in existence? They would be valued by many of us, on this side of the water, at least, as evidences of the attention which he gave to all his business. In return for the articles exported, it was his custom, twice in each year, to import, at that period, from London, the goods which he desired to use; and Mr. Sparks thus delineates how accurately he fulfilled his duties as an importer:—" He required his agent to send him, in addition to a general bill of the whole, the original vouchers of the shopkeepers and mechanics from whom purchases had been made. So particular was he in these concerns, that he recorded with his own hand, in books prepared for the purpose, all the long lists of orders and copies of the multifarious receipts from the different merchants and tradesmen who had supplied the goods. In this way he kept a perfect oversight of the business; ascertained the prices; could detect any imposition, mismanagement, or carelessness, and tell when any advantage was taken of him; of which, if he discovered any, he did not fail to remind his correspondents."

And all this, we must remember, was while he had the charge of the large estate of Mount Vernon, and while he was dispensing a large and generous hospitality.

When the French war had ended, it became his duty to attend to the settlement of the complicated military accounts of the colony of Virginia, a task arduous enough, but, like all the other duties of his life, faithfully performed.

The war of the Revolution left him no leisure for personal

attendance on his private business, but yet it was never neglected. He could not be personally present; but while the noises of the camp, the preparations for battle, the deliberations of councils were all shared in to the utmost, his correspondence about his home affairs was as thorough and minute as though he had been an absentee of leisure.

His accounts, while engaged in the service of his country, were so accurately kept, that to this hour they are an example held up before the nation. His habits of business enabled him, amidst the tumult of the Revolution —its fierce contests, its sufferings and disorders—to so methodize and record all the business incidents of each day that the end of the war found him prepared to lay before Congress an exact statement of his expenditure. There was about him a pervading principle of order, not of a lifeless, sluggish caste, but life-like and energetic; so that, while everything was well done, it was done in time and in earnest.

Let any one read his will, and they will rise up from the perusal with the conviction that a more thorough man of business never lived. There have been many documents of a similar kind, drawn up with wonderful care and labour, and at vast remuneration, by gentlemen learned in the law, but none where every incident is so carefully attended to— not in the spirit of fearfulness of flaws and evasions, and all the thousand munitions of attack to which they resort who "break" wills—but in the orderly, sound, business-like manner in which a Gresham might have written his projection of an exchange.

But we need point to no isolated instance. His whole life establishes the fact that a more perfect man of business never lived than George Washington.

Valueless, indeed, in the comparison, had they stood alone, would all this method and order and industry be—a merchant may have all these, and yet be but sagacious, and—unprincipled; but of this man a nobler record is left to us. I quote only what Thomas Jefferson has said, and *he* spoke certainly with no improper bias:—" HIS INTEGRITY WAS MOST PURE."

To the merchant of the United States the example of *Pater Patriæ* has not been, and will not be lost. So prompt to do—so exact in doing—so wise to know what was to be done—so prudent as to what should *not* be done—such unsullied honesty—such pure integrity. These are the qualities that, combined, make up the good and great merchant; and as they were eminent in George Washington, may he not be claimed as well by the merchants as by the soldiers, or farmers, or statesmen?

This same writer thus expressed himself regarding the Sharples Washington portraits:—

"Criticism of these noble portraits may be said to be exhausted; their excellence is on a par with their national importance, and this is beyond estimate. It is not easy to set aside portraits in sight of which the nation has been built up; time alone, therefore, will yield the place they must eventually take relatively with the Stuarts. No one will deny the Sharples revelation, it is of incomparably more force and strength, and must rank in the future as conveying more powerfully the dignity and greatness of our Chief. Well may the Washington family have commended these portraits as 'by far the most truthful likenesses of Washington ever taken:' a conviction enforced on all who behold them, so far as innate feeling can entertain it."

CHAPTER XII.

Object of the Memorials—Washington joins Braddock—Early discouragements—Mary Phillipse—Rochambeau at Mount Vernon—English description of Washington—Rebukes Lund Washington—Labour in founding the City of Washington—Visits his mother at Fredericksburg—Declines State money aid—Course of life at Mount Vernon—Organization of Congress—Washington elected President—Proceeds to New York—Ovations *en route*—Sworn in as President—Seat of Government removed to Philadelphia—The Philadelphia Mansion—Washington's English carriage described—also his presentation china—Equipages and plate described—Loss of valuable correspondence between Sharples and Robert Fulton greatly to be deplored—Eventful occurrences of 1794 and 1795—Jefferson's retirement—and requested resumption of office—Vaughan, a London merchant, presents chimney-piece at Mount Vernon.

THE design of this volume being to place before the world much deeply interesting matter in the lives of Washington and his mother never before made known, and which the writer feels will help to make valuable history, as additional evidences of the grandeur of their characters, it has been a necessitous duty to weave into the narrative of these important revelations much that has come down through the biographies by the many writers honoured in contributing each a stone towards building up the edifice of Washington's life. So far as the main facts are concerned, much is found to be a repetition of preceding writers. To such an extent is this with records of the Great Patriot's life, as to render it frequently difficult to trace and quote the original author. Without these narratives, however, his work would be even less connected than he fears it will with such helps prove. Far be it from the writer's wish to adopt as original that which has emanated from others. It is, however, difficult to say who was the author of much even of the most interesting and ably recorded materials forming the life of

Washington. The writer of this volume aspires to no merit whatever in his work. His duty has been to present facts coming down through one deservedly honoured in Washington's confidence, and to combine with this labour of love the high privilege of gratifying his readers in possessing them with the only known portrait of Mary Washington. In itself, this is enough; apology for unworthy matter of the surrounding frame will not be required. The additional honour of giving through this volume worthily executed presentments of the Sharples portraits of Washington himself, his wife, and the many remarkable women whose characteristics, beauty, and grace throw such additional charms on the eventful period and life of him of undying fame, will, he feels, be allowed to atone for his own shortcomings in these Memorials.

Examination of Cary's papers proves that, like Martha Washington, Cary had been requested to destroy all letters having reference to the events in which he had so faithfully served his friend. These letters were very numerous. The worthy London merchant construed the command more literally than was necessary. Every scrap of his own having reference to the Patriot is couched in terms of deepest affection and respect. One passage fairly illustrates all—thus: "Who can fail to see in Washington a creation vouchsafed for purposes which only future generations can realize. May not the follies of the old world at some distant day inter all the pride of its power and the pomp of its civilization, and may not human nature find her destined renovation in the Empire created by Washington! May not the glory of past great ones prove to be legendary traditions! The monumental record of natural rise and natural ruin proclaims that no splendour of achievement, no solidity of success, can ensure to Empire the permanence of its possession. Troy thought so once, yet the land of Priam lives only in song! Thebes thought so once, yet her hundred gates have crumbled, and her tombs are as the dust they were destined to commemorate. So thought Palmyra! Where is she? So thought Demosthenes and the Spartans, but Leonidas is trampled by the timid slave. The rays of their glory are as if they never had been, and the island that was then a mere speck, rude and neglected in the barren ocean, now rivals all the wealth of their commerce, the glory of their names, the fame of their philosophy, the eloquence of their senate, and the inspiration of their bards."

During the war between the French and English, that commenced in 1755, when Braddock served as commander-in-chief of the British forces in America, until the close of the campaign of 1758, Washington was almost continually in the public service. He had been promoted to colonel in 1754, but on account of new military arrangements by a narrow-minded governor he had left the service with disgust, and retired to Mount Vernon, with a determination to spend his life there in his loved pursuits of agriculture.

General Braddock came to America in 1758 to arrange a campaign against the French. Braddock soon heard encomiums of the character of Colonel Washington, and invited him to Alexandria. Mount Vernon was little more than an hour's ride distant, and Washington's military ardour was aroused to obey the summons. From Mount Vernon he looked upon the ships-of-war on the bosom of the Potomac that bore Braddock and his troops, and the thought that close to his dwelling preparations were in progress for a brilliant campaign, under the command of an experienced general of the British army, stirred the depths of his soul, and made him yearn to go again to the field.

At Jonathan Carey's residence, Braddock's headquarters, the young provincial colonel and the veteran general first met, at the close of March. Carey's was then the finest house in Alexandria, surrounded by a noble lawn that was shaded by lofty forest trees, and its gardens extending down a gentle slope to the shore of the Potomac. Now it stands within the city, hemmed in by buildings and paved streets, a conversion natural to New World cities. The convention of governors met in it in April, and there the ensuing campaign was planned.

Braddock invited Washington to join his military family, as aide, with the rank he had lately borne. The mother of the young colonel hastened to Mount Vernon to persuade him not to accept it. She urged the claims of his and her own affairs upon his attention, as strong reasons for him not to enter the army again, and for two days she held his decision in abeyance, for filial obedience was one of the strongest sentiments of his nature. But it was not strong enough to restrain him on this occasion—or rather God's will must be obeyed—and he left Mount Vernon for Alexandria, after her departure for the Rappahannock, and was welcomed into Braddock's family with joy by Captains Orme and Morris.

On the 9th of July following, we behold him upon the bloody field of the Monongahela, shielded by God's providence, untouched by ball or bayonet, arrow or javelin, while carnage was laying its scores of victims around him, and his commander was borne mortally wounded from the field —we behold him riding from point to point, bringing order out of confusion, and leading away from that *aceldama* the shattered battalions of the proud army of the morning to a place of safety and repose. Then he returned to Mount Vernon, weak from recent sickness and exposure in the field. In his little library there, he wrote to his brother, then a member of the House of Burgesses at Williamsburg, and thus summed up his military career :—

"I was employed to go a journey in the winter, when I believe few or none would have undertaken it, and what did I get by it? My expenses borne! I was then appointed, with trifling pay, to conduct a handful of men to the Ohio. What did I get by that? Why, after putting myself to a considerable expense in equipping and providing necessaries for the campaign, I went out, was soundly beaten, and lost all! Came in, and had my commission taken from me; or, in other words, my command reduced, under pretence of an order from home. I then went out a volunteer with General Braddock, and lost all my horses, and many other things. But this being a voluntary act, I ought not to have mentioned it; nor should I have done it, were it not to show that I have been on the losing order ever since I entered the service, which is now nearly two years."

But what wonderful and necessary lessons for the future had Washington learned during that time!

Mount Vernon saw but little of its master during the next four years; for the flame of war lighted up the land from Acadia and along the St. Lawrence, away down to the beautiful Cherookee country, in Western Georgia and Carolina, and Washington was most of the time in camp, except from December, 1757, until March, 1758, when he was an invalid at home.

In February, 1756, we find him, accompanied by two aides, journeying to Boston, to confer with General Shirley concerning military rank in Virginia. Little did he then think that twenty years later he would again be there, directing a siege against the New England capital, in command of rebels against the crown he was then serving! The life even of Washington had its share of romance.

We find him lingering in New York. On his return, writers of the time record how the young soldier, apparently invincible to the mortal weapons of war, was sorely smitten there by the "sly archer" concealed in the bright eyes, blooming cheeks, and winning ways of Mary Phillipse, the heiress of a broad domain stretching many a mile along the Hudson. The young soldier lingered in her presence as long as duty would permit, and he would fain have carried her with him to Virginia as a bride, but his natural diffidence kept the momentous question unspoken in his heart, and his fellow aide-de-camp in Braddock's family, Roger Morris, bore away the prize. Mary Phillipse did not become the mistress of Mount Vernon, but reigned as beauteous queen in a more stately mansion on the bank of the Harlem River, where, twenty years later, Washington, as leader of a host of Americans in arms against the king, held his headquarters, the master and mistress of the mansion being proscribed as " enemies to their country ! "

But three years later there was a presiding angel over the mansion on Mount Vernon. Meanwhile, the tramp of steeds, the clangour of arms, and every sound betokening warlike preparations were heard there, and the decisive campaign of 1758 was opened.

Lonely was the mansion at Mount Vernon without the master during the seven years and more that the war lasted. Yet it was by no means deserted. The only child of Mrs. Washington, John Parke Custis, with his wife and growing family, were there much of the time.

On the 9th of September, 1781, the master of Mount Vernon paid his home an unexpected visit. The allied French and American armies were then on their march towards Virginia, to assist Lafayette and his compatriots in driving the invading Cornwallis from that state. Washington came from Baltimore late at night, attended only by Colonel Humphreys (one of his aides) and faithful Billy. They had left the Count de Rochambeau and the Marquis de Chastellux— one at Alexandria and the other at Georgetown—to follow

MARY PHILLIPSE.

Reproduced by the Autotype Company

them in the morning. Very soon the whole household was astir, and the news flew quickly over the estate that he had arrived. At early dawn the servants came from every cabin to greet him, and many looked sorrowfully upon a face so changed by the storms of successive campaigns, during more than six years that he had been absent.

On the morrow the French noblemen, with their suites, arrived—Rochambeau first, and De Chastellux afterward— and all but the chief made it a day of rest. For him there was no repose. He was not permitted to pass even an hour alone with his wife. Public and private cares were pressing heavily upon him. He was on his way to measure strength with a powerful enemy, and his words of affection were few and hurried. All the morning of the 10th he was closeted with his manager, and before dinner he wrote to Lafayette the first letter that he had dated at Mount Vernon since early in May, 1775, saying, "We are thus far on our way to you. The Count de Rochambeau has just arrived. General Chastellux will be here, and we propose, after resting to-morrow, to be at Fredericksburg on the night of the 12th. The 13th we shall reach New Castle; and the next day we expect to have the pleasure of seeing you at your encampment." These calculations were correct; they arrived at the camp of Lafayette, at Williamsburg, on the evening of the 14th.

Rochambeau and Chastellux were guests worthy of such a host.

On the second day after Washington's arrival at Mount Vernon, the 11th of September, the mansion was crowded with guests; and at dinner were met gentlemen and ladies from the country for miles around, who had not been at the festive board with the master of the feast since the war broke out. And there were children, too—tiny children, whom the master loved as his own, for they were the grandchildren of his wife. There were four of these. The eldest was a beautiful girl, five years old, who afterwards married a nephew of Lord Ellenborough; and the youngest was a boy-baby, only six months old, who was afterward adopted as the child of Washington, became one of the executors of his will, and lived until 1857. These were the children of John Parke Custis and his fair young wife, Eleanor Calvert, and had all been born during the absence of the master from his home at Mount Vernon. His appearance about this time was thus described by a writer in the English *London Chronicle* paper, who had then seen him:—

"General Washington is now in the forty-seventh year of his age, a handsome man, over six feet in height, rather large-boned; his features manly and bold, his eyes of a bluish cast, his hair a deep brown, his face rather long, his complexion sunburnt, and without much colour; his countenance sensible, composed, and thoughtful. There is a remarkable air of dignity about him, with a striking degree of peacefulness. He has an excellent understanding; is strictly just, vigilant, and generous; an affectionate husband, a faithful friend, a father to the deserving soldier; gentle in his manner, in temper reserved; a total stranger to religious prejudices; in morals irreproachable; and never known to exceed the bounds of the most rigid temperance. In a word, all his friends and acquaintances allow that no man ever united in his own person a more perfect alliance of the virtues of a philosopher with the talents of a general. Candour, sincerity, affability, and simplicity seem to be the striking features of his character, and when occasion offers, the power of displaying the most determined bravery and independence of spirit."

Domestic felicity and social enjoyment were, at that time, secondary considerations with Washington, and on the morning of the 12th of September he departed with all his military guests from his delightful dwelling-place, journeyed to Fredericksburg to embrace his aged mother and receive her blessing, and then hastened on towards Yorktown, where Cornwallis had entrenched himself with a view of overrunning Virginia.

In the early part of 1781 Mount Vernon very narrowly escaped destruction by the enemy. General Phillips had been operating in the country immediately around it, and some of his smaller vessels had carried on a plan of plunder and devastation in several of the rivers emptying into the Chesapeake Bay, setting fire to the houses where they met with resistance. One had ascended the Potomac and menaced Mount Vernon. Lafayette had been operating against General Phillips, and had used the opportunity of being in the neighbourhood to pay a hurried visit to Washington's mother at Fredericksburg. Lund Washington, who had charge of the estate at the time, met the flag which the enemy sent on shore, and saved the property from pillage by furnishing the vessel with provisions. Lafayette, who heard of the circumstance, and was sensitive for the honour of Washington, immediately wrote to him on the subject. "This conduct on the part of the person who represents you on your estate must certainly produce a bad effect, and contrast with the courageous replies of some of your neighbours, whose houses in consequence have been burnt. You will do what you think proper, my dear General, but friendship makes it my duty to give you confidentially the facts."

Washington, however, had previously received a letter from Lund himself, stating all the circumstances of the case, and had immediately written him a reply. He had no doubt that Lund had acted from his best judgment, and with a view to preserve the property and buildings from impending danger; but he was stung to the quick by the idea that his agent should go on board of the enemy's vessels, carry them refreshments, and "commune with a parcel of plundering scoundrels," as he termed them. "It would have been a less painful circumstance to me to have heard," writes he, "that in consequence of your non-compliance with their request they had burnt my house and laid my plantations in ruins. You ought to have considered yourself as my representative, and should have reflected on the bad example of communicating with the enemy, and making a voluntary offer of refreshments to them, with a view to prevent a conflagration." In concluding his letter he expresses his opinion that it was the intention of the enemy to prosecute the plundering plan they had begun, and that it would end in the destruction of his property, but adds that he is "prepared for the event." He advises his agent to deposit the most valuable and least bulky articles in a place of safety. "Such and so many things as are necessary for common and present use must be retained, and must run their chance through the fiery ordeal of this summer." Such were the steadfast purposes of Washington's mind when war was brought home to his door, and threatening his earthly paradise of Mount Vernon.

Washington, like every other lover of nature, had been charmed with the beautiful holly-tree, which in England does so much to add to the charms of shrubberies from the month of October until the end of February, by its exquisite red berries, and which throughout England, from time immemorial, has been universally availed of for Christmas decorative purposes. North of Virginia it is unable to resist the severe winters; but in Virginia, and south of it, this exquisite shrub grows well, though not as luxuriantly as in England. He managed to raise them from berries, and many trees thus produced now exist on the place. He had learnt the policy of clothing his ornamented grounds as much as possible with evergreens, which resist the rigours of winter, and maintain a cheering verdure throughout the year. Like a true gardener, he had been most charmed with the holly for this purpose, though in his day he could hardly have seen the exquisite variegated varieties now found throughout England.

It must not be imagined that Washington found the hoped-for haven in his retreats to Mount Vernon. On each occasion of seeking rest there he had to endure the lot common to men who have been harnessed to the chariot of earnest, patriotic service of his country. It afforded him little relaxation of any continuance. Irving pathetically asks, "Was a soldier's dream realized? Is he in perfect enjoyment of that seclusion from the world and its distractions which he had so often pictured to himself amid the hardships and turmoils of the camp?" Alas, no! The "post," that "herald of a noisy world," invades his quiet, and loads his table with letters, until correspondence becomes an intolerable burden. He looks in despair at the daily accumulating mass of unanswered letters. "Many mistakingly think," writes he, "that I am retired to ease, and to that kind of tranquillity which would grow tiresome for want of employment; but at no period of my life, not in the years I served the public, have I been obliged to write so much myself as I have done since my retirement." So wrote he to Richard Henry Lee. Again—"It is not the letters from my friends which give me trouble, or add aught to my perplexity. It is references to old matters, with which I have nothing to do; applications which often cannot be complied with; inquiries which would require the pen of a historian to satisfy; letters of compliment, as unmeaning, perhaps, as they are troublesome, but which must be attended to; and the commonplace business which employs my pen and my time often disagreeably. These, with company, deprive me of exercise, and, unless I can obtain relief, must be productive of disagreeable consequences." At length he found faithful help in the willing and efficient services of Mr. Tobias Lear, who for some years acted as his private secretary, and who was thoroughly desirous of doing his utmost to relieve him of as much of the drudgery as could be deputed. Lear was a graduate of Harvard University, an able and accomplished young man, and who, in addition to his secretarial duties, assisted in the education of the two children of Mr. Parke Custis, whom Washington had adopted.

Mount Vernon was ever a loved retreat to its illustrious owner. Just subsequent to his tour in the Eastern States, at the time when Rhode Island had adopted the constitution, and he had avoided going there because it had not then joined the union under the new government, his dear home proved productive of convalescence to his worn mind and wearied body. His health had been impaired by severe disease and constant application to business, and he determined to take advantage of the recess of Congress, and throw off for a brief space the burden of public cares, and seek repose and recreation in his own quiet home at Mount Vernon. His letters show how he always returned to that spot with delight; and at that time of prostration it proved doubly dear to him, as it promised rest from labour, refreshment to his weary spirit and debilitated body, and a few days of leisure—alas! too short, as he observed with a sigh to his trusty and beloved Hamilton—to ride over his farms, view his gardens, orchards, and fields, and observe the progress of his agricultural operations. These had been carried on under great disadvantage, in fits and snatches, as it were. The labour and public cares which throughout life had fallen to him utterly prevented any regular and systematic care of his farm. No sooner had he determined on a plan of work, than some public duty or irresistible call interfered to place it in abeyance. The determining the permanent seat of government, he told Sharples when wandering with him at early morn over the Mount Vernon lands, had given him an immensity of labour and correspondence. Congress had been for a long time divided on the point. Local interests, and other considerations, made it difficult to agree on the place best adapted for the purpose. It was at length resolved it should be removed for ten years to Philadelphia, and then be established at some place on the Potomac River. Ultimately the position was selected—afterwards named the District of Columbia—and the territory was surveyed, the city planned, and the public buildings commenced under the direction of Washington—this duty devolving on him as President.

In viewing that magnificent city, probably some day to be second to few on the globe, how rarely is it remembered the hand he had in all these laborious preliminaries! He told Sharples, "They were about the heaviest duties of my life." For fully five years they occupied a good deal of his time and mechanical toil. In this, as in every other trust, was shown the same undeviating compliance with the laws, and minute exaction of all accounts, which marks all business acts of his life. During this lengthened period he carried on a voluminous correspondence with the commissioners he had appointed to manage the business, and who fell back on him for directions on points of detail he might well have been spared. The willing horse need never despair of a rider.

Late in the autumn of 1781 Washington again visited Mount Vernon for a brief season. It was when he was on his journey to Philadelphia, in November, bearing the laurels of a victor. He was accompanied as far as Fredericksburg by a large retinue of American and French officers; and there, after an interview with his mother, he attended a ball given in honour of the occasion. The aged matron went with him to the assembly, and astonished the French officers by the plainness of her apparel, and the quiet simplicity of her manners, for they expected to see the mother of the great chief distinguished by a personal display such as they had been accustomed to behold among the families of the great in their own country. They thought of the Dowager Queen of France, of the brilliant Maria Antoinette, and the high-born dames of the Court of Louis XVI., and could not comprehend the vision.

Washington retired with his mother from the gay scene at an early hour, and the next morning, attended by two aides and Billy, he rode to Mount Vernon. His stay there was brief. Public duties beckoned him forward. "I shall remain but a few days here," he wrote to General Greene, "and shall proceed to Philadelphia, when I shall attempt to stimulate Congress to the best improvement of our late success, by taking the most vigorous and effectual measures to be ready for an early and decisive campaign the next year."

Gallant as he was in the society of the softer sex, it is not to be wondered at that he should wish Mount Vernon to be honoured by a visit from the wife of a beloved and faithful friend, such as Lafayette had ever proved. Under such desire we find him subsequently, in a letter to the Marchioness de Lafayette, inviting her to America to see the country, "young, rude, and uncultivated as it is," for the liberties of which her husband had fought, bled, and acquired much glory, and where everybody admired and loved him, and he adds, "I am now enjoying domestic cares under the shadow of my own vine and my own fig-tree, in a small villa, with the implements of husbandry and lambkins about me. . . . Come, then, let me entreat you, and call my cottage your own, for your doors do not open to you now with more readiness than mine would. You would see the plain manner in which we live, and meet with rustic civility; and you shall taste the simplicity of rural life. It will diversify the scene, and may give you a higher relish for the gaieties of the Court when you return to Versailles."

At times during these periods of rest, he allows free run to his dreams of enlarged hospitality. He indulges in dreams of desired descents of old comrades, and especially during the winter storms, we find him anticipating those times when the return of the sun will enable him to welcome these his friends and companions-in-arms to partake of his hospitality, and lays down his unpretending plan of receiving the curious visitors who are likely to throng in upon him. "My manner of living," writes he to a friend, "is plain, and I do not mean to be put out of it. A glass of wine and a bit of mutton are always ready, and such as will be content to partake of them are always welcome; those who expect more will be disappointed."

Warm and generous as his heart ever was, yet he was never known to have indulged in expenditure beyond his private means. The war had somewhat crippled his income, but he earnestly endeavoured to equalize expenditure and income by careful abstinence from luxuries. Some degree of economy was necessary. His financial concerns had always been carefully looked into, and although the products of his estate had fallen off during his long absence, yet there was never at any time any curtailing savouring of parsimony.

In the meantime, the Supreme Council of Pennsylvania, properly appreciating the disinterestedness of his conduct, and aware that popular love and popular curiosity would attract crowds of visitors to Mount Vernon, and subject him to extraordinary expenses, had instructed their delegates in Congress to call the attention of that body to these circumstances, with a view to produce some national reward for his eminent services. Before acting upon these instructions, the delegates were directed to send a copy of them to Washington for his approbation. He received the document while buried in accounts and calculations, and when, had he been of a mercenary disposition, the offered intervention in his favour would have seemed most seasonable; but he at once most gratefully and respectfully declined it, jealously maintaining the satisfaction of having served his country at the sacrifice of his private interest.

Few men could throw off the manners of the tented field and adopt that of the political ruler, or even the retirement of a simple country home with such dignity as was his in the former, or with the ease and content evidenced by him in the latter enviable condition.

As the spring of 1784 advanced, Irving tells us " Mount Vernon, as had been anticipated, began to attract numerous visitors. They were received in the frank, unpretending style Washington had determined upon. It was truly edifying to behold how easily and contentedly he subsided from the authoritative commander-in-chief of armies into the quiet country gentleman. There was nothing awkward or violent in the transition. He seemed to be in his natural element. Mrs. Washington, too, who had presided with quiet dignity at headquarters, and cheered the wintry gloom at Valley Forge with her presence, presided with equal amenity and grace at the simple board of Mount Vernon. She had a cheerful good sense that always made her an agreeable companion, and was an excellent manager. She has been remarked for an inveterate habit of knitting. It had been acquired, or at least fostered, in the wintry encampments of the Revolution, where she used to set an example to her lady visitors, by diligently plying her needles, knitting stockings for the poor destitute soldiers.

During the most trying years devoted to his country, Washington had never ceased having his home before him. Therefore, in re-entering upon the outdoor management of his estate at Mount Vernon, he was but doing in person what he had long been doing through others. He had never virtually ceased to be an agriculturist. Throughout all his campaigns he had kept himself informed of the course of rural affairs at Mount Vernon. By means of maps on which every field was laid down and numbered, he was enabled to give directions for their several cultivation, and receive accounts of their several crops. No hurry of affairs prevented a correspondence with his overseer or agent, and he exacted weekly reports. Thus his rural were interwoven with his military cares, the agriculturist was mingled with the soldier; and those strong sympathies with the honest cultivators of the soil, and that paternal care of their interests to be noted throughout his military career, may be ascribed, in a great measure, to the sweetening influences of Mount Vernon. Yet as spring returned, and he resumed his rides about the beautiful neighbourhood of this haven of his hopes, he must have been mournfully sensible, now and then, of the changes which time and events had effected there.

There is a certain degree of sadness traceable in most of Washington's visits to his loved home. The longed-for repose never came. The relentless pursuer of notabilities was constantly on his track, intruding into his presence with an importunity and assurance beyond all endurance. Alas for public men in America, repose, or even the veriest morsel of privacy, is denied them; the hideous nightmare spreads its murky wings with greater persistence than in

Washington's time, and has gained an ascendancy beyond mortal power of combat. Washington Irving had occasion to write: "My life is a burden, the harpies close in on every side. Would there was a cave at Sunnyside to which I could retreat!"

So tardily did the members of the Federal Congress assemble, that a quorum was not present at the capital in New York until the beginning of April, when the votes of the electoral college were counted, and Washington was declared to be elected President of the United States by the unanimous voice of the people. That delay was a source of pleasure to him. In a letter to General Knox, he compared it to a reprieve; "for," he said, "in confidence I tell you (with the *world* it would obtain little credit) that my movements to the chair of government will be accompanied by feelings not unlike those of a culprit who is going to the place of execution." "I am sensible," he continued, "that I am embarking the voice of the people, and a good name of my own on this voyage, but what returns will be made for them heaven alone can foretell. Integrity and firmness are all I can promise. These, be the voyage long or short, shall never forsake me, although I may be deserted by all men; for of all the consolations which are to be derived from them, under any circumstances the world cannot deprive me."

The Senate of the United States was organized on the 6th of April, and John Langdon, a representative therein from New Hampshire, was chosen its president *pro tempore*. As soon as the votes of the electoral college were opened and counted, he wrote a letter to the illustrious farmer at Mount Vernon, notifying him of the fact of his election. This letter, with an official certificate, was conveyed to the chief magistrate elect by the venerable Secretary Thomson, who arrived at Mount Vernon on Tuesday, the 14th, between ten and eleven o'clock in the morning. Washington was making the usual tour of his farms, and the secretary was cordially received by Mrs. Washington, who had enjoyed his friendship and the hospitality of his house at Philadelphia.

On his return from the fields at a quarter before one, Washington greeted Mr. Thomson with much warmth, for their friendship was most sincere. They had gone through a long struggle for their country's liberation hand in hand, one in the field, the other in the senate; and the bond of

MOUNT VERNON (REAR VIEW).

sympathy, strengthened by retrospection, was powerful. Thomson was soon invited to the library, where he revealed the object of his visit, and delivered the letter of President Langdon. Public affairs at once became the topic of conversation, and long did the two patriots linger at the table that day, after Mrs. Washington, Colonel Humphreys, Mr. Lear, and two or three guests had withdrawn. Only for a few minutes were they separated, when Washington, in his private study in an upper room, wrote the following letter to Mr. Langdon, and placed it in the hands of a servant to be conveyed to the post-office at Alexandria:—

"Mount Vernon, 14th April, 1789.

"Sir,—I had the honour to receive your official communication by the hand of Mr. Secretary Thomson, about one o'clock this day. Having concluded to obey the important and flattering call of my country, and having been impressed with the idea of the expediency of my being with Congress at as early a period as possible, I propose to commence my journey on Thursday morning, which will be the day after to-morrow."

Toward evening Washington left Mount Vernon on horseback, accompanied by his faithful servant Billy, and rode rapidly towards Fredericksburg, where his aged and invalid mother resided. He went to embrace her and bid her farewell before leaving for the distant seat of government. She was suffering from cancer, and the weight of more than fourscore years was upon her. The interview between the matron and her illustrious son was full of the most touching sublimity. "The people, madam," said Washington, "have been pleased with the most flattering unanimity to elect me to the chief magistracy of the United States; but before I can assume the functions of that office I have come to bid you an affectionate farewell. So soon as the public business which must necessarily be encountered in arranging a new government can be disposed of, I shall hasten to Virginia, and—" Here she interrupted him, saying, "You will see me no more. My great age, and the disease that is rapidly approaching my vitals, warn me that I shall not be long in this world. I trust in God I am somewhat prepared for a better. But go, George, fulfil the high destinies which

Heaven appears to assign you; go, my son, and may that Heaven's and your mother's blessing be with you always."

The mother and son embraced for the last time, for before he could return to Virginia, she was laid in the grave.

Washington returned to Mount Vernon on the evening of the 15th, and found everything in preparation for the journey toward New York the following morning. Nothing essential to the master's comfort and convenience was omitted by the faithful Billy.

There was a great stir at Mount Vernon on the morning of the 16th. Before sunrise a messenger had come from Alexandria, and departed; and that evening Washington wrote in his diary: "About ten o'clock I bade adieu to Mount Vernon, to private life and to domestic felicity, and with a mind oppressed with more anxious and painful sensations than I have words to express, set out for New York, in company with Mr. Thomson and Colonel Humphreys, with the best disposition to render service to my country in obedience to its call, but with less hope of answering its expectations."

Washington's neighbours and friends at Alexandria had invited him to halt and partake of a public dinner on the way. This manifestation of friendship touched his heart; but still deeper were his tenderest emotions awakened when, as he and his travelling companions ascended a little hill about a mile from his home, and came in view of the lodges at his gate, he saw a cavalcade of those friends, waiting to escort him to the town. The scene was one of marvellous interest. It was the first of a series of ovations that awaited him on his journey.

The President elect was anxious to proceed to New York with as little parade as possible, but the enthusiasm of the people could not be repressed. His journey was like a triumphal march. At Alexandria he partook of a public dinner, when the mayor said, "The first and best of our citizens must leave us; our aged must lose their ornament, our youth their model, our agriculture its improver, our commerce its friend, our infant academy its protector,[1] our poor their benefactor. * * * Farewell!" he said, turning to Washington, "go, and make a grateful people happy; a people who will be doubly grateful when they contemplate this new sacrifice for their interests."

Washington's feelings were deeply touched. He could say but little. "Words fail me," he said; "unutterable sensations must then be left to more expressive silence, while from an aching heart I bid all my affectionate friends and kind neighbours—farewell."

The President was greeted by the Marylanders at Georgetown; and at Baltimore he was entertained by a large number of citizens at a public supper. When leaving the city the next morning at half-past five, he was saluted by discharges of cannon, and attended by a cavalcade of gentlemen, who rode seven miles with him. At the frontier of Pennsylvania he was met early on the morning of the 19th by two troops of cavalry and a cavalcade of citizens at the head of whom were Governor Mifflin and Judge Peters; and by them he was escorted to Philadelphia. Upon that frontier Washington left his carriage, and mounting a superb white charger, he took position in the line of procession, with Secretary Thomson on one side and Colonel Humphreys on the other.

At Gray's Ferry, on the Schuylkill, they were joined by an immense number of citizens, led in order by General St. Clair. A triumphal arch was erected on both sides of the river, covered with laurel-branches and approached through avenues of evergreens. As Washington passed under the

[1] Washington had given funds for the establishment of an academy at Alexandria, and was its patron.

last arch, Angelica Peale, daughter of the artist and a child of rare beauty, and whose portrait was a few years later painted by Sharples, was concealed in the foliage, and let down a handsomely ornamented civic crown of laurel which rested upon the head of the patriot. The incident caused a tumultuous shout. The procession moved on into the city, its volume increasing every moment. At least twenty thousand people lined its passage-way from the Schuylkill to the city; and at every step the President was greeted with shouts of "Long live George Washington!" "Long live the father of his country!"

The President was entertained at a sumptuous banquet, given by the authorities at the City Tavern, and the next morning the military were paraded to form an escort for him to Trenton. But heavy rain frustrated their designs. Washington was compelled to ride in his carriage, and he would not allow an escort of friends to travel in the rain.

When the President and suite approached Trenton in the afternoon, the clouds had disappeared, and in the warm sunshine he crossed the Delaware, amid the greetings of shouts and cannon-peals, and the *feu de joie* of musketry. His route lay across the same bridge over the little stream which flows through the town, where, twelve years before, he had been driven across by Cornwallis on the evening previous to the battle at Princeton. Upon that bridge, where he was thus humiliated, was now a triumphal arch, twenty feet in height, supported by thirteen pillars twined with evergreens.

With joyous greetings at every step, Washington proceeded through New Jersey, over which he had once fled with a half-starved, half-naked army, before a closely pursuing foe, and at Elizabethtown Point he was met on the morning of the 23rd by a committee of both houses of Congress, and several civil and military officers. They had prepared a magnificent barge for his reception, which was manned by thirteen pilots, in white uniforms, commanded by Commodore Nicholson. In New York harbour the vessels were all decked with flags in honour of the President, and gaily-dressed small boats swarmed upon the waters, filled with gentlemen and ladies. The Spanish ship-of-war *Galveston*, lying in the harbour, was the only vessel of all nations that did not show signs of respect. The neglect was so marked that many words of censure were heard, when, at a given signal, just as the barge containing Washington was abreast of her, she displayed, on every part of her rigging, every flag and signal known among the nations. At the same moment she discharged thirteen heavy guns, and these were answered by the grand battery on shore. In the midst of this cannonade, and the shouts of the multitude on land and water, the President debarked, and was conducted by a military and civic procession to the residence prepared for his use, at No. 10, Cherry Street, near Franklin Square.

Such was the reception of the first President at the capital of the Union.

On Thursday, the 30th of April, 1789, Washington was inaugurated the first President of the United States. The ceremonies were preceded by a national salute at Bowling Green, the assembling of the people in the churches to implore the blessings of Heaven on the nation and the President, and a grand procession. The august spectacle was exhibited upon the open gallery at the front of the old Federal Hall, at the head of Broad Street, in the presence of a vast assemblage of people. Washington was dressed in a suit of dark-brown cloth, and white silk stockings, all of American manufacture, with silver buckles upon his shoes, and his hair powdered and dressed in the fashion of the time. Before him, when he arose to take the oath of office, stood Chancellor Livingstone, in a suit of black broadcloth; and near him were Vice-President Adams, Mr. Otis, the Secretary of the Senate, who held an open Bible upon a rich crimson cushion, Generals Knox, St. Clair, Steuben, and other officers of the army, and George Clinton, the Governor of the State of New York.

Washington laid his hand upon the page containing the fiftieth chapter of Genesis, opposite to which were two engravings, one representing *The Blessing of Zebulon*, the other, *The Prophecy of Issachar*. Chancellor Livingstone then raised his hand for the multitude to be silent, and in a clear voice read the prescribed oath. The President

BIBLE USED AT THE INAUGURATION OF WASHINGTON.

said, "I swear," then bowed his head and kissed the sacred volume, and with closed eyes, as he resumed his erect position, he continued with solemn voice and devotional attitude, "So help me God!"

"It is done!" exclaimed the Chancellor, and with a loud voice shouted, "Long live George Washington, President of the United States!"

Mrs. Washington did not journey to New York with her husband. Her reluctance to leave Mount Vernon and the quiet of domestic pursuits was quite equal to his. She loved her home, her family, and friends, and had no taste for the excitements of fashionable society and public life. She was, in every respect, a model Virginia housekeeper.

She was a very early riser, leaving her pillow at dawn at every season of the year, and engaging at once in the active duties of her household. Yet these duties never kept her from daily communion with God in the solitude of her closet. After breakfast she invariably retired to her chamber, where she remained an hour reading the Scriptures, and engaged in thanksgiving and prayer. For more than half a century she practised such de-

WASHINGTON'S SECRETARY AND CIRCULAR CHAIR.

votions in secret; and visitors often remarked that when she appeared after the hour of spiritual exercises her countenance beamed with ineffable sweetness.

All day long that careful, bustling, industrious little housewife kept her hands in motion. " Let us repair to the old lady's room, which is precisely in the style of our good old aunt's—that is to say, nicely fixed for all sorts of work On one side sits the chambermaid with her knitting; on the other a little coloured pet learning to sew. An old, decent woman is there, with her table and shears, cutting out the negroes' winter clothes, while the good lady directs them all, incessantly knitting herself. She points out to me several pairs of nice coloured stockings and gloves she has just finished, and presents me with a pair half done, which she begs I will finish and wear for her sake. It is wonderful, after a life spent as those good people have necessarily spent theirs, to see them in retirement assume those domestic habits that prevail in our country."

Mrs. Washington always spoke of the time when she was in public life, as wife of the President of the United States, as her "lost days." She was compelled to be governed by the etiquette prescribed for her, and she was very restive under it. To the wife of George A. Washington, the general's nephew, who had married her niece, and who was left in charge of domestic affairs at Mount Vernon when her husband assumed the presidency, she wrote from New York, saying:—

"Mrs. Sims will give you a better account of the fashions I saw. I live a very dull life here and know nothing that passes in the town. I never go to any public place; indeed I think I am more like a state prisoner than anything else. There are certain bounds set for me which I must not depart from; and as I cannot do as I like, I am obstinate, and stay at home a great deal."

At that time the etiquette of the President's household was not fully determined on. In his diary, on the 15th of November, Washington wrote: "Received an invitation to attend the funeral of Mrs. Roosevelt (the wife of a senator of this state—New York), but declined complying with it: first, because the propriety of accepting any invitation of this sort appeared very questionable; and secondly (though to do it in this instance might not be improper), because it might be difficult to discriminate in cases which might hereafter happen."

The establishment of precedents and the arrangement of etiquette were of more importance than might at first thought appear. The plan of having certain days and hours when the President would receive calls, was a measure of absolute necessity, in order that the chief magistrate might have the control of his time, and yet it offended many who were of the extremely democratic school.

The precedents of monarchy might not be followed in a simple republic, and yet a certain dignity was to be preserved. The arrangement of official ceremonies, connected with the President personally, was finally left to Colonel Humphreys, who had been abroad, and was a judicious observer of the phases of society under every aspect. The customs which were established during Washington's administration concerning the *levées*—the President not returning private visits, &c.—have ever since prevailed, and the chief magistrate of the republic is never seen in the position of a private citizen.

The seat of the federal government was removed from New York to Philadelphia in 1790, by Act of Congress. That body adjourned on the 12th of August, and Washington immediately thereafter made a voyage to Newport, Rhode Island, for the benefit of his health. Close application to public business had caused a nervous prostration, that threatened consequences almost as serious as those with which he had been menaced by a malignant carbuncle the year before. He had also suffered severely from violent inflammation of the lungs.

The sea voyage was beneficial, and on the 30th of August, the President and his family set out for Mount Vernon, there to spend the few months before the next meeting of Congress at Philadelphia. They left New York for Elizabethtown in the splendid barge in which they had arrived, amid the thunders of cannon and the huzzas of a great multitude of people.

In a few days Washington was again beneath the roof he loved so well, at Mount Vernon, but the coveted enjoyment of his home was lessened by the weight of public cares that pressed upon him. The old feeling of deep responsibility,

MOUNT VERNON.

which it was so difficult for him to lay aside at the close of his military career, returned; and in his library, where he loved to devote his morning hours to reading, and the labours of the pen in recording facts connected with his pursuits as a farmer, he might be seen with slate, maps, plans, and everything that indicated the weighty cares of a public man.

The Congress then just closed had been a most important one, and the labours of every conscientious officer and employée of the government had been very severe. Upon them had been laid the responsible and momentous task of putting in motion the machinery of a new government, and laying the foundations of the then present and future policy of that government, domestic and foreign. As the chief magistrate of the republic, the chief officer of the government, the chief architect of the new superstructure in progress, Washington felt the solemnity of his position, and the importance of the great trusts which the people had placed in his hands; and the sense of all this denied him needful repose, even while sitting within the quietude of his home on the banks of the Potomac.

There were some Philadelphians who were as afflicted because Congress was coming there, as New Yorkers were in having the government leave their city. As soon as it was ascertained that the government would reside there ten years, rents, and the prices of every kind of provision and other necessaries of life, greatly advanced. "Some of the blessings," said a letter-writer at Philadelphia, quoted by Griswold, "anticipated from the removal of Congress to this city, are already beginning to be apparent. Rents of houses have risen, and I fear will continue to rise, shamefully; even in the outskirts they have lately been increased from fourteen, sixteen, and eighteen pounds, to twenty-five, twenty-eight, and thirty. This is oppression. Our markets, it is expected, will also be dearer than heretofore."

THE HOUSE IN WHICH WASHINGTON RESIDED.

It was a view of these changes, and anticipated extortion, that made Washington so anxious to know beforehand how much rent he must pay for his house in Philadelphia.

When Oliver Wolcott, of Connecticut, was appointed first auditor of the treasury, he, like a prudent man, before he would accept the office, went to New York to ascertain whether he could live upon the salary of $1500 a year. He came to the conclusion that he could live upon $1000 a year, and he wrote to his wife, saying: "The example of the President and his family will render parade and expense improper and disreputable." This sentence speaks powerfully in illustration of the republican simplicity of Washington's household in those days.

The rent of Morris's house was fixed at $3000 dollars a year, and on the 22nd of November Washington left Mount Vernon for Philadelphia, accompanied by Mrs. Washington and family, in a chariot drawn by four horses. They were allowed to travel quietly, without any public parade, but receiving at every stopping-place the warm welcome of many private citizens and personal friends. None gave the President a heartier shake of the hand on this occasion, and none was more welcome to grasp it, than Tommy Giles, a short, thick-set man, of English birth, who kept a little tavern a short distance from the Head of Elk (now Elkton) on the road from Baltimore. His tavern-sign displayed a rude portrait of Washington; and the President, on his way to and from Mount Vernon, never passed by until he had greeted the worthy man.

Tommy had been a fife-major in the Continental army, and had been employed a long time by Washington, as his confidential express in the transmission of money from one point to another. In this business he was most trustworthy. Mrs. Giles was a stout Englishwoman, but republican to the core. Washington always shook hands with her as heartily as with her husband, and frequently left a guinea in her palm.

The President and his family reached Philadelphia on

the 28th of November. The first of Mrs. Washington's public receptions was on the 25th of December—Christmas Day. It is said that the most brilliant assemblage of beautiful, well-dressed, and well-educated women that had ever been seen in America, appeared at that *levée*. The Vice-President's wife mentioned in a letter that the dazzling Mrs. Bingham and her beautiful sisters (Misses Willing), the Misses Allens, the Misses Chew, and in short a constellation of beauties, were present.

The season opened very gaily, and balls, routs and dinners of the most sumptuous kind succeeded each other in rapid succession. "I should spend a very dissipated winter," wrote Mrs. Adams, "if I were to accept one-half the invitations I receive, particularly to the routs, or tea and cards." Philadelphia had never seen or felt anything like it, and the whole town was in a state of virtual intoxication for several weeks. But Washington and his wife could not be seduced from their temperate habits by the scenes of immoderate pleasure around them. They held their respective *levées* on Tuesdays and Fridays, as they did in New York, without the least ostentation; and Congressional and official dinners were also given in a plain way, without any extravagent displays of plate, ornament, or variety of dishes.

From Meade's "Old Churches, Ministers, and Families in Virginia" we learn that Washington was not indifferent to externals becoming his office and position. Soon after his arrival in New York to assume the duties of the presidency, he imported a semi-state carriage from England, in which towards the close of the time of his residence there, and while in Philadelphia, he often rode with his family, attended by outriders. On these occasions it was generally drawn by four, and sometimes by six fine bay horses.

The imported vehicle, one of the best of its kind, is described as heavy and substantial. The body and wheels were a cream colour, with gilt mouldings, suspended upon heavy leathern straps and iron springs.

WASHINGTON'S ENGLISH COACH.

Upon the door Washington's arms were emblazoned, having scroll ornaments issuing from the space between the shield and the crest; and below was a ribbon with his motto upon it.

Upon each of the four panels of the coach was an allegorical picture, emblematic of one of the seasons. These were painted upon copper by Cipriani, an Italian artist. The ground was a dark green—so dark that it appeared nearly black; and the allegorical figures were executed in bronze. One was emblematical of spring.

Washington and his family travelled from Elizabethtown to Philadelphia in this coach when on the way from New York to Mount Vernon, in the early autumn of 1789. Dunn, his driver, appears to have been quite incompetent to manage the six horses; and almost immediately after leaving Elizabethtown Point, he allowed the vehicle to run into a gully, by which it was injured. At Governor Livingston's, where they dined, another coachman was employed.

In a letter to Mr. Lear, written at a tavern in Maryland, while on his way to Mount Vernon, Washington said:— "Dunn has given such proof of his want of skill in driving that I find myself under the necessity of looking out for some one to take his place. Before we reached Elizabethtown we were obliged to take him from the coach and put

PANEL OF WASHINGTON'S COACH.

him on the wagon. This he turned over twice, and this morning he was found much intoxicated. He has also got the horses into the habit of stopping."

In a letter to Mr. Lear, soon after arriving at Mount Vernon, Washington mentions the fact that he had left the carriage and harness with Mr. Clarke, a coach-maker in Philadelphia, for repairs, and requests him to see that they are well done, when he shall reach that city, Mr. Lear being then in New York. Clarke built the coach in England, came over with it, and another precisely like it (which was imported by Mrs. Powell, of Philadelphia), and settled in business in that city.

From Mount Vernon, during the recess, Washington wrote several letters to Mr. Lear, who was charged with the removal of the effects of the President from New York, hiring a house for his residence in Philadelphia, and arranging the furniture of it. Previous to his arrival in Philadelphia from New York, the corporation of the latter city had hired for his use the house of Robert Morris, in Market Street, on the south side of Sixth Street, the best that could be procured at that time. Washington had examined

WASHINGTON'S CAMP CHEST.

it, and found it quite too small to accommodate his household as he could wish, even with an addition that was to be made.

This is stated in his letter to Mr. Charles Carter, mentioning Middleton's portrait of his mother. "There are good stables," he said, "but for twelve horses only, and a coachhouse which will hold all my carriages." He clearly maintained considerable state and various equipages. There was a fine garden, well inclosed by a brick wall, attached to the mansion.

The State Legislature had, at about the same time, appropriated a fine building for his use on South Ninth Street, on the grounds now covered by the University. But he declined accepting it, not choosing to live in a house hired and furnished at the public expense.

There were other considerations that caused him to decline the liberal offers of the state and city authorities, to relieve him of any private expense for the support of his personal establishment. The question of the permanent locality of the seat of the federal government was not then fairly settled, and the Philadelphians were using every means in their power to have it fixed in their city.

WASHINGTON'S INKSTAND.

Washington was aware of this, and as he was more favourable to a site further south, he was unwilling to afford a plea in favor of Philadelphia.

This matter gave him some trouble. He was willing to rent Morris's house on his own account, and, with his accustomed prudence, he directed Mr. Lear to ascertain the price; but for some months Mr. Lear was unsuccessful in his negotiations with Morris, who evidently sought to drive a good bargain. At length Mr. Lear arranged rent and needed alterations, but Washington, the first President, was never satisfied with the Philadelphia official residence. He wrote thus of it,—

"When all is done that can be done, the residence will not be so commodious as that I left in New York, for there (and the want of it will be found a real inconvenience at Mr. Morris's) my office was in the front room below, where persons on business immediately entered; whereas, in the present case, they will have to ascend two pairs of stairs, and to pass by the public rooms as well as the private chambers to get to it."

In making suggestions to Mr. Lear about the proper arrangement of the furniture, even in minute detail, Washington said: "There is a small room adjoining the

WASHINGTON'S SÈVRES CHINA, PRESENTED BY "THE CINCINNATI."

kitchen that might, if it is not essential for other purposes, be appropriated to the Sèvres china, and other things of that sort, which are not in common use." He undoubtedly referred to sets of china which had been presented, one to himself, and the other to Mrs. Washington, by the officers of the French army. The former was a dull white in colour, with heavy scroll and leaf ornaments in *bandeaux* of deep blue, and having upon the sides of the cups and tureens, and in the bottoms of the plates, saucers, and meat-dishes and other pieces, the Order of the Cincinnati, personated by a winged woman with a trumpet. These designs were in delicate colours.

These sets of china were presented to Washington and his wife at the time the elegant and costly Order of the Cincinnati was sent to him. That Order cost 3000 dollars. The whole of the eagle, except the beak and eye, was composed of diamonds. So, also, is the group of military emblems above it, in which each drum-head is composed of one large diamond.

MRS. WASHINGTON'S CHINA.

The set of china presented at the same time by the French officers to Mrs. Washington was of similar material, but more delicate in colour than the general's. The ornamentation was also far more delicate, excepting the delineation of the figure and Cincinnati Order on the former. Around the outside of each cup and tureen, and the inside of each plate and saucer, were in delicate colour a chain of thirteen large and thirteen small elliptical links. Within each large link is the name of one of the original thirteen states. On the sides of the cups and tureens, and in the bottom of each plate and saucer, is the interlaced monogram of Martha Washington—M. W.—inclosed in a green wreath, composed of the leaves of the laurel and olive. Beneath this is a ribbon, upon which is inscribed, in delicately traced letters, DECUS ET TUTAMEN ABILLO. From the wreath are rays of gold. There is also a coloured stripe around the edges of the cups, saucers, and plates. A few pieces of this set of china were preserved at Arlington House, but probably shared the sad fate of that mansion in the late war. The engraving on previous page represents a cup and saucer, and plate.

A writer of the time remarked of the first President that he had not lost "the genteel taste for fine cloathes," as Walton expresses it in speaking of George Herbert, which marks his commissions to his London agents before the war; or for fine equipages, as when, in the precincts of the viceregal court at Williamsburg, in the days of the old *régime*. Colonel Washington's bays vied with Colonel Byrd's grays, as is abundantly proved by the cream-coloured English coach, with panels painted by Cipriani with groups of the Seasons, and its six shining bay horses, which was one of the sights of Philadelphia; and the purple satin dress, or rich black velvet, with diamond knee-buckles, scrupulously japanned shoes and buckles, ruffles, powder, bag and dress-sword of his presidential days; all being adorned by a manner most courteous without being formal, a singularly attractive smile, eyes which could flash and glow on occasion, and an expression of countenance, grave, but not stern, which no painter could catch, and by a form declared by Lafayette to be the most superb he had ever beheld. The internal arrangements of his household were all decorous and dignified. There was no useless parade or expense; he always himself scrupulously inspected his weekly accounts; but there was, at the same time, nothing sordid; and though not of a disposition to diminish needlessly his patrimony, he freely spent the produce of the sale of a very considerable estate to eke out the State salary. We find amusingly described in the "Recollections" the awful neatness of the President's stables; the horses enveloped, the night before they were to be ridden, in a white paste; the ostlers hard at work rubbing this off before dawn; the overseer with a muslin handkerchief in his hand, on which, when applied to the animals' coats, if the slightest stain were perceptible, down came the whip; then Fraunces, the steward of magnificent ideas, who, to reproaches on the score of waste, would

SPECIMENS OF WASHINGTON'S SILVER PLATE.

reply with tears and the exclamation, " He may kill me if he will; but while he is President, and I have the honour to be his steward, his establishment shall have the best of everything"—even the solitary shad of the season, at three dollars the fish, though the master's indignation at the cost might consign the luxury to the servants' hall; and Uncle Harkless, the chief cook, sauntering with the dandies up Market Street, in silk, with cocked hat and gold-headed cane, to glorify the presidential establishment.

Washington knew how to preserve simplicity of manner

and thought amid some magnificence of living. Some few might murmur at, for instance, his *levées* and his wife's drawing-rooms as verging on monarchical etiquette and formality; but, on the whole, the nation approved and liked to have a chief who could live like a prince, and feel and talk like a citizen among citizens. The voluntary celebration of his birthday by a ball in every great town showed that the endurance of presidential ceremonials was not deemed by Republican America a forced discharge of the debt of gratitude due to its great liberator.

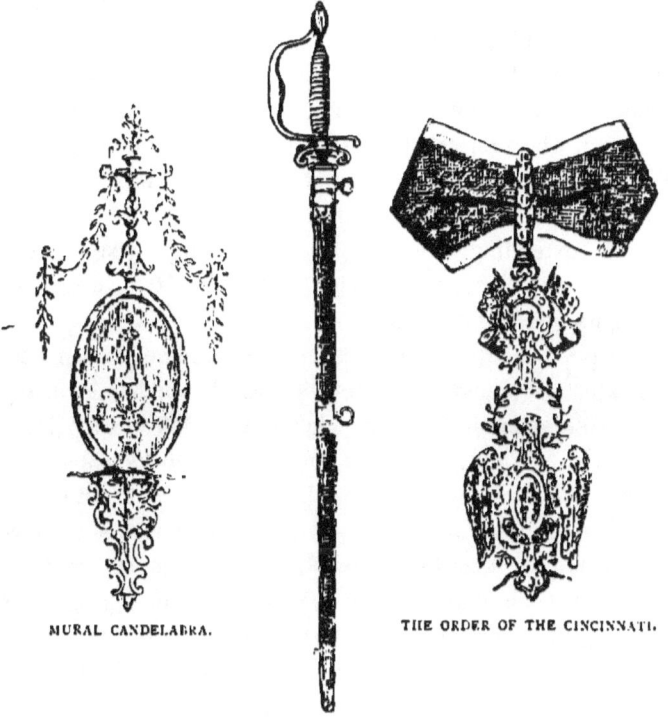

MURAL CANDELABRA.   THE ORDER OF THE CINCINNATI.

WASHINGTON'S DRESS SWORD.

The papers left by Sharples, together with such as were in Mr. Cary's possession at the time of his death, when the division of the portraits occurred, and all were for a time scattered, are of a fragmentary character, the result probably of carelessness in search, and through lack of interest at the time on the part of Mr. Cary's inheriting brother—a man utterly indifferent to American affairs, and worse than all, unequal to the great duty of grasping the importance of everything bearing on lives destined hereafter to be eagerly dwelt upon by the whole world. This lamentable carelessness applies equally to Sharples' widow as to Robert Cary's executors, and unfortunately the consequences are equally lamentable in both cases. Washington and Robert Fulton —the world's peerless Patriot, and the great practical engineer, who first applied steam to purposes of navigation. Where shall we seek greater men? There was evidently an active correspondence on the part of Sharples and Fulton, extending over a period of eventful years; both were men of science as well as artists, constantly exchanging thoughts one with the other.

The precise date of Sharples' visit, or as some of his papers indicate, several stays at Mount Vernon, is not defined in any of these memoranda; neither did those in his wife's holding state this. Happily, he seems to have been entirely absorbed in the revelations made to him by the illustrious sitter, and to have been so impressed with their import, as to have caused him to record these recollections of the occurrences, and of Washington's conversations with him during early morning walks before breakfast, and during his prolonged sittings, at much length in writing, and to have transmitted them to his wife, then in Philadelphia, at the joint home of the Franklins. All that are saved indicate that many others existed. Such papers did not assume the form of letters, but were the actual memoranda written in a book he usually carried in his pocket when journeying from place to place executing his crayon portraits. He did not transcribe from his memorandum book, but tore the leaves out and enclosed them to his wife. Such of these as were transmitted to her from Mount Vernon point clearly to events occurring in 1794 and 1795.

The mischievous activity and audacity of the French minister, Genet, combined with the defection of hitherto relied-on men at home, had worried Washington, causing deep mental anxiety; the self-control usually his, had in a degree forsaken him, and no wonder, if memory is allowed to recall that John Adams had marked the hour in words of no common portent. "No prospect of peace in Europe, therefore none of internal harmony in America. We cannot well be in a more disagreeable situation than we are with all Europe, with all Indians, and with all Barbary rovers. Nearly one-half of the Continent is in constant opposition to the other, and the President's situation, which is highly responsible, is very distressing."

That Washington had been greatly agitated at the time of making this admission is clearly seen from a further statement of Adams, that he had two hours' conversation with him alone in his cabinet, and that he "*could not reveal the purport of it, even by a hint.*" Who can overstate the importance and solemnity of an occasion, calling from a man of Adams' cautiousness and generally undemonstrative nature, these burning words? At such a moment, when witnessing his bitter grief at trusty men's falling away, and the fickleness of those who had hitherto been his supporters, Adams found the occasion to deepen more than ever his confidence in Washington's purity of heart and patriotism. He was entirely built up in his desire to do right; his close application to discover it, and his deliberate and comprehensive view of his country's affairs with all the world.

Writing at that time, and speaking of men he characterized as "the anti-federalists and the Frenchified zealots," Adams said: "These have nothing now to do that I conceive of, but to ruin his character, destroy his peace, and injure his health. He supports all their attacks with firmness, and his health appears to have been very good." Under the apparent calmness there was bitter chafing of spirit which the discernment of his counsellor and friend failed to see, but which, alas! existed in great intensity. Amid these hours of sad reflection and intense anxiety, the great Chief had to endure what appears to have bordered on studied coldness on the part of one whose counsel might in the emergency have been most helpful. Jefferson more than stood aloof; he manifested an utter lack of sympathy, and to the heart of him whose trials he should have shared, his action must have borne the semblance of cold indifference. Irving tells us that, "While Washington was endeavouring to steer the vessel of State, amid the surges and blasts which were threatening on every side, Jefferson, who had hauled out of the storm, writes serenely from his retirement at Monticello, to his friend, Tenche Cox, at Paris:—

"Your letters give a comfortable view of French affairs, and later events seem to confirm it. Over the foreign powers I am convinced they will triumph completely, and I cannot but hope that that triumph, and the consequent disgrace of the invading tyrants, is destined, in order of events, to kindle the wrath of Europe against those who have dared to embroil them in such wickedness, and to bring at length, kings, nobles, and priests to the scaffolds which they have been so long deluging with human blood. I am still warm whenever I think of these scoundrels, though I do it as seldom as I can, preferring infinitely to contemplate the tranquil growth of my lucerne and potatoes. I have so completely withdrawn myself from these spectacles of usurpation and misrule, that I do not take a single newspaper, nor read one a month; and I feel myself infinitely the happier for it."

Irving remarks that "No one seemed to throw off the toils of office with more delight than Jefferson, or to betake himself with more devotion to the simple occupations of rural life. It was his boast, in a letter to a friend written some time after his return to Monticello, that he had seen no newspaper since he had left Philadelphia, and he should never take another newspaper of any sort. 'I think it is Montaigne,' writes he, 'who has said that ignorance is the softest pillow on which a man can rest his head; I am sure it is true as to everything political, and shall endeavour to estrange myself to everything of that character.' Yet the very next sentence shows the lurking of the old party feud. 'I indulge myself in one political topic only; that is, in declaring to my countrymen the shameless corruption of a portion of the representatives of the first and second Congresses, *and their implicit devotion to the Treasury.*'"

In endeavouring to trace history, justice is a paramount duty. It is but fair towards Jefferson to bear in mind that his able and comprehensive report of the state of American trade with outside countries, specifying the various restrictions and prohibitions which embarrassed, and in some instances almost ruined, its commerce, had as it were closed his labours as Secretary of State. He had been permitted to retire, and an act of Genet's transmitting to him translations of the instructions given him by the Executive Council of France, requesting that the President would lay them before both Houses of Congress, and proposing to transmit successively other papers to be laid before them in like manner, had enabled him to do so with dignity and grace worthy of the great statesman. On the last day of 1793, Jefferson was enabled to inform Genet that he had laid his letter and its accompaniments before the President. "I have it in charge to observe," added he, "that your functions as the missionary of a foreign nation here, are confined to the transaction of the affairs of your nation with the Executive of the United States; that the communications which are to pass between the Executive and legislative branches cannot be a subject for your interference, and that the President must be left to judge for himself what matters his duty or the public good may require him to propose to the deliberations of Congress. I have, therefore, the honour of returning you the copies sent for distribution."

Irving has rightly said, "Such was Jefferson's dignified rebuke of the presumptuous meddling of Genet; and, indeed, his whole course of official proceedings with that minister, notwithstanding his personal intimacy with him and his strong French partialities, is worthy of the highest approbation. Genet, who had calculated on Jefferson's friendship, charged him openly with having a language official and a language confidential; but it certainly was creditable to him, as a public functionary in a place of high trust, that, in his official transactions, he could rise superior to individual prejudices and partialities, and consult only the dignity and interests of his country."

A page from Sharples' memorandum record, inscribed at Mount Vernon, is sorrowfully reminding as to the weariness of spirit endured by Washington at the time of Jefferson's retirement. It runs thus:—

"During our walk from the cottage to Mount Vernon this morning, the Chief's conversation was mainly on what he termed 'Jefferson's desertion of me in an hour of more than perplexity, when everything seemed to run in wrong currents, and, above all, at a time when there were but few friends at hand whose judgment could have been relied on even if they themselves had been trustworthy. I was almost alone, left to bear the studied taunts of men who had been elevated into positions of which they were utterly unworthy, whose aspirations were as limitless as other mere self-seekers, and who in the hour of peril were to be found sneaking under cover, yet ready at any moment to inflict a stab whenever it could in secrecy be ventured.'"

These were indeed piteous words from so great a man, especially from him who had rendered such services to his country. They should, however, be heard, if only to show the greatness of his nature; how in the hour of deep trial he could comfort himself under a good conscience and a serene external placidity—though racking under torture as wholly undeserved as it was uncalled for. But for these outpourings to Sharples, who had evidently more than won his confidence, and to whom it seems to have been a relief to disburden himself, his countrymen would not have had revealed to them his heart's secrets; for history relates that he had been especially sensible of the talents and integrity displayed by Jefferson during the closing year of his secretaryship, and particularly throughout this French perplexity, and had recently made a last attempt, but an unsuccessful one, to persuade him to remain in the cabinet. On the same day as his letter to Genet, Jefferson addressed one to Washington, reminding him of his having postponed his retirement from office until the end of the year. "That term being now arrived," he wrote, "and my propensities to retirement becoming daily more and more irresistible, I now take the liberty of resigning the office into your hands. Be pleased to accept with my sincere thanks for all the indulgences which you have been so good as to exercise towards me in the discharge of its duties. Conscious that my need of them has been great, I have still ever found them greater, without any other claim on my part than a firm pursuit of what has appeared to me to be right, and a thorough disdain of all means which were not as open and honourable as their object was pure. I carry into my retirement a lively sense of your goodness, and shall continue gratefully to remember it."

Washington's acknowledgment, which was as follows, evidences that he made unavailing efforts to induce his continuance in office. "Since it has been impossible to prevent you to forego any longer the indulgence of your desire for private life, the event, however anxious I am to avert it, must be submitted to. But I cannot suffer you to leave your station without assuring you that the opinion which I had formed of your integrity and talents, and which dictated your original nomination, has been confirmed by the fullest experience, and that both have been eminently displayed in the discharge of your duty."

In connection with Jefferson's retirement, which had occasioned such trial, it is gratifying to know that at the close of all, when death had removed the great Patriot from the scenes of mortification and strife, Jefferson, in a few measured and well-chosen words, sketched his comprehensive character, the result of long observation and cabinet experience, and written in after years, when there was no temptation to insincere eulogy:—

"His integrity was most pure; his justice the most inflexible I have ever known; no motive of interest or consanguinity, of friendship or hatred, being able to bias his decision. He was, indeed, in every sense of the word a wise, a good, and a great man."

The action of the Congress which assembled in December 1793, was generally hostile to Washington's intents. At its first meeting there were various causes of irritation acting in the public mind. Genet was busy with his perpetual intrigues; England did not show herself friendly, the old leaven was working in her more than suspicious dealing with America, and there was every indication of approaching war. Washington manifested his fears. In stating the measures he had taken in consequence of the war in Europe to protect the rights and interests of the United States, and maintain peaceful relations with the belligerent parties, he felt it his duty to press upon Congress the necessity of placing the country in a condition of complete defence. How solemn a lesson England has to learn from the ever-to-be-remembered words of the great Patriot, then uttered before the then newly-assembled Parliament of America! If they were needed to such ears, how tenfold applicable to "the old country," not only then, but in all future time. Let every son of Britain hold them near at heart.

"The United States," said he, "ought not to indulge a persuasion that, contrary to the order of human events, they will for ever keep at a distance those painful appeals to arms with which the history of every nation abounds. To avoid insult, we must be able to repel it; to secure peace —one of the most powerful instruments of our prosperity —we must be at all times ready for war."

Washington was the ardent desirer of universal peace. Himself a British subject, forced from her yoke, he saw with British eyes the danger of somnolent unpreparedness, and gives expression to needs peculiarly applicable to the country which so recently had suffered misfortune in being deprived of his citizenship.

Quaint old London has ever been foremost in the van of sympathizers with freedom. Robert Cary, who would have given his life in the cause of Washington, did not stand alone in his deep sympathies with the great Patriot so dear to his soul. One Robert Vaughan, who at eventide smoked the calumet of peace in Cary's quaint dining-room, practically illustrated his devotion by shipping to Mount Vernon a marble chimney-piece, and which now stands there a speaking evidence of the old burgher love of the cause of freedom. Daniel Webster wandered among the haunts of deceased London worthies, where he found food for reflection, and could gauge popularity at its real worth. Who among us does not now realize that we who are removed by the vista of years from the petty passions of his day, reverse the decision arrived at in the lifetime of many public men, and as

CHIMNEY PIECE AT MOUNT VERNON, PRESENTED BY ROBERT VAUGHAN.

we place Webster by the side of Hamilton, we wonder that one age gave being to both?—the interpretation of our day is that the nation, by a fatality of judgment, seemed to have exiled from the insignia, the form, the robe of power, men who ruled without it, causing as it were a dual government to be put in operation—that of place and that of mind.

ROBERT FULTON.

CHAPTER XIII.

Robert Fulton and Sharples, as artists and men of science, close friends during many years—Sketch of Fulton's steam and torpedo discoveries—Sharples' death—The unfinished oil portraits and sketches of female beauties left by Sharples—Vicissitudes through which many passed—Articles from the Boston papers—Testimony of the Rev. Henry Ward Beecher and Dr. Poole, Librarian of Chicago—The portraits' reception at Chicago, St. Paul, Cincinnati, and Philadelphia—Articles from the Chicago, Philadelphia, and Cincinnati papers—Testimony of Charles Henry Hart and W. G. Baker, of Philadelphia—Washington's high sense of duty in dealing with public appointments—Defence of Washington in the case of André from the charges preferred by historians—Washington's illness and death—Proceedings in the National Legislature consequent on his death—Rev. Dr. Bancroft on Washington.

AMERICA has allowed the name of Fulton to drop in a degree through the gridiron by which she usually tests her greatest sons. Undoubtedly he was the pioneer in the application of steam power to purposes of navigation, and therefore ranks among the highest of the world's discoverers. He was a man of the greatest practical genius, and despite that a hundred years have passed into the abyss since he made his discoveries, yet in the matter of torpedoes the nations of the world are only just waking up to the knowledge that he lived. In the most important feature, that of a submarine vessel for war purposes, he was entirely successful; and it is matter of history that he produced a torpedo which destroyed a vessel anchored in the Bay of New York. The French and English Governments, in common with that of his native country, failed in realizing the true nature and power of his inventions, though they were none the less important through their obtusity. At the time, his torpedo was looked upon, not as a substitute for the ordinary modes of warfare, but as a useful and powerful addition to the black-beetle ravages had to be transferred to new canvases; and one, a portrait of Mrs. Roger Morris, the Mary Phillipse, Washington's early love, was painted by Middleton, and is possessed of remarkable beauty. It is not known how it came into Sharples' possession; most probably for requested purpose of restoration. Sharples worked upon it, Maclise completing.

In the instance of these heads of female beauties said to have been "rubbed in" by Sharples during visits to Governeur Morris, the Van Ransalaers, and also in Philadelphia and Baltimore, which "rubs in" were at his death, as stated, taken to England and sold by his widow; very successful transfers to new canvases were accomplished under the advice of Maclise given by Macready in regard to them. Sharples himself never attached money value to these, for the reason that the amount of work needed to make *pictures* of them always loomed as a spectre before his eyes. But for his love of Hamilton, and not a little through happy remembrance of the handsome women themselves—he being a man very alive to the charms of the "form divine" and "fascination of the witching countenance"—the "rubbings" would most likely have given place to other heads on the canvases. As Maclise said of these beautiful women, "Any one will recognize them as in the best manner of Romney. The painter Sharples evidently aimed to follow his master, Romney. Each head is treated in thorough Romney style." Fond associations running back to Washington and to Hamilton, greatly endeared these to him, as they recalled to mind many happy balls at Philadelphia, Baltimore, and New York,—hence these little else than skeleton sketches being held on to in the manner evidenced to the day of his death. Robert Cary must have purchased them of Mrs. Sharples; they do not appear to have fallen under the cruel hammer of the auctioneer who disposed of the American historian

Dunlap for the equivalent of a few dollars. In themselves, the "rubbings" were of little value. Washington Irving had seen them when in England; he too was amenable to female beauty, and probably when away from home felt that Sharples had done well in selection as in promise of intention. Washington Irving felt that something could be done with them. Macready knew Irving well when in America, and was enabled to enlist his deepest sympathy in the interesting work. Charles Leupp, of New York, at that time well off in the world, persuaded Macready to interest himself in the "rubbings," and Maclise stood more than a friend in working them up as he did.

It seems little short of a miracle that these charming relics of an eventful historical past, of ever-increasing interest and value in hereafter time, should have escaped, and be in condition for perfect handing down. Maclise's beautiful work upon them, though retaining all the bold and classic style of Sharples' master Romney, is strongly evidenced in each; they are as fresh as though of yesterday's execution, and the beauteous ones themselves seem to look out of the canvases overjoyed at their renewed existence. It seems sad to dream of dividing them. They, as girls and women, loved each other after the fashion of rivals in ball assemblies, they voyaged together across the seas, and passed through Maclise's fickle mint ordeal without a murmur, and are now a collection of charming women, discoursing eloquently of one of the most eventful periods of the world's history. Marvellous has been the providence watching over them. Dunlap in his History complains of Sharples' widow having ruthlessly sold his portrait with a lot of others of his countrymen by auction, at Bath, in England. Who cares for Dunlap having passed under the hammer, so long as posterity has been bequeathed the precious legacy of the portraits this volume brings under notice? To have knocked down these fair houris would have been cruelly ungallant, and a national calamity.

In Boston the Sharples' portraits met with great honour at the hands of General Loring, the able and accomplished President of the Art Museum, who with the earnestness for which he is proverbial, collected as companions for the occasion the well-known portraits of the Chief by Peale, Copley, and other artists, hanging the entire collection together, chivalrously awarding the place of honour to the newly arrived visitors, who were ranged side by side with the prized paintings by Stuart; the whole forming a galaxy such as had never before been seen in the city of art and refinement. Among the earliest visitors was Charles Wendell Holmes, who was intensely charmed with the Sharples' revelation, and was almost a daily visitor during the period of their stay. Mr. Clements, the editor of the *Boston Transcript*, was the first of the eager throng, and on the following morning thus heralded the new-comers :—

A NEW WASHINGTON.

(From the Boston Transcript.)

"What rejoicing would there not be if a new portrait of Shakspeare, which Shakspeare's wife pronounced the best ever taken and which bore the inherent evidence of being the work of a trained and able artist, should be brought to light! What joy must patriotic Americans feel over a new portrait of George Washington, similarly well attested! We realize this in the Sharples' portraits of Washington. The fame of these pictures of Pater Patriæ and his wife has occasionally reached this country through the reports of cultivated travellers; but here we now have for a short while— it should be for ever—all three of these precious paintings, a full front and a profile of General Washington, and a profile of Mrs Washington.

All portraits of Washington must fight their way to popular favour against the familiar one of Stuart. So ingrained is this in the affections and veneration of generations, that it is the ideal Washington—the standard, in fact, by which all others are estimated. The Sharples portraits have the good fortune to 'fit in' with the standard Stuart—to supplement it, in effect, with realistic detail, and hence to carry conviction that it is near the truth as to its subject. There are some obvious allowances to be made for Stuart's original—the high colour, for instance; nobody's cheeks were ever so rosy or eyes so blue as Washington's are portrayed in the Stuart. Again, the expression is preternaturally majestic, a fortunate and a noble fault, to be sure. In this age, however, art seeks more and more to come at the very facts, and too much of dignity and ideality is apt to bring upon itself a reaction of scoffing. But let it be understood that Sharples' Washington is not lacking in the blended loftiness, purity, and sweetness of Stuart's, while adding thereto a visible element of virile force and human energy which must have belonged to the victorious general of our desperate arms, but which has to be imagined under the serene exterior Stuart has left us.

Ample evidence exists that Mr. Sharples had a habit of succeeding both in art and in society. He was evidently the fashion in the American high life of the beginning of the century."

The *Boston Traveller* was equally marked in its treatment:—

"The Sharples pictures of Washington have created a very proper sensation. We have never cared for the counterfeit presentments of the Father of his Country. They generally represent him as a man who might go through life saying 'prunes and prisms.' In most of his pictures the unlying youth is represented as having developed himself into a great master of moral deportment. He always is made to look 'fixed up'—features and all. He wears his nose as if it was only by a tremendous muscular effort that he kept it from turning up at the rest of humanity. His lips generally have the pursed-up look of a man who is always spitting out tiny shreds of morals. Now the Sharples portraits do nothing of the kind. General Washington unbent to Sharples; and Sharples was artist enough to fix the likeness of the unbent President on to canvas. The portrait of Martha Washington in her every-day clothes is a profile, and full of sweetness and dignity. As likenesses, these portraits were considered in their day the best ever made of the Washingtons. They certainly give one a stronger impression of life behind them than do the delicious pink-and-white portraits by Stuart."

From the Boston Courier.

"The Sharples Washington pictures as works of art are invaluable, the flesh-tints good, the modelling excellent, and the general execution, if possibly a thought formal, beautifully clear and direct As portraits the three pictures are simply inestimable, and the comparison between the pictures of Sharples and those of Stuart, by the side of which they are now at the Museum placed, is in the highest degree interesting. Whatever be the ultimate decision which artist has best portrayed his sitter, the fact is indisputable that the Sharples full-face view is far more human, alive, and vivacious than the Stuart. In Washington Irving's words, 'the Sharples portrait gives a better idea of the innate energy of Washington's character.'

It is to be hoped that by some happy circumstance they may ultimately be owned in this country."

From the Boston Herald.

"The Sharples paintings show the trained and practised artist but they are also marked by an individuality which speaks eloquently of their faithfulness as likenesses. Compared with the Stuarts they are bolder, more solid, and more grey in tone. The full-face of Washington shows him to be a man of force, dignity, and strength. There is none of the narrowness which the face by Stuart has always seemed to us to indicate. If true, it seemed brought into offensive prominence, or what may be termed, in a certain sense, priggishness. Stuart, too, in his love of colour, may well be supposed to have exaggerated the ruddy hue of Washington's face. In the Sharples portraits, however, this excess of colour is less marked, and the whole tone of the head is rather grey and harmonious. For a strong, heroic manhood, one would prefer the Sharples type to the Stuart, and, indeed, it seems more consistent with the life, career, and acts of the man. As to the portrait of Lady Washington, the Sharples profile, it is simple, charming, and characteristic; yet we cannot put it before the Stuart, with its exquisite delicacy of complexion and feature, and its suggestion of a gentle mien, united with a firm and lofty nature. There is a like indication of this character in the Sharples picture. It is unmistakable in the carriage of the head and the expression of the small part of the face that is visible. This picture is supplementary and emphatically corroborative of the Stuart. The typical Lady Washington lace cap and muslin neckerchief appear in the Sharples portrait. They are painted with skill and grace, and give a charm to the picture which no change of fashion can ever destroy."

From the Boston Post.

"The portrait of Martha Washington, a profile, is a picture of rare sweetness and purity, a face to admire and to love. It is painted with a nicety and delicacy of touch that is in the highest degree charming. The whole three are certainly very fine works of art. In some respects they are not inferior—heresy though it be to say it—to our much admired and much loved Stuarts. One cannot fail, however, to notice in general characteristics the striking similarity of likeness between the works of the two artists, and this would seem to be pretty conclusive evidence of the faithfulness of the portraiture in both cases. The work of Sharples lacks somewhat in the grace and the pure, charming quality inherent in the Stuarts, but it presents us with fully as striking likenesses. The faces are firmly and carefully modelled, and while the flesh tones give an indication of the ruddiness of the Stuart portraits, it is in a greatly modified degree, that seems much more natural, life-like, and pleasing. The full-face portrait is very impressive. The features are strongly marked, the expression is very pronounced, and we are shown a man of vigour, of determination, of dignity almost amounting to austerity. The real man seems revealed to us as in no other portrait that we have seen. These Sharples pictures would be a priceless acquisition to our art museum, to hang for ever beside the Stuarts, and would grow in value, interest and attractiveness as the years go by. They would be an inspiration in art and in patriotism that would far out-value any sum of money that might be paid for them."

Arrived at Chicago, they were welcomed by the late Thomas Hoyne, one of the pioneers in Chicago's greatness. The fair city Hoyne had so zealously aided to re-create from the fire of annihilation, never boasted of a nobler or more patriotic citizen. They were introduced with great honour by N. K. Fairbank, Franklin MacVeagh, Professor

Fraser of the University, ex-Governor Bross, W. G. Hibbard, F. D. Gray, and others. The Rev. Professor David Swing, one of the most gifted pulpit orators living, was their willing sponsor in the Western Metropolis, receiving the paintings at his own residence, which he threw open for a whole day to guests specially invited by him to a reception in their honour. Edgar L. Wakeman, representative in Chicago of the *Louisville Gazette*, manifested an earnestness in their behalf not exceeded by any of the many warm adherents who flocked to their standard. He was unceasing in urging friends to attend the *levées* and enjoy the presence of the paintings, from which, as he publicly expressed, he had himself derived gratification exceeding anything he had ever before experienced. Edgar Wakeman was as warm in his devotion to their English representative, a stranger, as to the portraits themselves.

It was during their stay in Chicago that the Rev. Henry Ward Beecher, of New York, visited the portraits, he being there lecturing at the time. They were specially for him placed under the electric light. His inspection was a prolonged one, and he expressed himself in terms of warmest delight, remarking, "*I have enjoyed these portraits far more than I can express. Here, indeed, we see Washington! They must never be permitted to leave the country. No other has any right in them. I am not as much impressed with the profile as with Martha, but neither can ever die so long as these portraits exist. Whoever looks upon them must feel in the actual presence of the living man.*"

W. F. Poole, LL.D., Librarian of the Chicago Public Library (author of the wondrous volume, "Index to Periodical Literature," a monument of the untiring patience, industry, and great ability of the writer), who for many years had charge of the Stuart Portraits of Washington at the Athenæum, Boston, issued the following :—

"Public Library, Chicago, Dec. 24, 1882.

"I have examined the original portraits of Washington and Mrs. Washington, by Sharples, with delight, and with a feeling of surprise that pictures of so great merit, often seen and described by travellers in England, are so little known in this country, even by persons who have given special attention to the portraits of Washington. It is, indeed, a great privilege that we are able to see them in Chicago.

Our ideas as to the faces of Washington and his wife are derived chiefly from the portraits by Stuart, the celebrated originals of which, owned by the Boston Athenæum, are now deposited in the Art Museum in Boston. For thirteen years, when Librarian of the Boston Athenæum, the Stuart originals were in my charge, and, in my supreme admiration of their merits, I had not imagined that any portraits could challenge comparison with them. As an artistic and almost inspired treatment of the subjects, I still think that the Stuart pictures have no rivals; but as actual portraits of a real man and a real woman, I am ready to confess that the Sharples portraits are the more satisfactory. The latter, besides having great artistic merits, are a commentary on and interpretation of the former. The mouth of Washington in the Stuart is vague and uncertain; in the Sharples, taken earlier in life, it is distinct and well-formed, giving a thoughtful and energetic expression to the face. The colouring of Stuart is so brilliant as to suggest the query whether roses and lilies were ever so blended in the human countenance as in that of the Father of his Country. In Sharples we see precisely what his complexion was. The same treatment of Stuart in Mrs. Washington's picture we accept without a question; for we are glad to believe that in her face she was the most brilliant of her sex, as she was confessedly in character and accomplishments, the most lovely woman in her day. Sharples' treatment of her complexion was less gallant, and in a lower key; but, doubtless, and alas! as it looked to his English and realistic eye—a beautiful woman, nevertheless.

In standing before the Sharples portraits, and vividly remembering the Stuart pictures, I was especially gratified to see that each of these great painters confirms the other, though painting at different times, with different national sentiments, and from different standpoints. The Sharples portraits ought to find a permanent home in the United States.   W. F. POOLE."

In common with all other places in which the portraits were exhibited to the citizens, the Press of Chicago was unanimous as to their merits and historical value. A few only of the articles can now be reproduced.

From the Chicago Tribune.

" Lovers of art and of their country will be glad to learn that Chicago is honoured in a visit of the celebrated Sharples portraits of General Washington and his wife Martha, painted by the English artist of that name in 1796. They have already been exhibited in New York and Boston, and excited the admiration of connoisseurs, particularly in the latter city, where they were given place among other notable portraits of the Father of his Country hung in the Boston Fine Art Museum. The paintings are three in number, two of them being portraits of the General, one a full face, the other a profile. The former presents him in full military uniform, giving animated expression to his native dignity and majesty of carriage and bearing; while the other represents him in ordinary evening dress, and commends itself at once for its combined simplicity and manly energy and conspicuous force of character. The portrait of Martha, his devoted wife, alike the sharer of his trials and his honours, is eminently winning and gracious, representing her in quiet and matronly garb, full of mingled sweetness and light, and seemingly transfusing into the surrounding atmosphere some of her own womanliness and tender affection and grace."

From the Inter Ocean.

"The celebrated Sharples portraits of General and Lady Washington, now brought to this country, recommend themselves warmly to the interest and affection of our people. There are two likenesses of the General, one a face picture, one a profile. The latter is perhaps a finer picture, artistically considered, and appeals more to our appreciation of Washington. It is the former picture which comes into direct comparison with the pictures of him engraved from the Stuart, Peale, and other portraits which we are accustomed to see. There is always something a little aggravating in the benignity of the usual pictures of Washington. While one acknowledges fully their strength and beauty, they give one an idea of intrusiveness in his benignity. Before them one remembers instinctively the little boy who never told a lie. The feeling comes unbidden of a sort of assertion of virtue. 'He poses,' as the French say. In the Sharples portrait there is none of this misinterpretation. The full force and grace of his noble and dignified manhood is felt.

Engravings of this picture should go into every home and school-room in this country, to give new impulse to the patriotic reverence which we feel for the Father of his Country.

The portrait of Lady Washington is marked by singular sweetness and dignity, and accompanies most fittingly the portrait of her husband. These portraits ought never to be allowed to leave Chicago, if there is money enough in the pockets of one or more public-spirited citizens to buy them. These are the best portraits of Washington, and would form a noble nucleus for that collection which is certain to be formed here within the next decade or two. It would be a gift to the city which might make some man's name always gratefully remembered."

From the Chicago Weekly Magazine.

"Who that has looked upon those grand old portraits of General and Lady Washington, and then gone out into the busy thoroughfare, but has felt the better for the half hour in their presence! Painted from life by the acute, observing artist, they give back to us something more than we can get from any of the counterfeit presentments which have made the face of our first President familiar to every schoolboy. Walk through the gallery of old Independence Hall at Philadelphia, where the portraits of the men illustrious in Continental times are enshrined, or the Museum in Boston where the Stuart pictures of Washington hang, and those pink and white faces in powdered wigs that look out of faded frames do not make us feel as if we would like to have known the men. In the Sharples portraits the artist caught the General when 'off duty.' We see the man, not the President, and exclaim, as Emerson did: 'I would gladly have crossed the Atlantic to behold these inestimable paintings—our true Washingtons! Future ages will glory in their existence!'

What enthusiasm Longfellow and Washington Irving and Bryant felt at sight of these portraits is attested in autograph letters. President Arthur placed the grand drawing-room at the White House at their disposal, where they drew such a coterie of guests as any queen might be proud of; poets, artists, historians, critics, lawyers, jurists, preachers and eminent citizens, all came to honour and admire the Father of his Country, who lives again in these canvases."

During the period of the paintings' stay in Chicago, they received several visits from Colonel the Honourable William F. Vilas, the great orator of the North-West, a loyal worshiper at their shrine, who eagerly avails of every opportunity to pay reverent duty. Colonel Vilas is a New Englander, and has been wisely selected by President Cleveland to be of his Cabinet. Since the days of the mighty Daniel Webster, America has not produced any man of higher oratorical power than Vilas. Associated with him in the earliest acquaintance and appreciation of the Sharples Washingtons was Colonel James-Knight, of Madison, Illinois, a man of high culture and refinement, who has rendered his country good service in the regular army.

President Cleveland, desirous of marking the period of his Presidency, hoped to secure in Washington city a grand display of the portraits of the fair charmers who in the Patriot's day graced his Court. The realization is deferred, pending the hoped-for acquisition of the portrait of Robert Fulton. Whenever it comes off, it must prove attractive beyond precedent.

Great appreciation fell to the portraits in Philadelphia

during a short rest in Earle's Gallery. On arrival they were welcomed by Charles Henry Hart, Wm. S. Baker, and others, and during their Court holding were visited by many thousands of persons.

Charles Henry Hart, an eminent lawyer and writer of Philadelphia, gifted as a scholar and literary man of highest refinement, a leader in the Council of the Pennsylvania Art Academy, and a recognized authority throughout America in everything appertaining to Washington portraiture and history, proved their loving henchman in this delightful city of culture and refinement. Charles H. Hart has recorded of the Sharples as follows:—

"Philadelphia, 5 mo. 4, 1883.

Familiar as I am with the portraiture of Washington, and well acquainted with the pastel portraits made by Sharples, I feared that though I might find some interest in the Sharples oil paintings of Washington and his wife (known to have been in England since the time of their execution by Sharples for his friend, Mr. Cary, in London), yet that I should find them so deficient in artistic merit that their value as likenesses would necessarily be greatly diminished. I am glad to say that in this I was agreeably surprised, as they are decidedly meritorious as works of art, and the three-quarter face portrait in military costume gives especially every indication of being *a likeness*. In its lines it is not very dissimilar to the Houdon bust, the Pine portrait, and that by Savage, which, to my mind, is good evidence that *it is like the living man;* in other words, it is a life-like portrait. Its unlikeness to the *ideal* Boston Athenæum portrait by Stuart is no argument against its correctness; for that picture can impress no calm, thoughtful student of the subject with the feelings that it is *a likeness* of the man. Stuart's Washington is a great painter's one great failure. CHARLES HENRY HART."

W. S. Baker, of Philadelphia, author of a handsomely printed volume of over 200 pages in royal quarto, "The Engraved Portraits of Washington, with Notices of the Originals and brief Biographical Sketches of the Painters," published by Lindsay and Baker, Philadelphia; and also author of "The Antiquity of Engraving, and the Utility and Pleasure of Prints," and of a work, "William Sharp, Engraver, and his Works;" also, "American Engravers and their Works,"—a literate who has devoted his time to matters bearing on Washington, has thus publicly observed in regard to the Sharples Washingtons:—

"Philadelphia, April 21, 1884.

The sight of the autotypes of the two portraits of Washington and that of Martha Washington, by Sharples, renews the pleasant surprise of twelve months ago when I examined the originals.

While the profile was familiar to me through pastel copies made by the painter, the military portrait was entirely new, and I found both to be much superior in artistic merit to what I had expected. The profile I have always considered an admirable likeness, and the full-face not only impressed me as a decided portrait, but as the work of an artist of no mean pretensions, simple in treatment, and harmonious in colour.

I regret that these canvases are not retained in this country, as they would be a valuable addition to our knowledge of Washington portraiture, which, so far as the public is concerned, is limited in painting to the Stuart head; something to admire, but we imagine not so faithful in presentment as the Sharples, the Pine, or the Savage, all which profess similar characteristics and traits in common with the Houdon bust, an undoubted portrait.

WILLIAM S. BAKER."

The *Philadelphia Record*, speaking of the portraits' arrival in that city, observed:—

"How deeply interesting is everything bearing upon the Sharples Washington portraits. How Sharples, a successful English portrait painter, being here in 1796, was commissioned by Robert Cary, Washington's confidant and English agent, to put the General's face and form on canvas, in order that the Cary family might have them to all time; how Washington gave the artist sittings at Mount Vernon, dressed in his Continental uniform, and how successful Sharples was. He finished the first portrait late one afternoon, Washington sitting to the end. Then Washington dressed for dinner. When he returned, Sharples, who was touching his portrait here and there, struck by his æsthetic costume, asked to be allowed to paint him in it. The good-natured hero consented, and the result was another good portrait—this time in profile. Mrs. Washington had taken a great interest in the artist's work. When it was finished she was so well pleased with it that she paid him a handsome fee to paint a portrait of herself, to be sent to England with those of her husband. Sharples was as successful with this as with the others. They were excellent portraits, realistic to the last degree, and better in some respects than that of Stuart. The Cary family has exhibited them ever since with great pride. Many distinguished Americans who have been abroad have seen and approved them. Washington Irving declared that he had never known the great General until he saw these portraits. He wanted to make drawings of them for his 'Life of Washington,' but a clause in their deed of settlement prevented it. Emerson, when beholding these portraits in their English home, quietly remarked, *apropos* of the portrait of Mrs. Washington, 'What a blessing, Martha, you unexpectedly conferred on your country;' and so said the rest. But, by-and-by, the Cary family settlement ran out through efflux of time, and the famous portraits came home to America to see and be seen. They are out West now, giving the pork packers and the grain brokers a chance to bid for them. It wouldn't be such a bad investment for a pork packer. He would become famous in the art world in a day. The first man who saw the portraits on their return to this country was President Arthur. The English gentleman who brought them out called on the President. He told the President their story, and then said that he would like to have his Excellency see them. 'I shall be glad to,' said the President. 'But,' urged the representative, 'you must receive them in state. They have been owned in England well-nigh a hundred years, and now that they're here I have made it my first business to come and see you, and we expect you to receive them formally, that is, in a manner befitting your high office and becoming their position in the eyes of the world.' 'H'm,' said the President, adding, doubtfully, 'I don't know about my engagements.' 'Well, then,' said the gentleman, 'if unfortunately it should be inconvenient to your Excellency to render the honour their English owners consider to be their due, they will have to voyage back to England without being unboxed.' 'That's pretty stiff,' said the President thoughtfully; 'but I like your manner, and I'll do what you ask.' And he did it, like the true patriot and gentleman he is; and President Arthur has the satisfaction and pleasure of having given them a right royal welcome. They were exhibited in the Blue Parlour, and the President and members of the Cabinet paid their respects to these grand memorials of the nation's early days."

A story went the round of the papers at the time, stating that the President had a grand supper for a select party of friends in this said Blue Parlour, on the evening with the

Washingtons, and that the gratification of himself and guests was unbounded. On the night following, his Excellency passed some hours alone with the pictures; the number of cigar stumps said to have been collected in the morning was clear evidence that President Arthur's interview with the father of his country was a prolonged one. This was the newspaper gossip at the time of the pictures being in Washington.

To meet the wishes of one of America's most gifted sons, J. A. Wheelock, editor and co-proprietor of the *Pioneer Press*, the portraits journeyed on to St. Paul and Minneapolis, resting awhile in Milwaukie. Providentially, their departure had been accidentally delayed, or they would have been burnt up in that horrible human holocaust fire in the Milwaukie Hotel, where they would just have arrived. Happily a better fate awaited them in a worthy reception at the hands of the Honourable C. L. Colby, William Plankinton, R. G. Frackelton and their gifted wives. St. Paul and Chicago were, perhaps, of the few cities to which they journeyed, the places in which they seemed most at home; certainly they were nowhere more appreciated. In St. Paul especially they enjoyed an ovation from first to last. J. A. Wheelock may be said to have been their Grand High Chamberlain from the hour of entering the railway depôt until they finally took leave. He received them, and officiated at their departure. He was daily in the presence chamber, and afterwards, having voyaged to England, looked in at their English home in Sussex, hoping to render further homage. J. A. Wheelock, a man of rare attractions and loving character, admittedly one of the most finished writers of the great North-West, rejoices in a treasured wife of marked attractions, of the family of the mighty orator, Daniel Webster. It was Wheelock's influence that drew the portraits so long a distance from their base, well rewarded, however, in the enthusiastic reception experienced in the beautifully located and stirring city owing him so much, where they rejoiced to tarry, and where they enjoyed the bounteous hospitality of that truly public-spirited and true patriot, President J. J. Hill, owner of the Sharples portraits of Jefferson, Adams, and Munroe. President Hill and his earnestly patriotic wife paid great honour to the Father of his Country and Martha during their sojourn in St. Paul, and it is matter of much regret that the occasion could not then be availed of to exhibit the portraits in company with the several ex-Presidents whose portraits by Sharples President Hill is the worthy owner.

The good Bishop Whipple, of Minnesota, yielded to no man in his veneration for the portraits. When in St. Paul, they proved an almost daily attraction to him; he was unceasing in urging friends to seize the opportunity of viewing them. Bishop Whipple wrote very earnestly regarding them, especially pointing out in forcible language that none of the other portraits of Washington disclosed to him the religious light of the Patriot's character, and which he realized so vividly in the Sharples portraits.

Murat Halstead, one of the most brilliant writers in America, was their sponsor in Cincinnati. As chief editor he heralded their arrival in a leading article in the *Cincinnati Gazette*:—

" He who sees the portraits of Washington by Sharples feels that he is looking upon a true likeness of the Father of his Country. In like manner does the portrait of Martha Washington impress the beholder with its life-like truth. And this, in its naturalness, and in the quaint cap and kerchief, is a nobler face than any which the artists have made in the idealizations of her portrait. She looks like the peer of so great a man, and as if every inch a queen.

There is a lack of confidence in the universal pictures of

Washington, in the feeling that the disposition of artists to improve on the portrait of a great man to equal his fame, has made it a process of evolution; but in these portraits, taken by an English artist of high character, at the time when each was sixty-four years of age, and with their authenticity beyond all question, the beholder can see the man and the woman as they looked living.

They are also of the high art of portrait painting, lifelike in expression, admirable in colouring, and the features standing out from the canvas like sculpture. Two paintings of Washington, one in front, the other in profile, complete the view. To the American these must be the most interesting of all portraits, and this interest will increase with time. The fame of Washington will never die, and succeeding generations will more and more desire to see how the Father of his Country looked.

Nor is this interest American alone. The whole world recognized the greatness of Washington's character. It is hardly less esteemed by the English, to whose Government he was a rebel, than by his countrymen. This happy fortune in fame among political enemies has no parallel. By the civilized world Washington is recognized as the grandest character of his century, if not of all history.

Nor is this greatness the evolution of tradition. It was recognized by his contemporaries and by the whole world while he lived. It is established by contemporary history. We have records of what was charged upon him by truculent party hostility in times of hot excitement. Out of all this does he come with a pure and more exalted character.

His country is the monument of his greatness, alike in its independence and in its National Union. No one can say with confidence that the first could have been gained without the confidence in Washington which held the troops when the feeble Government had almost abandoned them, or without the military ability which achieved much with small means; nor that the last could have been established without Washington's statesmanship and unbounded popularity. The people's confidence in him overcame their jealousy of newly written forms of government.

In a larger sense than we think when we repeat the familiar ascription, was Washington the Father of his Country, and First in War, First in Peace, and First in the Hearts of his Countrymen. The affection and admiration of his countrymen have a solid foundation in the greatness of his character. Every American wants to look upon his likeness. In these portraits he can feel that he sees the veritable man, and the woman who was a fitting mate. They should be owned in America, and placed where generation after generation of Americans may come to behold them."

This eminent writer, recurring to the subject in a second leading article in the same journal, further wrote:—

"One's interest and enthusiasm are increased by a familiarity with these portraits, and to those who have never seen a veritable painting of Washington from life, the present opportunity is one for which they may be highly grateful. The feeling is one of agreeable disappointment, that of seeing the 'Father of his Country' (we speak of the three-quarter view) in a plain, every-day expression of face, not the least forbidding to the humblest member of his great democratic family, yet full of noble dignity and sweetness, to command equally respect and love. Stuart's Washington is a 'Father' for 'State occasions,' to which suspicion attaches that the artist had induced an attitudinizing of features of the 'prunes and prisms' order which he never truly wore. That his mien upon occasion was more grave and mysterious than here represented, is possible; but the intense honesty of this portrait, removed from the faintest pencil stroke of flattery, and yet so lofty and so tender, touches the heart of the natural man as we had never thought possible. A hundred years are annihilated, and he is—an undreamed-of pleasure—our own flesh and blood Washington of to-day.

That there is not all in this face in point of character that Washington possessed, we may concede. It requires a very great master to accomplish so much as to give the highest expression of character with the literal features of his subject; nevertheless, it is, while simple in expression, noble in character and artistic in treatment. The soft depth of the eyes, in colour and in feeling, is quite unusual. The frills and pale yellow collar of the charming old Continental coat and the yellow epaulettes, give a touch of colour not in either of the other portraits, each of which are profiles. The steely-gray of the high cap and neckerchief of plain Mrs. Washington give a severity in tone that would be very trying to a less kindly face; and even for her, pleased as one may be to see her, as well as the General, in the *pendant* portrait, in every-day costume, yet one could wish a silver touch of colour in the soft head- and neck-wear. The familiarity of the profile of Washington comes from the fact that it is like a photograph of the Houdin statue of Washington at Richmond, Va. All in all, one is quite willing to believe, with the members of the Washington family, that 'the Sharples portraits were by far the best and truest representations' of the noble pair. We may esteem ourselves most fortunate that these portraits should remain where they fitly belong—in our own country. They should be the property of the nation most emphatically."

From the "Philadelphia Press."

Opportunities for public benefaction are constantly arising, and the family of Dives, more than ever in the history of humanity, are awaking to the fact that, since they cannot take their treasures with them into the unseen, they can make no better disposition of them than to dedicate them to some public interest. The time is coming when, instead of waiting for death to bring an uncertain issue to their projected posthumous plans, they will see the infinitely greater pleasure to be gained by taking charge of their own donations. Suppose some public-spirited man should build a really beautiful bridge across the Schuylkill, what better monument could he raise for his own glory and the glory of his city?

Every day, fashionable people squander small fortunes in giving dinner-parties, the only fruit of which are indigestions and headaches. A hundred citizens of Philadelphia might spend only their surplus in wise charity, instead of heaping it up to be dissipated by spendthrift heirs.

At the present time there is a peculiarly tempting chance for some philanthropist. There are on exhibition at Earle's galleries three paintings which ought to find a permanent home in this city. They are the portraits of George Washington and his wife, painted by Sharples in 1796. One of the three represents the general in military dress; the other in that of the civilian. The third is a delightful picture of Martha Washington, in simple home attire in mob cap and lace. It is the universal testimony of all who have seen these portraits, that they are the most attractive of all that have been painted. Washington Irving, thirty years ago, wrote that it was a matter for national regret that the Sharples Washington portrait, which was exhibited in New York at that time, could not be allowed to rest in America. The legal difficulties which then stood in the way have been removed, and the English family into whose possession they have come are willing to part with them for a fair consideration.

America is certainly " the natural home " for such masterpieces, and they ought to be so placed that they should be familiar objects to the rising generations. It would at first thought seem appropriate to have them at the National Capitol, but in many respects this would be inadvisable. The risk of destruction or damage is too great. No better place could be found for them than in the Philadelphia Academy of the Fine Arts. Why should not some wealthy citizen, or a few wealthy citizens, prevent the further wandering of these noble works of art? The gain to the city would be obvious, and the fame that would result to the donors would be enduring.

From the " Cincinnati News."

The Sharples Washingtons are truly nationals. The principal portrait represents almost a full front view of the Father of his Country in his general's uniform. The second is a profile in the evening dress of the period. The portrait of Lady Washington is also a profile. In all the modelling is beautifully soft, without losing anything of the character or precision of line which makes one feel that these portraits must be likenesses. The colouring is not high, but impresses one with the same sense of exactness and truth that is felt in the drawing. The accessories, draperies, and background are finely simple and subordinated to the faces. In fact, each portrait, as a whole, is so simply and unpretentiously painted that it takes a conscious effort to direct the attention to the way the work is done. The best description of the pictures would be the effect which they produce upon the beholder, were that describable. One hardly feels like sitting in the presence of these pictures. Looking at these calm, benignant, gracious faces, with their evidences of thought, experience, culture, and power, one can realize something of human perfectibility, the possibility of fully rounded manhood and womanhood, of which the fractional lives most of us lead seem but the shadow. Here is the best that the old world has of blood, culture, and power, with the superadded influence and incitement of a new world at its most eventful period. It is not a difficult matter, looking at this portrait, to understand why Washington—like Cæsar in the act, but purer and more sincere in the motive—had to put aside a kingly crown. If ever there was an uncrowned king, this was he. We earnestly trust there is every prospect of these grand old national portraits being left to rest in America, their proper home. The English owners are presumed to prefer the pictures continuing to be held there, though we confess it appears to us on narrow, prejudiced grounds. The pictures were painted in America, and if Mr. Cary had lived to see their universal appreciation here, he would gladly have restored them to this nation. It seems to be an act of barbarism to withhold these portraits from the people of this country, and we hesitate to believe in their probable return. There are thousands of individual patriots in this, the native home of the portraits, who are ready and willing to buy them, ay, and give more dollars for them than the entire British nation could get subscribed for the purpose. Any city in America will find the money. To talk of their going back to England is idle nonsense. What do we care about the British National Portrait Gallery being without a Washington? Let it get one where it can, but it must not be allowed to annex the Sharples portraits.

The writer feels he would be wanting in duty if he omitted recording in this volume Washington's high sense of honour and rectitude in reference to public appointments, so abundantly evidenced by his letter to Mr. Carter, who had married his niece.

In another letter to a gentleman, soliciting an appointment for a friend, he wrote:—

"From the moment when the necessity had become more apparent," said he, "and as it were inevitable, I anticipated, with a heart filled with distress, the ten thousand embarrassments, perplexities, and troubles to which I must again be exposed in the evening of a life already nearly consumed in public cares. Among all these anxieties, I will not conceal from you, I anticipated none greater than those that were likely to be produced by applications for appointments to the different offices, which would be created under the new Government. Nor will I conceal, that my apprehensions have already been but too well justified. Scarcely a day passes in which applications of one kind or another do not arrive; insomuch that, had I not early adopted some general principles, I should before this time have been wholly occupied in this business. As it is, I have found the number of answers, which I have been necessitated to give in my own hand, an almost insupportable burden to me."

"The points in which all these answers have agreed in substance are, that, should it be my lot to go again into public office, I would go without being under any public engagement of any nature whatsoever; that so far as I know my own heart, I would not be in the remotest degree influenced, in making nominations, by motives arising from the ties of family or blood; and that, on the other hand, three things, in my opinion, ought principally to be regarded, namely, the fitness of characters to fill offices, the comparative claims from the former merits and sufferings in service of the different candidates, and the distribution of appointments in as equal a proportion as might be to persons belonging to the different States in the Union. Without precautions of this kind, I clearly foresaw the endless jealousies, and possibly the fatal consequences, to which a Government, depending altogether on the good will of the people for its establishment, would certainly be exposed in its early stages. Besides, I thought, whatever the effect might be in pleasing or displeasing any individuals at the present moment, a due concern for my own reputation, not less decisively than a sacred regard to the interests of the community, required that I should hold myself absolutely at liberty to act, while in office, with a sole reference to justice and the public good."

In practice he verified these declarations, acting in every case with perfect independence, looking first to the national interests, and next to the best means of promoting them, and admitting no other ground of preference between candidates, whose pretensions were in other respects equal, than that of former efforts and sacrifices in serving their country.

WASHINGTON'S SEALS, WATCH, AND MORTAR.

THE CASE OF MAJOR ANDRÉ CONSIDERED.

The writer feels it a duty to refer to Washington's action in the case of André, it having been dealt with most unfairly, and in the teeth of unquestionable evidence, by more than one writer, American as well as English. His hope and desire is to set the painful matter at rest for ever, so that no man desiring that truth shall prevail may ever question the great Patriot's humanity.

More than a century of years has rolled by since Major André expatiated his crime; one of the clearest, as it is one of the most indefensible, cases of human treachery afforded by any history annals, and which, had it been successful in accomplishment, could not have failed of the direst effect on the cause of the American Revolution. Justice to Washington in this case has hitherto been too generally withheld, and it is not uncommon to find, even in America, and at this distance of time, intelligent men endorsing the sentimental calumny of the day, questioning the humanity of the great patriot. English writers at the time could hardly be expected to deal other than *ex parte* with the case, and it must be remembered there existed, from the hour of the Revolution outbreak to its successful accomplishment, a numerous community in the country itself, openly as well as covertly, opposed to the revolt against the mother country. There was no stronger trait in the character of Washington than humanity; the misfortunes and sufferings of others touched him keenly, and on all hands it is admitted that his feelings were deeply moved at the part he was compelled to act in consenting to the death of André; yet justice to the office he held, and to the cause for which his countrymen were shedding their blood, left him no alternative. Lord Mahon, like many other writers, has most unjustly stigmatized Washington's character and action in the André case. At this distance of time, and with the evidence before him, Lord Mahon should have known better. It is a fashion thus to deal with the sad event; the habit arose in past days from utter ignorance of the real facts and circumstances of the case. Washington was utterly incapable of acting in a manner implied by the stigma. At the time of this unfair and unworthy conclusion, charging Washington with worse than indifference to André's fate, England was naturally excited and stirred by the event, not unreasonably so, looking at the admitted bravery, character, and antecedents of the youthful sufferer. The case was at the time put before the world in a semi-romantic light, and without any regard to the truth and actual facts. The Honourable Erastus Brooks has well gathered up and sifted in masterly manner the evidence in the painful case.

André was unquestionably a spy—he was fairly tried as one—he was justly condemned as one, and met the fate accorded to such by every nation under heaven. There was no haste manifested in the formation or action of the tribunal. He was taken red-handed. A board of officers was summoned to inquire into the case, report the facts, and give opinion, both in regard to the nature of his offence and to the punishment that ought to be awarded. All available papers were laid before the board, and André himself was questioned, and desired to make such statements and explanations as he chose. After the fullest possible investigation, the board reported, that the prisoner came on shore in the night, to hold a private and secret interview with Arnold; that he changed his dress within the American lines, and passed the guards in a disguised habit, having in his possession several papers, which contained intelligence for the enemy; and that he ought to be considered as a spy, and according to the law and usage of nations, to suffer death. General Washington, as became his solemn duty, approved this decision, and Major André was executed at Tappan, on the 2nd of October, 1780. While André's case was pending Sir Henry Clinton used every effort in his power to rescue him from his fate. He wrote to Washington, and endeavoured to show that he should not be regarded as a spy, inasmuch as he came on shore at the request of an American general, and afterwards acted by his direction; but connected with all the circumstances, this argument could not, in reason or commonsense, be allowed to have any weight. That he was drawn into a snare by a traitor did not make him the less a spy. Bancroft, in his grand, exhaustive, and impartial history, says:—"At the request of Clinton, who promised to present 'a true state of facts,' the execution was delayed till the 2nd day of October, and General Robertson, attended by two civilians, came up the river for a conference. The civilians were not allowed to land, but Greene was deputed to meet the officer. Instead of presenting facts, Robertson, after compliments to the character of Greene, announced that he had come to treat with him. Greene answered, 'The case of an acknowledged spy admits of no official discussion.' Robertson then proposed to free André by an exchange. Greene answered, 'If André is set free, Arnold must be given up,' for the liberation of André could not be asked for except in exchange for one who was equally implicated in the complot. Robertson then so far forgot himself as to deliver an open letter from Arnold to Washington, in which, in the event André should suffer the penalty of death, he used these threats, 'I shall think myself bound by every tie of duty and honour to retaliate on such unhappy persons of your army as may fall within my power. Forty of the principal inhabitants of South Carolina have justly forfeited their lives; Sir Henry Clinton cannot in justice extend his mercy to them any longer if Major André suffers.'

"Meantime, André entreated with touching earnestness that he might not die 'on the gibbet.' Washington and every other officer in the American army were moved to the deepest compassion; and Hamilton, who has left his opinion that no one ever suffered death with more justice, and that there was in truth no way of saving him, wished that in the mode of his death his feelings as an officer and a man might be respected. But the English themselves had established the exclusive usage of the gallows. At the beginning of the war their officers in America threatened the highest American officers and statesmen with the cord. It was the only mode of execution authorized by them. Under the orders of Clinton, Lord Cornwallis in South Carolina had set up the gallows for those whom he styled deserters, without regard to rank. Neither the sentence of the court nor the order of Washington names death on the gallows; the execution took place in the manner that was alone in use on both sides."

Bancroft, with the eloquent power and strict impartiality and justice characterizing his noble monumental history, closes this sad chapter on human treachery in these truthful words, to which no honourably-minded Englishman can take exception:—" Tried by the laws of morals, it is one of the worst forms of dissimulation to achieve by corruption and treachery what cannot be gained by honourable arms. If we confine our judgment within the limits of the laws of war, it is a blemish on the character of André that he was willing to prostitute a flag, to pledge his word, even under the orders of his chief, for the innocence and private nature of his design, and to have wished to make the lives of faultless prisoners hostages for his own. About these things a man of honour and humanity ought to have had a scruple; but the temptation was great, let his misfortunes cast a veil over his errors. The last words of André committed to the Americans the care of his reputation; and they faithfully fulfilled his request. His king did right in granting pensions to his mother and sisters, but not in raising a memorial to his name in Westminster Abbey. Such honour belongs to other enterprises and deeds. The tablet has no fit place in a sanctuary dear from its monuments to every friend to genius and mankind."

Mild as is the rebuke of America's gifted historian, Bancroft, it is as just as it is deserving. No true lover of his country would desire to see deeds such as that of André held up for approval and fitting as hero-worship. The writer of these memorials of Sharples Washington does not hesitate to confess that he has never known a British officer who questioned the justice of André's sentence or Washington's action and entire humanity evidenced in the whole case. He has had it from the lips of more than one distinguished heroic son of Britain, whose honoured remains now repose in the sacred fane of Westminster, that the "storied urn" to André never should have been set up in the venerable pile.

Inasmuch as these memorials of Washington refer mainly to a limited period of his life, it is just to the Great Apostle of Liberty, whose heart was incapable of the least act of inhumanity, to narrate somewhat fully the circumstances of André's treachery. The three peasant-militiamen, Paulding, Williams, and Van Wart, who captured André, and whose work in the most trying period of the Revolution is so wrought into the history of the nation that it has become one of its chief transactions. It is enough to say that the three men proved to be above temptation, if the best evidences of the time are credible. We must, however, regret that men like André, and his friend Major Tallmadge, ever doubted the integrity of the captors; and regret also that the record was published more than once that "they were self-appointed to the office of stopping well-dressed travellers, and men who perhaps would have rifled a traveller." It is a duty to say that Paulding had been twice captured by the British army, that Williams was but twenty-two years old, and the eldest of his three companions. Though young in years and poor in purse, they were rich in mature judgment, and in their work performed a service of immense value.

The charges of Major Tallmadge on the floor of Congress in 1817, grew out of the application of Paulding for an increased pension. The request gave rise to the debate which started the accusation that the captors were undeserving men, who for money would have released André. As it was they took his watch, which was afterwards redeemed by Colonel Smith for thirty guineas, his horse, saddle, and bridle, and for their service to the country they were rewarded by the State and by Congress. It is due to Major Tallmadge to say that his opinion of the bad character of André's captors grew in part out of the statement of André himself, that he would have been released at the time of his arrest if he had had money with him sufficient to meet the demands of his captors. There is no evidence of the truth of this statement. Looking at the good work done, and the temptations offered, it is a pleasure to accord the most honourable intentions as well as the grandest possible results to the timely and needed arrest of one in whose hands for a time were the destinies of the nation.

A scene of dramatic interest attaches to the time and place of André's arrest. The spy came upon his captors, galloping upon a large brown horse, upon one of whose shoulders was branded the initial letters, "U. S. A." He found them engaged in a game of cards. Before dismounting he was taken to a whitewood or tulip-tree—long known as André's tree—its girth of twenty-six feet and its gnarled limbs reaching almost to the earth, making it an object of intense interest, at times almost of reverence, and especially so after the tree was struck with lightning. Here André, as in the very shadow of death, stood with a marked countenance, a man about five feet seven inches in height. Here he was again questioned, and protested that he had no letters—perhaps, under the circumstances, and as wilful deceivers value the truth when in danger, a pardonable lie. Piece by piece he threw off his clothing. His long boots, the first object of attraction on the highway— for boots were rare and valuable at that time—proved that André was no common man. If, as was alleged thirty-seven years later, the captors were looking for money, they found in the stockings in André's boots treasure far more valuable than all the gold and silver in the colonies. The cry came at once and with an oath, which might also be pardoned in the Heavens: "*Here it is!*" "HE IS A SPY!" And the prisoner was borne twelve miles off to Lieutenant-Colonel Jamieson, in command of the nearest quarters of the American army. With no suspicion of treason the first order of Jamieson was to send André to Arnold; but a good providence changed the intent as to the prisoner, but not as to information sent, to Arnold of the capture of a spy. The escape of Arnold was a cruelty to the cause he had both served and betrayed: to the country at large, and in its example to mankind. He told the story of his villainy in a few hurried words to his devoted and agonized wife, who, with her infant child in her arms, fell fainting to the floor, as it were, dead; but now, alas! the life-long companion of the basest of ingrates and traitors, and far worse than dead. She was, be it said to her honour, and in sympathy with her great misfortune, innocent of all knowledge of her husband's infamy, and of all offence against her country; and Washington, at the request of Arnold, sent her in safety to her parental home in Philadelphia.

General Greene, on the 26th of September, 1780, stated that "this was the first instance of treason of the kind where many were from the nature of the dispute to be expected." But this one example was upon the mind of Washington most distressing. "Whom," he was tempted to exclaim even to his friend Lafayette, in view of the confidence reposed in Arnold, and who, after earnest importunities growing out of his wounds and alleged weakness, he had placed in supreme command at West Point, "WHOM CAN WE TRUST NOW?"

The prisoner was at this time under the care of Major Tallmadge, when the latter, in answer to a question as to the possible fate of André, reminded him of the fate of his own classmate and friend, Nathan Hale, near the commencement of the war. "Yes," said Tallmadge, he was hanged as a spy!" "Surely," quoth André, in reply, "you do not consider his case and mine alike?" "They are precisely similar, and similar will be your punishment," was the prompt answer of his keeper, and of a man in deep sympathy with his fate. It was the result of this free intercourse no doubt which prompted Tallmadge to declare in Congress that the captors of Arnold were "cowboys, or persons who traded with both camps and drove cattle for profit between the two armies." Major Biddle treated this statement, as did many in Congress when it was made, as ungenerous and unjust.

It should be borne in mind, in reference to this case of André's execution, so unjustly adduced as reflecting on Washington's character and humanity, that one Nathan Hale, a classmate and friend of André, was publicly hanged for treason in 1776, on the morning of the Revolution. After but one night's imprisonment he was executed, without trial, without mercy, and as a dying man was even denied the use of a Bible. Like André he was a spy. His letters to his mother and the lady he loved were torn to pieces before his eyes. Even his last recorded words of love and final remembrance failed to move the stony heart of the miscalled man and officer before him. Young Hale entered the enemy's lines at the request of Washington, who needed light as to the number of the enemy on Long Island. With the purest motives and for the most patriotic services he met the wishes of his Commander-in-Chief. He was detected as he was leaving the enemy's camp, and was betrayed by his own kinsman. The time of his execution was at break of day, while the great fires of September 21st, 1776, were smouldering in the distance, and where the conflagration heightened the anger of the British occupants of American territory. His execution was upon the order of Sir William Howe, and the manner of it was the most brutal official act of the seven years' war. The treatment and trial of André, in contrast, not only won the sympathy and approval of André himself, but the respectful recognitions of the entire country. Whatever the differences of opinion as to the act of execution upon the gibbet, there were none as to the fairness of the trial. Nor was there any division of sentiment as to the gentlemanly and courageous bearing of the prisoner. André was but twenty-nine at the time of his execution, and Hale but twenty-one. While André in his death was calm, silent, and self-possessed, almost beyond precedent, the last and glowing words of Hale were his regrets that "he had but one life to give for his country." In contrast to Hale's manner of death, André wrote to Sir Henry Clinton, September 29th, less than three days before his execution, as follows : " I receive the greatest attention from his Excellency General Washington, and from every person under whose charge I happen to be placed." The spot where Hale was buried no one knows, while André received the respect of his enemies, the honours of his country, and to remove the taint of hanging, the King of England knighted one of André's brothers.

Washington burst into tears when he heard of the treason of Arnold, and said, "I had no more suspicion of Arnold than I had of myself." André also once burst into tears when he counted the cost of a sacrifice which, beginning in Arnold's foul treason, ended in his own death upon the gibbet. André's tears, it is proper to say, grew out of his great distress for the feelings of Clinton, whose orders he had exceeded, whom he sincerely loved, and in whom Clinton seemed to repose more confidence, and to give more power, than to any other officer on his staff or under his command.

One other scene recorded in the drama of André's seizure should not be forgotten in judging the case. Hitherto all had been well with him, especially his many miles of midnight travel with muffled oars from King's Ferry to Teller's Point and back from the Vulture to Long Cove. He had left behind him all the guards, sentries, and patrols of his enemies, and was looking forward to the meeting of friends in a place of safety, when he was confronted by his three captors with three cocked muskets aimed at his person. As a means of safety he was clothed in part in the dress of Arnold's confidential, if not traitorous, companion, Smith. The dress worn by him was a tall beaver hat, crimson coat, and pantaloons and waistcoat of nankeen. He also bore upon his person the order of Arnold "to pass André where he would within the American lines." Edmund Burke's Register has said of the offender, that "his open bravery, high ideas of candour, and disdain of duplicity, unfitted him for the mechanical boldness, dissimulation, and circumspection of a spy." When discovered he thought the three men he encountered on the highway belonged either to his own country, or if not that they were friendly to it. Paulding had been only four days out of a British prison, and one of his keepers had compelled him to change his own better dress for that of a Briton or Hessian. In this recognized dress André's eyes fell first upon Paulding and then upon his companions. Some ambiguous word of one of the captors brought out the response which betrayed the spy: "You are from *below*. I, too, am from BELOW. I am a British officer, on urgent business; do not detain me a minute." Then came the presentation of Arnold's pass, and the vain threat of Arnold's name and vengeance if it was not respected. The boots, the boast, the urgency of manner, and the promise of money, made duty plain, and brought out the reply of Paulding, which, like Nathan Hale's last words, will live for ever: "If you gave us ten thousand guineas, you should not stir a step."

General Arnold has been compared to General Monk, whose bad example the American traitor copied, but with none of Monk's success. George III. was Arnold's friend; while reason was enthroned in the brain of the king he was in high favour with his Majesty, but when the mind of the king was lost by a fatal insanity, the Government re-called the man who had brought neither honour to himself nor profit to their country; and they also remembered him as one whose crimes to his own country, as well as to the British colonies in America, had caused the death of one now esteemed and honoured through all the realm. Lord Surrey said in Parliament, "I will not speak while that man is in the House." Lord Lauderdale was equally offended when he saw Arnold familiar with the king. Then came the plague-spot in Arnold's life. Despised in England, detested in America, and wretched in his own existence, we are told in a family tradition, possibly true, that his last words were, "Bring me, I beg you, the epaulettes and sword-knots which Washington gave me; let me die in my old American uniform, the uniform in which I fought my battles, and God forgive me," he added, "for ever putting on any other." The death of this man took place in 1801, but where buried in the wilderness of London no man knows. When Arnold and his wife looked upon the remains of André in Westminster Abbey, then, indeed, he might have felt and said all this, and more than this, especially when he remembered that his, in high places, if not in the lowest estate, was the solitary treason of his country,—

"One grateful truth he left to glad mankind,
That in a war so long, his crime alone
Should stain the annals of recording time."

We recall also as a part of the events of the time in hand, the impudent threats of Arnold in his letters to Washington in behalf of André, and the persistent but more honourable demands of Clinton and his friend Robinson for his release, because André, as alleged, but without truth—André himself writing to the contrary—was under "a flag of truce" when he left the *Vulture*, and rightly named the *Vulture* for the mischief done both to André and Arnold. The court which tried the offender, the chief of the army, who felt deep pity for André's youth, and respect for his manly bearing—and it was in every way deserving of respect and sympathy—and the general feeling of the country was that there could be no pardon for such an offence. It was said at the time that "men are not to be reckoned as we reckon animals, and that one camel is worth no more than another, but the man who is before us is worth an army."

Nor was the sentence and execution one of retaliation as has been more than once stated, for since the hanging of Nathan Hale in 1776, at least eight British spies had been hung. The reply of Israel Putnam to General Tryon expressed the spirit of the times and the duties of the occasion. He wrote as follows:—

"SIR,—Nathan Palmer, a lieutenant in your king's service, was taken in my army as a *spy*, he was tried as a *spy*, he was condemned as a *spy*, and you may rest assured, sir, that he shall be hanged as a *spy*.

"I have the honour to be, &c.,

"ISRAEL PUTNAM.

" P.S.—Afternoon. He is hanged."

The disloyalty of the period, and the great number of loyalists even in that part of the country, made some terrible example a necessity. André was not only a spy in 1780, but it is stated, and is believed, that he was a successful spy, in the disguise of a cattle-driver, in the fall of Charlestown, one of the greatest disasters of the war, compelling as it did the surrender of General Lincoln with his army of nearly 7000 troops. The fact of André's presence disguised as a spy in the South, as well as at the North, is upon the evidence of one of Clinton's own officers who so stated in 1822, and of one of André's intimate friends. He was fond of adventure, and by talent and study, by art and address, was fitted for the work before him. He found pleasure in danger. Like Arnold he could run with the hare or hunt with the hounds. He was in the upper story of Smith's house in the grey of the morning and through the night. He left Arnold, we are told, who detained him through the night, depressed in spirit and sad in countenance, but recovered rapidly as he passed beyond what he regarded as points of danger. All commend his self-possession from the hour of his arrest to the moment of his execution. He shuddered, but only for a second of time, as he glanced at the gibbet which in a moment was to launch him into the presence of the Almighty; but with recovered composure he calmly said, "It will soon be over." It may be said of him without exaggeration and hardly in the figure of speech, that "he smiled at the drawn dagger and defied its point."

It is due to his gentle nature also to say that in the presence of women and children he was every inch a manly man. When practically second in command in New York he came to the rescue of a lad fifteen years of age, a boy of true Yankee grit in the fight, but not so plucky in defeat. The boy had been caught while fighting, with children of a larger growth, a body of men on the British side engaged in a foraging party. The party were taken to the city jail, where André, richly dressed in his uniform, approached the lad, and said to him, "My dear boy, what makes you cry?" The natural and childish answer, in sight of the prison, was, "My mother and my sister at home!" And André then said, "Well, my dear child, don't cry any more;" and after seeing Clinton he came again to the scared and weeping youth, and said, "My boy, I've good news for you! The General has given you to me to dispose of as I choose, and now you are at liberty. So run home to your parents, and be a good boy. Mind what they tell you. Say your prayers, *love one another*, and GOD ALMIGHTY WILL BLESS YOU."

Inside or outside of the gospel of peace for men, women, or children, State or country, no better sermon nor nobler example than this was ever heard.

There is abundant evidence of André's kindness to American prisoners of war when under his care. All who were near him were kindly treated. Washington the Chief, his aide-de-camp, Hamilton, then at about the age of twenty-three, who was much with him, Major Jackson, who had received André's kindness in prison, one and all indeed were deeply touched with the genuine manliness of the prisoner. Hamilton could not refrain from saying, while justifying the execution, in a long and memorable letter to his betrothed, " I confess to you I had the weakness to value the esteem of a dying man because I reverenced his merit;" and Hamilton would if he could have saved his life by receiving, life for life, Arnold in exchange. It is in evidence that Washington proposed this in a letter to Clinton under a flag of truce; but, as was natural, and in war and precedent proper, the offer was declined. No wonder that Lafayette, as one of the court who sentenced him to death, said, " All the court were filled with expressions of admiration for him. It is impossible to express too much respect or too deep regret for Major André." Tallmadge wrote, " I became so deeply attached to Major André that I could remember no instance where my affection was so fully absorbed by any man." No marvel then that tears fell from many eyes when André died upon the gibbet, with the courage of a hero and the philosophy of a sage.

The closing scene of all in André's life is one of the saddest recorded in history. He appealed to Washington to soften his last moments by allowing him to be shot instead of dying upon the gibbet. His brief words were, for I am limited by rapidly passing time to a paragraph:—

"TAPPAN, October, 1780.

"Sympathy towards a soldier will surely induce your Excellency and a military tribunal to adapt the mode of my death to the feelings of a man of honour. Let me hope, sir, if aught in my character impresses you with esteem towards me, if aught in my misfortunes makes me the victim of policy and not of resentment, I shall experience the operations of those feelings in your heart by being informed that I am not to die on a gibbet.

"JOHN ANDRÉ,
"*Adjutant-General to the British Army.*"

Washington's counsellors declared the request inadmissible, and Washington himself chose not to add a fresh pang to André's heart by any written denial to his earnest request. And hence the misconstrued studied silence where words would only have added more pain to the deepest sorrow. The heart of the great Patriot was tender as that of any woman, but it was just.

It was the mode of André's death which caused criticism in England, as it caused profound pity, and criticism in the United States. André was young in years and eleven years the junior of Arnold. He was born of Swiss parents in 1751, and educated in Europe. Arnold, the source and cause of all his public woes, an American by birth and education, had engaged a man of great address and of deliberate purpose to ruin the land against which he was in arms, and not now in the open field of war as at St. John's, near Lake Champlain, and elsewhere. The deed was done in the by-paths and concealments of a country road, at night time in part, and under a false flag of truce. But if Arnold could have been exchanged for André, the country and the world would have rejoiced, and André's life been saved. Delicate and refined in features, educated in books and arts, cultivated in manners, brave as a soldier, fond of painting, drawing, and music, which not alone in poetry to his loved one, but in rhyme and song and music to his enemies, he used all his arms and arts with skill and satire at the expense of America, and especially against General Wayne.

He was in love, too, and, saddest of all to a sensitive

mind and heart, he was a rejected lover, and this, as rarely happens, without love lost upon his own side. The woman he loved, Honora Sneyd by name, is presented to us at the time as graceful in person, beautiful in features, and as one whose expression heightened the eloquence of everything she said. Another memory or painting of her is that she was surrounded by virgin glories, beauty and grace, sensibility and goodness, superior intelligence and unswerving truth. It was said of André at home, and as a man worthy of this affection, that the better he was known the more he was loved, and certain it is that in many ways his was a gentle spirit. He failed in love, and he failed in war. At St. John's in November, 1775, he was captured, with six hundred troops, and for a time was quartered in Philadelphia, later at Lancaster and Carlisle, and was released by exchange near the close of 1776. Soon he was advanced in the British army, and so passed on honoured and respected, until the fatal months, eighteen of them in all, as I read, when he became, if not the companion, the counsellor and correspondent of a traitor. And so, as the good book tells us, it is always true that evil communications corrupt good manners.

Better a hundred times over André than Arnold. Better André upon the gibbet, than Arnold the American traitor Major-General, or the Major-General of the British army. Arnold, intellectually and physically, was brave, brilliant, capable of immense will power, and of great nervous activity. He knew as a soldier, as some men have known in political service, how to be the greatest, wisest, and meanest of mankind. He sold his honour and his patriotism to a bad ambition, a mean jealousy, and a spirit of revenge. In the history of mankind it would be hard to find a sadder example of the consequences of misguided thought and conduct than in the life of Benedict Arnold. Some of his name, related to him by blood, honourable as citizens, have felt the sting of his crime, and have tried at times to find some excuse for it in the seeming neglect of recognition for work performed by him when a successful soldier in the war of the Revolution, and especially for his valour at Saratoga and Quebec. We cheerfully admit his courage in battle, and in all that once belonged to the glories of the field his claim to higher military promotion, before he fell to the lowest depths of personal degradation. Whatever his wrongs, Washington nor his country were the wrong-doers; and if they had been, the man should have risen above revenge and treason, and proved to the country and to mankind that patience, forbearance, and endurance are the first duties of the patriot and the soldier. Arnold so felt in the end, and but for the sin by which the angels fell, a better fate might have saved his name and fame.

Arnold's greatest personal crime was to Washington himself. To him he was guilty of ingratitude, injustice, insincerity, and baseness in all their forms. Though Washington had placed him in the triple post of confidence, honour, and safety at West Point, to keep Clinton from the North and Burgoyne from the South, he sought from June to near the close of September, if not long before, to break this barrier of separation, and to place Washington, the army, and the country in possession of the enemy,—and all for a sum of money, and a place in power.

André was dealing with a man guilty of the double crime of treason to his country and treason to his commander in arms. To this end he sought and obtained command of the fortress which separated the two great forces of the enemy. He had given orders to his subordinate, Colonel Sheldon, to pass André through the American lines. He had carried on a secret and villainous correspondence with André, as one John Anderson, about " good speculations," " the price of tobacco," and "ready money." He had again and again violated the flag of truce. On the night of September 21st he dispatched Joshua H. Smith, if not an open criminal, an accomplice, to visit the British sloop-of-war *Vulture* at Teller's Point, twelve or fifteen miles below West Point, and to this vessel he was rowed by two labourers. He was in conference with André at Smith's house, the one an open foe to liberty and union, people, and country, and the other making terms with this foe as to the price to be paid for the betrayal of his country. He had completed a bargain, under six distinct heads, showing, one by one, the place and force of each corps at West Point, of each redoubt and battery, with a complete description of the place, of the condition and strength of all points of defence, and the confidential communication of Washington to Arnold. Two of these papers gave, in Arnold's handwriting, the strength of the garrison and the force necessary to man the works. André accepted all this information from Arnold secretly, willingly, on American soil, and for the direct purpose of destroying the country. It is also important to remember that Clinton would consent to nothing short of a knowledge of Arnold's purpose to tell all he knew of the forces at West Point and with the intent of their surrender. Well did King George III. say "the public never can be compensated for the vast advantages which must have followed from the success of his plan."

André also came from the *Vulture* to the shores of the Hudson in his own British uniform, covered only by an ordinary cloak, and he returned in clothes borrowed from Smith and with a pass from Arnold. Smith, his companion, parted with him on the left bank of the river to report to Arnold at West Point that "all was going well." Arnold also was to receive for his treason, if successful, "30,000*l*.

in money, and no loss of rank or pay. Clinton, for value received, was as willing to buy as Arnold was to sell; ready, indeed, to quote his own words, to close the bargain, "at every risk and at any cost." In the upper story of Smith's house, already mentioned, Arnold was paying, by betrayal of his country, the price agreed upon, and for several hours the spy and traitor, face to face, were engaged in these treacherous bargains. Arnold here laid before André, in Smith's upper chamber, the official plans of all the works at West Point, and the very plans prepared for Washington by the French engineer Duportail. These were the papers seized, and it was for this seizure that the three captors received their lands, medals, and pensions from the United States Government, from the State Government, the thanks of Congress, of the Legislature of New York, and of the City of New York, in a monument for Paulding, besides the thanks of Washington himself. The people at the time, and for two generations since, have recognized their patriotism and the great value of their services.

Of Arnold's thirty thousand pounds of blood-money, with pay and rank, which Clinton had promised him, it may be said with Vattel, the great expositor on the laws of war, that such bribes for seduction are not in accord with the laws of a moral conscience. The best law says that in "seducing a subject to betray his country, and practising on the fidelity of a governor, enticing him, persuading him to deliver up a place, is prompting such persons to commit detestable crimes;" and Vattel further asks, "Is it honest to incite our most inveterate enemy to be guilty of a crime?" He also says of spies, that "they are those who introduce themselves among the enemy to discover the condition of his affairs, penetrate his designs, and communicate them to him who employs them." The entire law of nations is in accord with this opinion, and hence when the conspirators of Clinton were engaged in the foul work of fomenting mutiny and treason among American troops at Princeton, they were seized and hung on the authority of the laws of war, or the law of nations.

General Washington, in his letter to Congress bearing date at Robinson's house in the Highlands, September 26th, 1780, declared, upon the instant of his knowledge of what these men had done, that "their acts do them the highest honour and prove them to be men of virtue," and, he added, in a letter to his court of six major-generals and eight brigadier-generals, that the men who tried him had performed their duty.

In the height of the war Arnold became weary of the war, and was eager for peace. His mind, like his body, was ill at ease. He complained of a ruined constitution and of a limb rendered useless in the war. In his letter to Joshua H. Smith, he says, "At the close of the war I look for compensation for such damages as I have sustained," and the same man wrote these foul words from the *Vulture* to Washington at West Point, October 1st, 1780, " I ca'l heaven and earth to witness that your Excellency will be justly answerable for the torrent of blood that may be shed " if André is executed.

André's remains were removed, with all the honours of war, from the place of his execution, and buried in his own country in 1821, under an order of George III. They were borne to the shores of his fatherland, and with renewed honours placed in Westminster Abbey, where upon his monument we read, " he fell a sacrifice to his zeal for his king and country." André for sixty years has had his chief monument in the great mausoleum of the Old World; and a monument to his memory, recording his execution as a spy, has been erected to him in America, the inscription on which does not in any way reflect upon the men who tried and convicted André, nor in any way upon the country whose very life he would have taken in its first struggle for independence, nor upon Washington himself who signed the sentence of death.

In this connection, reference should be made to the form of André's trial. The record reads as follows:—

"The Board having considered the letter from his Excellency, General Washington, respecting Major André, Adjutant-General to the British Army, the confession of Major André, and the papers produced to them, report to his Excellency the Commander-in-Chief the following facts which appear to them in relation to Major André:—

"Firstly, That he came on shore from the *Vulture*, sloop-of-war, on the night of the 21st September instant, on an interview with General Arnold in a private and secret manner.

"Secondly, That he changed his dress within our lines, and, under a feigned name and in a disguised habit, passed our works at Stony and Verplank's Point, the evening of the 22nd September instant, and was taken the morning of the 23rd September instant at Tarrytown in a disguised habit, being then on his way to New York, and when taken he had in his possession several papers which contained intelligence for the enemy.

"The Board having maturely considered these facts do also report to his Excellency General Washington that Major André, Adjutant-General to the British Army, ought to be considered as a spy from the enemy, and that, agreeable to the law and usage of nations, it is their opinion that he ought to suffer death."

Signed by Nathaniel Greene, M.G., president, and thirteen others, including Lafayette, Steuben, James Clinton, Knox, and Starke.

The letter of Washington, which preceded this trial, reads as follows :—

"GENTLEMEN,—Major André, Adjutant-General to the British Army, will be brought before you for your examination. He came within our lines in the night on an interview with Major-General Arnold, and in an assumed character, and was taken within our lines in a disguised habit, with a pass under a feigned name, and with the enclosed papers concealed upon him. After a careful examination you will be pleased as speedily as possible to report a precise state of his case, together with your opinion of the light in which he ought to be considered and the punishment that ought to be inflicted."

And when all was over, another letter read as follows :—

"PARAMUS, October 7, 1780.

" . . . This officer was executed in pursuance of the opinion of the Board on Monday, the second instant, at twelve o'clock, at our late camp at Tappan. . . ."

Arnold, like André and his captors, also has his monument, and Alexander Hamilton, as the aide-de-camp of Washington, inscribed upon it, in the form of the memories of the people, the undying record, that while "Arnold is handed down with execration to future times, posterity will repeat with reverence the names of Paulding, Williams, and Van Wart," and in the same paper he said of André, in connection with these men, " He tempted their integrity with the offer of his watch, his horse, and any sum of money they should name. They rejected his offer with indignation, and the gold that could seduce a man high in the esteem and confidence of his country had no charms for these simple peasants, leaning on their virtue and a sense of duty."

It was Sterne who said that "of all the cant in this

canting world, though the cant of hypocrisy may be the worst, the cant of criticism is the most tormenting." The severest criticisms have followed the part taken by Washington in the trial and execution of André. Had the offenders been either of the Howes, in command of the British army and navy, or Clinton in command when André was arrested, tried, sentenced, and executed, no deeper feeling could have pervaded Great Britain or impressed the colonies. The sentence and its execution proved at least that America, sink or swim, live or die, was in dead earnest for independence. It was the detestable treason of Arnold also which was, in part, punished in the sentence of André. The latter was in close communication with a man whose later avowal was the confident expectation that, with the British in possession of West Point, America was subdued. At times that communication was open, and when necessary it was confidential and secret. The officers selected by Washington to hear and determine his case were men whose reputations will live as long as the country lives as among the wisest, truest, and most patriotic men of the Revolution. The report of these fourteen officers was unanimous, after the fairest trial, and by men who felt the deepest sympathy for the guilty officer detected in a work which contemplated literally the surrender of the strongest fortress in the land, and the worst possible consequences to liberty and independence. The verdict was that "he ought to be considered as a spy from the enemy;" and that "he ought to suffer death." The next day, September 30th, 1780, the sentence of death being known, Washington, now acting as a judge, obedient to law, as the chief of the army which Arnold would have betrayed into the hands of André, as a patriot whose mind was pure as the air of heaven, whose heart in every fibre of its being was devoted to the love of country, wrote these words:—

"The Commander-in-Chief approves of the opinion of the Board of General Officers respecting Major André, and orders that the execution of Major André take place to-morrow at five o'clock p.m."

The execution was postponed until the 2nd of October. September 30th, the sentence was laid before Congress, whose judgment Washington would gladly have received; but, while there was intense feeling upon the subject of the trial and the sentence of death, there was no public debate nor any interference with the judgment of the court, nor any advice in regard to it. Washington is charged with "cold insensibility" for the mode of André's death. The answer is that the mode was a logical necessity for the crime committed, and even Walter Scott so held it before his countrymen.

The appeals made to Washington for an exchange of prisoners by Clinton and his representatives, and for a change of the manner of death, were unheeded but not unheard by Washington. He did what the military court who tried André decided to be just. He did what he thought it was right to do, in view both of the crime committed against the country and as a necessary example upon the people of the nation, many of whom were disloyal even in the midst of the country where the wrong was done. He followed the wisest military precedents all the world over. Napoleon, when on trial before the great triumvirate of British statesmen, Stockwell, Ellenborough, and Grant, thirty-four years after André was executed, was pronounced a pirate, a criminal, and a common enemy of mankind. There was a disposition even to hand him over as a traitor to Louis XVIII., and only a division of opinion—where there was none in the court that sentenced André—substituted an exile worse than death for death itself. The fate of André, ignominious as it was, was in the end better than that of many of his comrades, and hardly worse than that which befell his two American friends, Hamilton and Henry Lee—the one killed in a most shameful duel, and the other the inmate of a jail, the victim of a mob, the creature of malice and of the most terrible poverty. Chief Justice Marshall, pure and great among the wisest of the land, one of the most eminent jurists the country has ever produced, than whom a more humane man never lived, said that "André having been unquestionably a spy, his sentence consequently was just."

Death early or late is the common lot of all mankind; and it came to André a little beyond the morning of life, amidst the sincere regrets of his enemies and the esteem and lamentations of all whom he served on both sides of the ocean. "Unusually esteemed and unusually regretted," were the words of Alexander Hamilton in his record of the transaction, and this was the general feeling of all men. While Hamilton's sympathies for André were intense, they were every way manly. "Never, perhaps," he said, "did a man suffer with more justice, or deserve it less." He condemned André for what he had attempted against the country, and acquitted him because, as he said, "the authorized maxims and practices of war are the satire of human nature;" and because, as he also said, "these maxims permit the general that can make the worst traitors in the army of his adversary to be frequently most applauded." Like Washington, Hamilton felt, as upon reflection we all must feel, apart from our interest in talent, taste, and a generous nature, that it was "a blemish in André's fame that he once intended to prostitute a flag; and about this a nice honour ought to have had a scruple." Major Tallmadge also wrote as André's sympathizing friend, "Though he dies lamented, he dies justly." While André gave his true name to Washington, it is but a just inference to say that he did this partly in the interest of truth, but more in his own interest for his own fame. In the myth "John Anderson," there was nowhere any personal interest; as John André, Adjutant-General of the British army, though the same man, he was altogether a different person. The only particle of selfishness in his conduct after his arrest was in his letter to Washington, wherein he intimated a threat that "some gentlemen at Charleston," quoting his own words, "were engaged in a conspiracy against us" . . . "objects who may be sent in exchange for me, or persons whom the treatment I receive might affect." It was on this hint that Arnold wrote his threat to Washington, and Clinton also claimed André's release. The demand suggested acts of retaliation which if put in practice no doubt André would have deplored. The suggestion was ungenerous and unjust, since these Charleston men, then in confinement at St. Augustine, had both invited and demanded investigation.

The quaint old building known as Washington's Headquarters at Tappan, although associated with one of the most important events of the Revolution—the trial and execution of Major André—has little more than a local reputatation. And yet Americans will often scramble about all over the world in search of novelties possessing little or no real interest. It was erected in the year 1700, as is attested by figures some four feet in height set in the front brick wall of the building, The property was purchased by Johannes De Wint, a wealthy planter from St. Thomas, West Indies, about 1756, and continued in his possession up to 1790, the time of his death.

On the 28th September, 1780, Washington and his staff, who had been on a visit to the French General Rochambeau at Hartford, arrived at Tappan, and took up his quarters at Mr. De Wint's mansion, which is still well preserved.

With the exception of Major Blauvelt, the son-in-law of De Wint, all the family were loyalists; but the daughter, with the natural spirit of a woman and of the times, was proud of the honour of entertaining the Commander-in-Chief of the American army. During the trial of André, Washington followed strictly his habits of family worship in the parlour of the mansion. The orderly life of his early home was his practice then, and up to the last month of the last year of the last century, when he died. As an incident of the times it may be stated that a grandmother of Colonel Haring, of Rockland County, was in the habit of visiting the soldiers on errands of mercy while in the locality, and that in one of her visits she found a soldier under sentence of death for desertion. The poor fellow pleaded with her to intercede in his behalf. Calling at headquarters the following morning, she was informed by Major Blauvelt, the son-in-law of Mr. De Wint, that the General was conducting family worship, and that immediately after the service he would open the front door and walk through the hall. Biding her time she saw the Commander-in-Chief and made known her errand. "I am afraid he is a bad man, but for your sake I will see what can be done," said the General. After investigating the case he pardoned the man. Three weeks after he deserted again, and was captured and shot. Washington's almost single failure in his judgment of men was in the character of Arnold. Arnold's early life had proved his courage in the field and his devotion to the country.

Everything in the room occupied by Washington remains as he left it. The Dutch tiles, with their Scripture illustrations, adorn the mantel. The closet and its wooden pegs used by the General for hanging his clothes, are the same. It was in this room that Washington signed the death warrant of Major André, and from one of the windows he saw the preparations for André's execution upon the hill and ordered his servant to close the blinds. As we shall see in the end he looked upon this act as one of the necessary tragedies of war.

Major André left West Point on the morning of September 28th, with Major Tallmadge, and arrived at Tappan on the evening of that day. He was assigned quarters at a tavern then kept by Carparus Maybee, now known as the '76 House. At the same time Joshua Hett Smith was confined in the Dutch church, about 100 feet distant from the '76 House, where he heard most of the conversation during the trial of André. The Dutch church, where André was tried, was built in 1716, rebuilt and enlarged in 1788. At a later period it was demolished and the present edifice was erected in 1835.

The provisions supplied to Major André during his confinement were sent from Washington's private table. Mrs. De Wint would no doubt give all the delicacies which a sympathizing woman could provide for an attractive man doomed to die for his zeal to serve his country.

Washington's work was done. He had built up a nation destined, if it will but follow his example, to be the greatest upon earth. Since his retirement from the presidency his health had been remarkably good; and although advancing years had brought their infirmities, yet up to the very close of life he was able to endure fatigue, and make exertions of body and mind, with scarcely less ease and activity than he had done in the prime of his strength.

Washington Irving made many anxious efforts to have the Sharples portraits appear in his Life of the great Patriot. No miserable desire of gain on the part of the owners prevented this. Nothing but legal settlement of the paintings stood in the way of gratifying his wishes. The whole set are laid before the reader of these Memorials, who desires that the last scene in the noblest of all lives should here be recorded in the language of Irving himself, whose hand the writer so frequently grasped, on a first visit to America in 1848, and who holds it his highest honour to have been called his friend.

Irving tells us, in his simple language :—

"Winter had now set in, with occasional wind and rain and frost, yet Washington still kept up his active round of indoor and out-door avocations, as his diary records. He was in full heath and vigour, dined out occasionally, and had frequent guests at Mount Vernon; and, as usual, was part of every day in the saddle, going the rounds of his estates, and, in his military phraseology, 'visiting the outposts.'

About ten o'clock on the morning of the 12th of December, he mounted his horse, and rode out as usual to make the rounds of the estate. The ominous ring round the moon, which he had observed on the preceding night, proved a fatal portent. 'About one o'clock,' he notes, 'it began to snow, soon after to hail, and then turned to a settled cold rain.' Having on an overcoat, he continued his ride without regarding the weather, and did not return to the house until after three.

His secretary approached him with letters to be franked, that they might be taken to the post-office in the evening. Washington franked the letters, but observed that the weather was too bad to send a servant out with them. Mr. Lear perceived that snow was hanging from his hair, and expressed fears that he had got wet; but he replied, 'No, his great-coat had kept him dry.' As dinner had been waiting for him, he sat down to table without changing his dress. 'In the evening,' writes his secretary, 'he appeared as well as usual.'

On the following morning the snow was three inches deep

and still falling, which prevented him from taking his usual ride. He complained of a sore throat, and had evidently taken cold the day before. In the afternoon the weather cleared up, and he went out on the grounds between the house and the river, to mark some trees which were to be cut down. A hoarseness, which had hung about him through the day, grew worse towards night; but he made light of it.

He was very cheerful in the evening, as he sat in the parlour with Mrs. Washington and Mr. Lear, amusing himself with the papers which had been brought from the post-office. When he met with anything interesting or entertaining, he would read it aloud as well as his hoarseness would permit; or he listened and made occasional comments, while Mr. Lear read the debates of the Virginia Assembly.

On retiring to bed, Mr. Lear suggested that he should take something to relieve the cold. 'No,' replied he, ' you know I never take anything for a cold. Let it go as it came.'

In the night he was taken extremely ill with ague and difficulty of breathing. Between two and three o'clock in the morning he awoke Mrs. Washington, who would have risen to call a servant; but he would not permit her, lest she should take cold. At daybreak, when the servant woman entered to make a fire, she was sent to call Mr. Lear. He found the General breathing with difficulty, and hardly able to utter a word intelligibly. Washington desired that Dr. Craik, who lived in Alexandria, should be sent for, and that in the meantime Rawlins, one of the overseers, should be summoned to bleed him before the doctor could arrive.

A gargle was prepared for his throat; but, whenever he attempted to swallow any of it, he was convulsed and

almost suffocated. Rawlins made his appearance soon after
sunrise, but, when the General's arm was ready for the
operation, became agitated. 'Don't be afraid,' said the
General, as well as he could speak. Rawlins made an
incision. 'The orifice is not large enough,' said Washington. The blood, however, ran pretty freely, and Mrs.
Washington, uncertain whether the treatment was proper,
and fearful that too much blood might be taken, begged
Mr. Lear to stop it. When he was about to untie the string
the General put up his hand to prevent him, and as soon as
he could speak, murmured, 'More—more;' but Mrs.
Washington's doubts prevailed, and the bleeding was
stopped, after about half a pint of blood had been taken.
External applications were now made to the throat, and
his feet were bathed in warm water, but without affording
any relief.

His old friend Dr. Craik arrived between eight and nine,
and two other physicians, Drs. Dick and Brown, were
called in. Various remedies were tried, and additional
bleeding—but all of no avail.

'About half-past four o'clock,' writes Mr. Lear, 'he
desired me to call Mrs. Washington to his bedside; when
he requested her to go down into his room and take from
his desk two wills, which she would find there, and bring
them to him—which she did. Upon looking at them, he
gave her one, which he observed was useless, as being
superseded by the other, and desired her to burn it, which
she did, and took the other and put it into her closet.

'After this was done, I returned to his bedside and took
his hand. He said to me :—"I find I am going, my breath
cannot last long. I believed from the first that the disorder
would prove fatal. Do you arrange and record all my late
military letters and papers. Arrange my accounts and
settle my books, as you know more about them than any

one else; and let Mr. Rawlins finish recording my other letters which he has begun." I told him this should be done. He then asked if I recollected anything which it was essential for him to do, as he had but a very short time to continue with us. I told him that I could recollect nothing; but that I hoped he was not so near his end. He observed, smiling, that he certainly was, and that, as it was the debt which we must all pay, he looked to the event with perfect resignation.'

In the course of the afternoon he appeared to be in great pain and distress from the difficulty of breathing, and frequently changed his posture in the bed. Mr. Lear endeavoured to raise him and turn him with as much ease as possible. 'I am afraid I fatigue you too much,' the General would say. Upon being assured to the contrary, 'Well,' observed he gratefully, 'it is a debt we must pay to each other, and I hope when you want aid of this kind you will find it.'

His servant, Christopher, had been in the room during the day, and almost the whole time on his feet. The General noticed it in the afternoon, and kindly told him to sit down.

About five o'clock his old friend Dr. Craik came again into the room, and approached the bedside. 'Doctor,' said the General, 'I die hard, but I am not afraid to go. I believed, from my first attack, that I should not survive it—my breath cannot last long.' The doctor pressed his hand in silence, retired from the bedside, and sat by the fire absorbed in grief.

Between five and six the other physicians came in, and he was assisted to sit up in his bed. 'I feel I am going,' said he; 'I thank you for your attentions, but I pray you to take no more trouble about me: let me go off quietly; I cannot last long.' He lay down again; all retired, excepting Dr. Craik. The General continued uneasy and restless, but without complaining, frequently asking what hour it was.

Further remedies were tried without avail in the evening. He took whatever was offered him, did as he was desired by the physicians, and never uttered sigh or complaint.

BED AND BEDSTEAD ON WHICH WASHINGTON DIED.

'About ten o'clock,' writes Mr. Lear, 'he made several attempts to speak to me before he could effect it. At length he said, "I am just going. Have me decently buried, and do not let my body be put into the vault in less than three days after I am dead." I bowed assent, for I could not speak. He then looked at me again and said, "Do you understand me?" I replied, "Yes." "'Tis well," said he.

'About ten minutes before he expired (which was between ten and eleven o'clock) his breathing became easier. He lay quietly; he withdrew his hand from mine, and felt his own pulse. I saw his countenance change. I spoke to Dr. Craik, who sat by the fire: he came to the bedside.

The General's hand fell from his wrist: I took it in mine, and pressed it to my bosom. Dr. Craik put his hands over his eyes, and he expired without a struggle or a sigh.

'While we were fixed in silent grief, Mrs. Washington, who was seated at the foot of the bed, asked with a firm and collected voice, "Is he gone?" I could not speak, but held up my hand as a signal that he was no more. "'Tis well," said she in the same voice. "All is now over: I shall soon follow him; I have no more trials to pass through."'

Congress was in session in Philadelphia at the moment of Washington's death. A written message was received from the President, transmitting a letter from Mr. Tobias Lear (Washington's private secretary), "which," said the message, "will inform you that it had pleased Divine Providence to remove from this life our excellent fellow-citizen, GEORGE WASHINGTON, by the purity of his life, and a long series of services to his country, rendered illustrious through the world. It remains for an affectionate and grateful people, in whose hearts he can never die, to pay suitable honour to his memory."

On this mournful event the Senate addressed to the President the following letter:—

"The Senate of the United States respectfully take leave, sir, to express to you their deep regret for the loss their country sustains in the death of General GEORGE WASHINGTON.

"'This event, so distressing to all our fellow-citizens, must be peculiarly heavy to you, who have long been associated with him in *deeds of patriotism.* Permit us, sir, to mingle our tears with yours. On this occasion it is manly to weep. To lose such a man, at such a crisis, it no common calamity to the world. Our country mourns a father. The Almighty Disposer of human events has taken from us our greatest benefactor and ornament. It becomes us to submit with reverence to HIM who 'maketh darkness His pavilion.'

"With patriotick pride we review the life of our WASHINGTON, and compare him with those of other countries who have been pre-eminent in fame. Ancient and modern names are diminished before him. Greatness and guilt have too often been allied; but *his* fame is whiter than it is brilliant. The destroyers of nations stood abashed at the majesty of *his* virtues. It reproved the intemperance of their ambition, and darkened the splendour of victory. The scene is closed, and we are no longer anxious lest misfortune should sully his glory; he has travelled on to the end of his journey, and carried with him an increasing weight of honour; he has deposited it safely where misfortune cannot tarnish it, where malice cannot blast it. Favoured of heaven, he departed without exhibiting the weakness of humanity; magnanimous in death, the darkness of the grave could not obscure his brightness.

"Such was the man whom we deplore. Thanks to God, his glory is consummated. WASHINGTON yet lives on earth in his spotless example. . . . His spirit is in heaven.

"Let his countrymen consecrate the memory of the heroick general, the patriotic statesman, and the virtuous sage. Let them teach their children never to forget that the fruits of his labours and his example *are their inheritance.*"

To which the President made the following answer:—

"I receive, with the most respectful and affectionate sentiments, in this impressive address, the obliging expressions of your regret for the loss our country has sustained, in the death of her most esteemed, beloved, and admired citizen.

"In the multitude of my thoughts and recollections on this melancholy event, you will permit me to say that I have seen him in the days of adversity, in some of the scenes of his deepest distress, and most trying perplexities. I have also attended him in his highest elevation and most prosperous felicity, with uniform admiration of his wisdom, moderation, and constancy.

"Among all our original associates in that memorable *league* of *this continent* in 1774, which first expressed the sovereign will of a free nation in America, he was the only one remaining in the general government. Although with a constitution more enfeebled than his, at an age when he thought it necessary to prepare for retirement, I feel myself alone, bereaved of my last brother; yet I derive a strong consolation from the unanimous disposition which appears in all ages and classes to mingle their sorrows with mine on this common calamity to the world.

"The life of our WASHINGTON cannot suffer by a comparison with those of other countries, who have been most celebrated and exalted by fame. The attributes and decorations of *royalty* could only have served to eclipse the majesty of those virtues which made him, from being a modest *citizen*, a more resplendent luminary. Misfortune, had he lived, could hereafter have sullied the glory only with those superficial minds, who, believing that characters and actions are marked by success alone, rarely deserve to enjoy it. *Malice* could never blast his honour, and *envy* made him a singular exception to her universal rule. For himself, he had lived long enough to life and to glory. For his fellow-citizens, if their prayers could have been answered, he would have been immortal; for me, his departure is at a most unfortunate moment. Trusting, however, in the wise and righteous dominion of Providence over the passions of men, and the results of their councils and actions, as well as over their lives, nothing remains for me but *humble resignation.*"

On opening the House of Representatives the morning after Washington's death, Mr. Marshall addressed it in the following terms :—

"The melancholy event which was yesterday announced with doubt, has been rendered but too certain—our Washington is no more! The hero, the patriot, and the sage of America . . . the man on whom in times of danger every eye was turned and all hopes were placed, lives now only in his own great actions, and in the hearts of an affectionate and afflicted people.

"If, sir, it had even not been usual openly to testify respect for the memory of those whom Heaven has selected as its instruments for dispensing good to man, yet, such has been the uncommon worth, and such the extraordinary incidents which have marked the life of him whose loss we all deplore, that the whole American nation, impelled by the same feelings, would call with one voice for a public manifestation of that sorrow which is so deep and so universal.

"More than any other individual, and as much as to one individual was possible, has he contributed to found this our wide-spreading empire, and to give to the Western World independence and freedom.

"Having effected the great object for which he was placed at the head of our armies, we have seen him convert the sword into the ploughshare, and sink the soldier into the citizen.

"When the debility of our Federal system had become manifest, and the bonds which connected this vast continent were dissolving, we have seen him, the chief of those patriots who formed for us a Constitution which, by preserving the Union, will, I trust, substantiate and perpetuate those blessings which our Revolution had promised to bestow.

"In obedience to the general voice of his country, calling him to preside over a great people, we have seen him once more quit the retirement he loved, and in a season more stormy and tempestuous than war itself, with calm and wise determination, pursue the true interests of the nation, and contribute, more than any other could contribute, to the establishment of that system of policy which will, I trust, yet preserve our peace, our honour and independence.

"Having twice been unanimously chosen the Chief Magistrate of a free people, we have seen him, at a time when his re-election with universal suffrage could not be doubted, afford to the world a rare instance of moderation, by withdrawing from his high station to the peaceful walks of private life.

"However the publick confidence may change, and the publick affections fluctuate with respect to others, with respect to him they have, in war and in peace, in publick and in private life, been as steady as his own firm mind, and as constant as his own exalted virtues."

No truer or more faithful summary of Washington's character has appeared than the following, given to the world almost on the day of his death by the Rev. Dr. Bancroft:—

"His countenance was serene and thoughtful. His manners were graceful, manly, and dignified. His general appearance never failed to engage the respect and esteem of all who approached him.

Possessing strong natural passions, and having the nicest feelings of honour, he was, in early life, prone keenly to resent practices which carried the intention of abuse or insult; but the reflections of maturer age gave him the most perfect government of himself. He possessed a faculty above all other men, to hide the weaknesses inseparable from human nature; and he bore with meekness and equanimity his distinguished honours.

Reserved, but not haughty, in his disposition, he was accessible to all in concerns of business, but he opened himself only to his confidential friends; and no art or address could draw from him an opinion, which he thought prudent to conceal.

Above arms have, after much research, been ascertained to be those borne by the family in England. It will be seen closely to resemble the Virginian armorial bearings of the American settlers.

Above arms of Washington are from Washington's original book label, presented to Major James Walter by the poet Longfellow.

[In all that concerns the reproduction of the home of Washington, it has been deemed best to give such in the simplest and rudest possible style, as in the days in which the illustrious Patriot lived. The writer of the Memorials feels that his readers will prefer such primitive illustrations, especially seeing that they are accompanied by the beautiful portraits forming the great feature of the work.]

He was not so much distinguished for brilliancy of genius, as for solidity of judgment, and consummate prudence of conduct. He was not so eminent for any one quality of greatness and worth, as for the union of those great, amiable, and good qualities, which are very rarely combined in the same character.

His maxims were formed upon the result of mature reflection, or extensive experience; they were the invariable rules of his practice; and on all important instances, he seemed to have an intuitive view of what the occasion rendered fit and proper. He pursued his purposes with a resolution which, one solitary moment excepted, never failed him.[1]

Alive to social pleasures, he delighted to enter into familiar conversation with his acquaintance, and was sometimes sportive in his letters to his friends; but he never lost sight of the dignity of his character, nor deviated from the decorous and appropriate behaviour becoming his station in society.

He commanded from all the most respectful attention, and no man in his company ever fell into light or lewd conversation. His style of living corresponded with his wealth; but his extensive establishment was managed with the strictest economy, and he ever reserved ample funds liberally to promote schemes of private benevolence, and works of publick utility. Punctual himself to every engagement, he exacted from others a strict fulfilment of contracts; but to the necessitous he was diffusive in his charities, and he greatly assisted the poorer classes of people in his vicinity, by furnishing them with means successfully to prosecute plans of industry.

In domestic and private life, he blended the authority of the master with the care and kindness of the guardian and

[1] On York Island in 1776.

friend. Solicitous for the welfare of his slaves, while at Mount Vernon, he every morning rode round his estates to examine their condition; for the sick, physicians were provided, and to the weak and infirm every necessary comfort was administered. The servitude of the negroes lay with weight upon his mind; he often made it the subject of conversation, and revolved several plans for their general emancipation, but could devise none, which promised success, in consistency with humanity to them, and safety to the State.

The address presented to him at Alexandria, on the commencement of his presidency, fully shows how much he was endeared to his neighbours, and the affection and esteem in which his friends held his private character.

His industry was unremitted, and his method so exact, that all the complicated business of his military command and civil administration was managed without confusion and without hurry. Not feeling the lust of power, and ambitious only for honourable fame, he devoted himself to his country upon the most disinterested principles; and his actions were not the semblance, but the reality of virtue. The purity of his motives was accredited, and absolute confidence placed in his patriotism.

While filling a publick station, the performance of his duty took the place of pleasure, emolument, and every private consideration. During the more critical years of the war, a smile was scarcely seen upon his countenance; he gave himself no moments of relaxation; but his whole mind was engrossed to execute successfully his trust.

As a military commander, he struggled with innumerable embarrassments, arising from the short enlistment of his men, and from the want of provision, clothing, arms, and ammunition; and an opinion of his achievements should be formed in view of these inadequate means.

The first years of his civil administration were attended with the extraordinary fact that while a great proportion of his countrymen reprobated his measures, they universally venerated his character, and relied implicitly on his integrity. Although his opponents eventually deemed it expedient to villify his character, that they might diminish his political influence, yet the moment that he retired from publick life, they returned to their expressions of veneration and esteem, and after his death used every endeavour to secure to their party the influence of his name.

He was eminent for piety as for patriotism. His publick and private conduct evince that he impressively felt a sense of the superintendence of God and of the dependence of man. In his addresses while at the head of the army and of the national government, he gratefully noticed the signal blessings of Providence, and fervently commended his country to divine benediction. In private he was known to have been habitually devout.

In principle and practice he was a *Christian*—the support of an Episcopal Church in the vicinity of Mount Vernon rested principally upon him; and here, when on his estate, he with constancy attended publick worship. In his address to the American people, at the close of the war, mentioning the favourable period of the world at which the independence of his country was established, and enumerating the causes which unitedly had ameliorated the condition of human society, he, above science, philosophy, commerce, and all other considerations, ranked '*the pure and benign light of Revelation.*'

Supplicating Heaven that his fellow-citizens might cultivate the disposition and practise the virtues which exalt a community, he presented the following petition to his God: 'That He would most graciously be pleased to dispose us all to do justice, to love mercy, and to demean ourselves with that charity, humility, and pacifick temper of mind which were the characteristicks of the *Divine Author of our blessed religion;* without an humble imitation of whose example, in these things, we can never hope to be a happy nation.'

During the war he not unfrequently rode ten or twelve miles from camp to attend publick worship; and he never omitted this attendance when opportunity presented.

In the establishment of his presidential household, he reserved to himself the Sabbath, free from the interruptions of private visits, or publick business; and throughout the eight years of his civil administration, he gave to the institutions of Christianity the influence of his example.

Uniting the talents of the soldier with the qualifications of the statesman, and pursuing, unmoved by difficulties, the noblest end by the purest means, he had the supreme satisfaction of beholding the complete success of his great military and civil services, in the independence and happiness of his country."

THE WASHINGTON TOMB AT MOUNT VERNON.

www.ingramcontent.com/pod-product-compliance
Lightning Source LLC
Chambersburg PA
CBHW032018220426
43664CB00006B/283